PECULIAR ATTUNEMENTS

Peculiar Attunements

HOW AFFECT THEORY TURNED MUSICAL

Roger Mathew Grant

FORDHAM UNIVERSITY PRESS   NEW YORK 2020

Fordham University Press has no responsibility for the persistence or accuracy of URLs for external or third-party Internet websites referred to in this publication and does not guarantee that any content on such websites is, or will remain, accurate or appropriate.

Fordham University Press also publishes its books in a variety of electronic formats. Some content that appears in print may not be available in electronic books.

Visit us online at www.fordhampress.com.

Library of Congress Control Number:2019955796

Printed in the United States of America

22 21 20   5 4 3 2 1

First edition

Contents

Notes on Orthography and Translation

Quotations preserve the spelling and idiosyncrasies of the original wherever possible. All translations are my own unless otherwise indicated.

I had not heard any music for a few days, and I was all charged
up, glowing and gratified, so that my sense of everything was
heightened. I felt every phrase of the music in a physical way, as if I
had turned into a little orchestra myself.

— ALAN HOLLINGHURST, THE SWIMMING-POOL LIBRARY

Introduction

The music begins: Beethoven's Fifth Symphony. The orchestra roars the opening gestures with unsettling power. Your hands become clammy, and your heartbeat accelerates. Watching the stage with anticipation, you hear the pace of events quicken and the music hasten toward some conclusion that it cannot reach. Your breathing becomes heavy, your cheeks flush, the muscles in your back tighten, and your throat closes. A rush of pleasure washes over you.

Affect gives name to the dynamic transformation that is achieved in experiences like these. Contemporary theorists describe affect as corporeal, immediate, and nondiscursive.[1] Affect is said to relate conditions of feeling that cannot be adequately captured with the tools of language. Affect theory has recently benefited from a huge resurgence in interest among humanists

---

1. Brian Massumi, "Notes on the Translation," in *A Thousand Plateaus: Capitalism and Schizophrenia*, by Gilles Deleuze and Félix Guattari (Minneapolis: University of Minnesota Press, 1987), xvii. In the words of Massumi, affect is "a prepersonal intensity corresponding to the passage from one experiential state of the body to another and implying an augmentation or diminution in that body's capacity to act." Or take the definition that Nigel Thrift proposes in *Non-Representational Theory*: "Affect . . . refers to complex, self-referential states of being, rather than to their cultural interpretation as emotions or to their identification as instinctual drives." Thrift, *Non-Representational Theory: Space, Politics, Affect* (New York: Routledge, 2008), 221. See also Eve Kosofsky Sedgwick and Adam Frank, "Shame in the Cybernetic Fold: Reading Silvan Tomkins," *Critical Inquiry* 21, no. 2 (1995): 496–522; and Gilles Deleuze, "The Shame and the Glory: T. E. Lawrence," in *Essays Critical and Clinical*, trans. Daniel W. Smith and Michael A. Greco (Minneapolis: University of Minnesota Press, 1997), 115–125.

and social scientists, and whether the apex of this new popularity has already passed or is yet to come, it is safe to say that affect has not always attracted the attention it does today. As the story typically goes, critics have recently favored affect theory in their search for alternatives to the focus on discourse that characterized the linguistic turn. But this narrative is not exclusive to the twenty-first century; it is also the story of a less-well-known movement in intellectual history that occurred in the middle decades of the eighteenth, when European debates on music created a fundamental transformation within aesthetic theory. This is the story of how affect theory turned musical.

Inflecting our current intellectual moment through eighteenth-century music theory and aesthetics, this book reveals formal aspects of historical and contemporary theories of affect. It sets forth a way of thinking through affect dialectically, drawing attention to patterns and problems in affect theory that we have been given to repeating. Finally, it argues for renewed attention to the objects that generate affects in subjects.[2]

Affect has a long and rich intellectual heritage, and the locations of subject and object within it have been anything but uniform. In early modernity, the affects — or the passions, as they were also called — were important components of an elaborate semiotic system that explained the impact of aesthetic objects. Today, by stark contrast, affect is often explicitly opposed to theories of the sign and of representation; theorists construe affect as a matter of subjective reception that is fundamentally objectless or nonintentional, occasionally even contrasting affect with ideology.[3] This book narrates an eighteenth-century transformation during which affect was slowly separated

2. My call for renewed attention to the objects of affect theory owes much to David Halperin's thinking on the objects of love and erotic desire. See Halperin, "What Is Sex For?," *Critical Inquiry* 43, no. 1 (2016): 1–31, especially 28–29. I've also drawn inspiration from Sianne Ngai's *Our Aesthetic Categories: Zany, Cute, Interesting* (Cambridge, MA: Harvard University Press, 2012); and Katherine Behar's "An Introduction to OOF," in *Object-Oriented Feminism*, ed. Katherine Behar (Minneapolis: University of Minnesota Press, 2016), 1–36.

3. Gary Tomlinson has recently pointed out that in the work of recent affect theorists, "the sign often comes to seem synonymous with *representation*, a term, in this usage, opposed to embodiment and embodied experience; or with *conventionalization*, which seems to some of these writers to define the sign but of course is limited in Peircean semiosis to one (rare) type of signs, symbols; or even with *ideology*, an effect of human culture and society and their patterns." Tomlinson, "Sign, Affect, and Musicking before the Human," *boundary 2* 43, no. 1 (2016): 160. On the nonintentional nature of recent affect theory, see Ruth Leys, *The Ascent of Affect: Genealogy and Critique* (Chicago: University of Chicago Press, 2017), in particular "Introduction: Setting the Stage," 1–25.

from representations of aesthetic objects, and it draws attention to the central and surprising role that music played in this separation.[4]

Comparing two pivotal moments within affect theory's history, this book offers a reassessment of affect's common systems, processes, and dilemmas. It also aims to draw affect theory into conversation with another, equally vexed archive: the history of music theory. Affective experience and musical sound have created similar problems for theorists. Both are said to act on the body in a material fashion that can be explained with a certain degree of specificity, and yet both are also said to produce transformations within us that exceed and overspill linguistic or rational containment. Music theory and affect theory may yet have much to teach each other.

Music scholars have not completely neglected the early modern turn to affect within music theory; it used to be called the *Affektenlehre*, or the "doctrine of affections."[5] But work on this phenomenon came to a halt in the 1980s, when George Buelow and others decided that its documents contain too many internal contradictions to be considered a cohesive doctrine.[6] Buelow was correct about this, but he underestimated both the importance of those thorny, contradictory treatises and the scope of the intellectual movement they represent. The *Affektenlehre* was bigger and messier than we had previously thought, and it is now more pertinent to our contemporary discourse than we could ever have imagined. The time has come for a careful reconsideration of this vital and challenging intellectual moment. First, though,

4. This study builds, therefore, on the wealth of scholarship concerning affect and emotion in eighteenth-century culture, but it does so with critical and theoretical goals in mind. Taking an important cue from Stephen Ahern, the aim here is to "read affect theory through the age of sensibility," rather than interpreting the texts of that era with the tools of affect theory. Ahern, "Nothing More than Feelings? Affect Theory Reads the Age of Sensibility," *Eighteenth Century* 58, no. 3 (2017): 289. On affect and emotion in the eighteenth century, see in particular Ahern, "Nothing More than Feelings?"; and Joseph Roach, *The Player's Passion: Studies in the Science of Acting* (Ann Arbor: University of Michigan Press, 1993); William M. Reddy, *The Navigation of Feeling: A Framework for the History of Emotions* (Cambridge: Cambridge University Press, 2001); and Aleksondra Hultquist, "Introductory Essay: Emotion, Affect, and the Eighteenth Century," *Eighteenth Century* 58, no. 3 (2017): 273–280.

5. See for instance Frederick T. Wessel, "The Affektenlehre in the Eighteenth Century" (PhD diss., Indiana University, 1955); Willi Apel, *Harvard Dictionary of Music*, 2nd ed. (Cambridge, MA: Harvard University Press, 1972), s.v. "Affections, doctrine of"; and Manfred F. Bukofzer, *Music in the Baroque Era: From Monteverdi to Bach* (New York: Norton, 1947), 388.

6. The document most frequently cited in this connection is George J. Buelow, "Johann Mattheson and the Invention of the *Affektenlehre*," in *New Mattheson Studies*, ed. Buelow and Hans Joachim Marx (Cambridge: Cambridge University Press, 1983), 393–407.

some preliminaries on the intellectual context out of which that earlier turn to affect emerged.

Affect, Representation, Music

Contemporary affect theorists rely on a variety of sources from the history of philosophy, but by far the most important of these is the work of Baruch Spinoza. In the *Ethics*, Spinoza describes affect [*affectus*] as the body's capacity to respond to the world in a preconscious manner that either increases or decreases its power of activity.[7] His theory is particularly attractive to contemporary scholars because it postulates a mind-body union. Not often discussed are the commonalities between Spinoza's thought and the work of his important predecessor René Descartes. Despite the fact that these two thinkers conceptualized the mind-body relationship in radically different ways, Spinoza and Descartes authored remarkably similar theories of the affects. In addition to nearly identical lists of the basic affects, these thinkers also shared an important commitment to theorize the relationship between the affecting object and the affected subject. Both Spinoza and Descartes endeavored to describe the objects that create affective responses in subjects, especially when these things were reproductions or images of other affect-inducing objects.

For Spinoza, an object that creates an affective response of pleasure or pain in a subject could be anything that causes an increase or decrease in the body's power of acting. When you see an object that you love, your body's power of acting is increased, and you experience pleasure. Spinoza specifies that these objects themselves need not be present in order for us to experience an affective response. "From the mere fact that we imagine a thing to have something similar to an object that is wont to affect the mind with pleasure or pain, we shall love it or hate it, although the point of similarity is not the efficient cause of these emotions."[8] That is, if something resembles your be-

---

7. Baruch Spinoza, *Ethica*, in *Spinoza, Opera* im Auftrag der Heidelberger Akademie der Wissenschaften, ed. Carl Gebhardt (Heidelberg: Universitætsbuchhandlung, 1925), 139. See in particular *Ethics* III Definition 3: "Per Affectum intelligo Corporis affectiones, quibus ipsius Corporis agendi potentia augetur, vel minuitur, juvatur, vel coërcetur, & simul harum affectionum ideas." In *Spinoza: The Complete Works*, trans. Samuel Shirley, ed. with introduction and notes by Michael L. Morgan (Indianapolis: Hackett, 2002), 278. "By emotion [*affectus*] I understand the affections of the body by which the body's power of activity is increased or diminished, assisted or checked, together with the ideas of these affections."

8. In *Spinoza: The Complete Works*, 287. *Ethics* III Proposition 16: "Ex eo solo, quòd rem aliquam aliquid habere imaginamur simile objecto, quod Mentem Lætitiâ, vel Tristitiâ afficere

loved object enough—say, an image of it—you may love that object as well, and your body's power of acting may be increased. It is not the "point of similarity" or mimesis of the object that provides the efficient cause, but rather, he clarifies, "the thing which we perceive to have this said point of similarity will indirectly be the cause of pleasure or pain."[9] The similar object—or sign of the object—indirectly induces the affective response on the part of the subject.[10] In later elaborations, Spinoza takes an explicitly oculocentric turn in his emphasis on the image of affecting objects. "The body," he writes, "is affected by the image of the thing in the same way as if the thing itself were present."[11] Later he continues, "Images of things are affections of the human body."[12] For Spinoza, mimetically reproduced images of affecting objects have the ability to produce affects in the subject.

Descartes had gone even further to specify the nature of these affective transactions in *Les passions de l'âme* of 1649. "When we read of unusual adventures in a book or see them represented on a stage, this sometimes excites Sadness in us, sometimes Joy or Love or Hatred."[13] He explains this further when he writes, "one naturally takes pleasure in feeling moved to all sorts of Passions, even Sadness and Hatred, when these passions are caused only by the unusual adventures one sees represented on a stage or by other similar matters, which, not being able to harm us in any way, seem to titillate our soul in affecting it."[14] Descartes's more extensive theory separates out the im-

---

solet, quamvis id, in quo res objecto est similis, non sit horum affectuum efficiens causa, eam tamen amabimus, vel odio habebimus." Spinoza, *Ethica*, 153.

9. In *Spinoza: The Complete Works*, 287. *Ethics* III Proposition 16, Proof: "Consequenter res, quam hoc idem habere precipimus, erit (*per Prop.* 15. *hujus*) per accidens Lætitiæ, vel Tristitiæ causa." Spinoza, *Ethica*, 153.

10. As Rei Terada explains, "Literally impressions in the body, affections imply that encounters with other bodies, and, moreover, between parts of one's own body, are in themselves semiotic. They infect all of experience with interpretation, and thus are portrayed as corrupting; they are also in danger of infecting signification with corporeal opacity." She continues, "It is Deleuze who arranges Spinoza's thought about signs into a fundamental opposition between indication and expression with their modern connotations." Terada, *Feeling in Theory: Emotion after the "Death of the Subject"* (Cambridge, MA: Harvard University Press, 2001), 115.

11. *Spinoza: The Complete Works*, 288. *Ethics* III Proposition 18, Scholium 1: "Corpus ejusdem rei imagine eodem modo afficitur, ac si res ipsa præsens adesset." Spinoza, *Ethica*, 154.

12. *Spinoza: The Complete Works*, 292. *Ethics* III Proposition 27, Proof: "Rerum imagines sunt corporis humani affectiones." Spinoza, *Ethica*, 160.

13. "Et lors que nous lisons des avantures estranges dans un livre, ou que nous les voyons representer sur un theatre, cela excite quelquefois en nous la Tristesse, quelquefois la Ioye, ou l'Amour, ou la Haine." Descartes, *Les passions de l'âme* (Paris: Henry Le Gras, 1649), 202.

14. "On prend naturellement plaisir à se sentir émouvoir à toutes sortes de Passions, mesme à le Tristesse, & à la Haine, lors que ces passions ne sont causées que par les avantures estranges

mediate affective response from the subsequent pleasure we take in feeling it, providing the basis for a theory of art.

Eighteenth-century aesthetic theory built on the seventeenth century's theories of the affects, further elaborating the work of Spinoza, Descartes, and their contemporaries. Affect, in this doctrine, played an important role in systems of signification and representation, fulfilling a function that might seem completely foreign to contemporary affect theory. In eighteenth-century aesthetic theory, representation referred not only to artistic renderings of objects and events but also to the mechanism by which the soul came to know the objects in the world. Representation named what was then an unknowable connection between the soul and the sensorium; according to certain models, the soul was completely constituted by representation.[15] Affects resulted from re-presenting the world's external objects to the soul. The arousal of the affects and the subsequent pleasure obtained in their arousal was — as aesthetic theory saw it — the major goal of art. Jean-Baptiste Dubos, writing at the beginning of the century, could straightforwardly claim, "the principal merit of poems and paintings consists in imitating the objects that arouse real passions."[16] He went on to explain, "the copy of the object should, so to speak, excite in us a copy of the passion which the imitated object would itself have excited."[17] Alexander Gottlieb Baumgarten, often credited with naming the discipline of aesthetics in his *Meditations* of 1735, put it directly when he wrote, "representations are motions of the affects, therefore *to arouse affects is poetic*."[18] Dubos and Baumgarten contributed to a growing body of knowledge

qu'on voit representer sur un theatre, ou par d'autres pareils sujets, qui ne pouvant nous nuire en aucune façon, semblent chatoüiller nostre ame en la touchant." Descartes, *Passions*, 128–129.

15. As Michel Foucault put it, "This universal extension of the sign within the field of representation precludes even the possibility of a theory of signification. For to ask ourselves questions about what signification is presupposes that it is a determinate form in our consciousness. But if phenomena are posited only in a representation that, in itself and because of its own representability, is wholly a sign, then signification cannot constitute a problem." Foucault, *The Order of Things* (1966), English trans. (1970; repr., New York: Routledge, 2002), 72. On early modern representation see especially Gary Tomlinson, *Metaphysical Song: An Essay on Opera* (Princeton: Princeton University Press, 1999), 34–40; and David Wellbery, *Lessing's Laocoon: Semiotics and Aesthetics in the Age of Reason* (Cambridge: Cambridge University Press, 1984), 9–17.

16. In Jean-Baptiste Dubos, *Réflexions critiques sur la poésie et sur la peinture*, vol. 1 (Paris: Jean Mariette, 1719), 23, the title of the third chapter reads, "Que le mérite principal des Poëms & des Tableaux consiste à imiter les objets qui auroient excité en nous des passions réelles."

17. Dubos, *Réflexions*, 25. "La copie de l'objet doit, pour ainsi dire, exciter en nous une copie de la passion que l'objet y auroit excitée."

18. "Repraesentationes sunt motiones affectuum, ergo *movere affectus poeticum*." Alexander Gottlieb Baumgarten, *Meditationes philosophicae de nonnullis ad poema pertinentibus* (Halle: Grunert, 1735), § XXVI; modern ed., ed. Benedetto Croce (Naples: Vecchi, 1900), 14.

that construed affect as an essential component in the experience of art — one they endeavored to describe and explain.

Aesthetic theory in the eighteenth century was not only concerned with the soul's responses to the objects of the world; it also aimed to specify the qualities of objects that would elicit certain affective responses in subjects. One persistent line of inquiry concerned the aesthetic experience of pain and suffering. How is it that we take pleasure in witnessing the depiction of other people's misfortune, torment, or agony? A seminal example in this tradition — and an artwork returned to again and again in the history of affect theory — is the sculpture group *Laocoön and His Sons* (Figure 1), otherwise called the *Laocoön Group*. Specialists debate the origin and provenance of the work (which may be a Roman copy of an earlier Greek bronze), but eighteenth-century theorists took it be an ancient Greek work.[19] The sculpture depicts the death of the eponymous Trojan priest and his two sons as serpents surround and attack the trio. The treatment of Laocoön's face elicited considerable commentary. While Johann Joachim Winckelmann considered its relative calm to reflect the noble Greek soul of its creator, Gotthold Ephraim Lessing argued that the sculptor had moderated Laocoön's expression so that pain was tempered with beauty in order to evoke "the sweet feeling of pity" in the viewer.[20] "One should just imagine Laocoön with his mouth torn open," Lessing suggests, "and judge! Let him scream, and look!"[21] For Lessing, the portrayal of too much pain in the medium of sculpture would have meant too direct a transference of this affect to the viewer.

This transmission, from an object of art to the affective response of a subject experiencing it, constituted the basic framework of aesthetic theory in the eighteenth century. Broadly speaking, it was a paradigm of mimesis or, as the period sources put it, imitation. Mimesis and affect were two foundational parts of this basic architecture. While each theorist offered a slightly different account, the underlying assumption was that artworks imitate those things in

19. For critical commentary, chronology, and bibliography on the work itself, see "Laocoön," Digital Sculpture Project, Virtual World Heritage Laboratory at University of Virginia, accessed June 17, 2016, www.digitalsculpture.org/laocoon/.

20. Johann Joachim Winckelmann, *Gedanken über die Nachahmung der Griechischen Werke in der Malerey und Bildhauerkunst* (Dresden und Leipzig: Verlag der Waltherischen Handlung, 1756), 21–22; Gotthold Ephraim Lessing, *Laokoon: Oder über die Grenzen der Mahlerey und Poesie*, vol. 1 (Berlin: Christian Friedrich Voß, 1766), 20.

21. "Denn man reisse dem Laokoon in Gedanken nur den Mund auf, und urtheile. Man lass ihn schreyen, und sehe." Lessing, *Laokoon*, 20. On this point, see David Wellbery's discussion in *Lessing's Laocoon: Semiotics and Aesthetics in the Age of Reason* (Cambridge: Cambridge University Press, 1984), 164–165; I borrow the use of exclamation points in my translation from Wellbery.

Figure 1. *Laocoön and His Sons*, Museo Pio Clementino, Vatican Museums, Rome (Photo: Livio Andronico; used in accordance with the Creative Commons Attribution-Share Alike 4.0 International License, https://commons.wikimedia.org/wiki/File:Laocoon_and_His_Sons.jpg)

the world that evoke the affects in their beholders. Theorists described the mimetic capability of artworks in two different ways, with two principal types of signs: the natural sign (somewhat akin to C. S. Peirce's icon) reproduced something of the object it signified, like a flame to fire or a portrait to the sitter; the arbitrary sign (like Peirce's symbol) held an abstract, preestablished relationship to the object, like the word "fire" to the same. (Peirce's category of the index is missing from this eighteenth-century scheme.)[22] Natural signs,

22. If Hume's "impression" might have functioned in a way somewhat analogous to Peirce's index, Continental writers of the period seem not to have grasped onto it as a solution to the problem of musical signification. On eighteenth-century semiotic theory and musical semiotics,

in this system, were the domain of the fine arts such as painting and sculpture, whereas arbitrary signs were the material of the belles lettres. For many theorists, the natural sign both logically and historically preceded the arbitrary sign in art. Natural signs appealed more directly, more simply, or "without self-consciousness," as Moses Mendelssohn put it.[23]

How does music work in this theory of art? Until the eighteenth century, theorists had understood the art of musical sound as a vehicle for amplifying other mimetic representations. Music assisted in the mimetic work of poetry in song, or of stage drama in opera, or in other types of sacred or secular theatrical depictions. Musical sounds themselves were not considered proper objects for mimetic aesthetic theory. Indeed "music" as such was not yet conceptually cleaved apart from song and was not quite yet its own intellectual category, as Gary Tomlinson has persuasively argued.[24] But because of several interrelated processes that unfolded both within the world of musical performance and within the world of criticism, eighteenth-century thinkers slowly began to realize that the art of musical sound needed its own aesthetic language.[25] It was in the process of creating an aesthetic language for musical sound itself that both aesthetic theory and affect theory were forever changed.

Seventeenth-century composers of opera, still experimenting with this new art form, had already begun to systematize relationships between musical gestures and mimetic representations. Using stock musical figures, patterns, and recognizable musical styles, they created links between the poetry of the opera and the sounds of its music. A fanfare of trumpets and drums playing specific rhythms could signify a victorious celebration, for example, while a slowly descending bass line could indicate a lament. We now call these musical "topics."[26] Over the course of the seventeenth century and into the turn of

---

see Danuta Mirka, introduction to *The Oxford Handbook of Topic Theory*, ed. Mirka (Oxford: Oxford University Press, 2014), 1–57; also Wellbery, *Lessing's Laocoon.*

23. "Ohne Selbstbewußtseyn." Moses Mendelssohn, "Ueber das Erhabene und das Naïve in den schönen Wissenschaften," in *Moses Mendelssohns philosophische Schriften*, vol. 2 (Berlin: Christian Friedrich Voß, 1771), 226. Mendelssohn is here discussing what he calls "naïve expression."

24. Gary Tomlinson, "Early Modern Opera," in *Metaphysical Song: An Essay on Opera* (Princeton, NJ: Princeton University Press, 1999), 34–72; and Tomlinson, "Musicology, Anthropology, History," *Il saggiatore musicale* 8, no. 1 (2001): 21–37.

25. The narrative of historical music theory traced in this portion of the chapter bears some resemblance to one previously suggested by Martha Feldman, though with rather different conclusions. See Feldman, "Music and the Order of the Passions," in *Representing the Passions: Histories, Bodies, Visions*, ed. Richard Evan Meyer (Los Angeles: Getty Research Institute, 2003), 37–67.

26. The relationship between musical topics and the *Affektenlehre* is covered in greater detail in chapter 1.

the eighteenth, these stock musical figures and patterns became predictable enough to be identifiable. Two important developments sprang from this momentary stylistic regularity. The first was the development of a robust set of theoretical attempts to codify these relationships and their consequences for aesthetic theory: which bass lines, exactly, should be used to elicit sadness? Which dance rhythms should be used to create joy or gaiety? Although theorists could not agree on the specifics, they concurred at least that such connections were conventional and that some general observations could be made about them. The result was a set of documents on music theory — all conflicting in their attempts to do this work — that was once referred to as the *Affektenlehre*. In its effort to systematize relationships between musical materials and affective responses, this constituted the first stage in eighteenth-century musical affect theories: the mimetic *Affektenlehre*.

The other development, equally if not more important for the history of affect theory, was the emergence of comic opera. Comic opera began as a parodic, metatheatrical critique of its serious predecessor, and it mocked the formulaic conventionality of the older form with hyperbole. Comic opera used the stock gestures of serious opera, but it used them in exaggeration, in rapid succession, simultaneously on top of each other, and in ways that contradicted the poetry of the libretto — all to hilarious effect.

Both music theory's effort to taxonomize and comic opera's hyperbolic mockery drew attention to a system of conventions that composers had begun to rely on. It was the new legibility of this system of musical conventions that enticed eighteenth-century thinkers to develop an aesthetic language for the art of musical sound itself. Some critics were worried that the music of the opera was overstepping the poetry of the operatic drama and saw this as an unfortunate development. Others, newly impressed by the Italian style of opera buffa that was slowly spreading across the continent, thought that the art of music had been completely revitalized.[27] But no matter whether they loved or hated these developments, they had to admit that change was afoot in this form of art and that it required explanation. Specifically, critics felt as though they had to account for the role of musical sound in aesthetic experience. Music, therefore, had to be theorized along the lines of mimesis. How was it that music created mimetic representations that moved its auditors to various

27. This debate, the "Querelle des Bouffons," is the subject of Roger Mathew Grant, "Peculiar Attunements: Comic Opera and Enlightenment Mimesis," *Critical Inquiry* 43, no. 2 (2017): 550–569. See also Richard A. Oliver, *The Encyclopedists as Critics of Music* (New York: Columbia University Press, 1947); and Daniel Heartz, *From Garrick to Gluck: Essays on Opera in the Age of Enlightenment*, ed. John A. Rice (Hillsdale, NY: Pendragon, 2004), 213–254.

affects? Did music produce representations at all, or did music somehow create affects in listeners by some other means?

The attempts to fit music into the preexisting categories of signification within aesthetic theory were legion. Some critics, like Jean-Jacques Rousseau, insisted that music operated as a natural sign. In Rousseau's view, music was mimetic of the first plaints of primitive man, in which speech and song were one. It imitated those natural impassioned cries that were now inaccessible to humanity.[28] Others tried to imagine music as some sort of imperfect version of an arbitrary sign. Music without words, in particular, seemed to them some sort of ancient language for which we had lost the code. Johann Philipp Kirnberger, for instance, thought of instrumental music as an "incomprehensible language," whereas André Morellet likened it to a language written without consonants.[29] Jean le Rond d'Alembert also saw a problem with the intelligibility of musical sounds, likening the symphony to "a German discourse spoken before someone who understands only French."[30] If music was an arbitrary sign, it was one that was nearly impossible to interpret.

There is no more instructive document on the crisis that music caused for aesthetic theory — indeed, for all Enlightenment knowledge — than d'Alembert's "Discours préliminaire" to the *Encyclopédie*. D'Alembert's introduction systematically lays out the branches of the tree of human knowledge, coming finally to the arts at the conclusion of the taxonomy. He begins this section with painting and sculpture — arts associated with the natural sign — since "it

28. Jean-Jacques Rousseau, *Essai sur l'origine des langues*, published posthumously in *Œuvres completes de J. J. Rousseau, citoyen de Genève*, vol. 8 (Geneva, 1782), 137–231.

29. Johann Philipp Kirnberger, "Instrumentalmusik," in *Allgemeine Theorie der schönen Künste*, by Johann Georg Sulzer, 2 vols. (Leipzig: M. G. Weidmanns Erben und Reich, 1771–1774), 1:559; André Morellet, *De l'expression en musique* (Paris, 1770), 13. "La musique instrumentale toute seule sera au moins une langue a voyelles à laquelle nous n'aurons plus que les consonnes à ajouter." Note that the version of this essay that appears in the nineteenth-century compilation *Mélanges de littérature et de philosophie du 18e siècle*, vol. 4 (Paris: Le Bailly, Libraire, 1836), 382, has a different version of the quotation: "La musique instrumentale toute seule sera au moins une langue qui s'écrit sans voyelles, comme quelques langues orientales." This is the version translated in *Musical Aesthetics: A Historical Reader*, ed. Edward A. Lippman, vol. 1 (Hillsdale, NY: Pendragon, 1986), 269–284. Oddly enough, the 1770 print of Morellet's text in the British Library has "voyelles" crossed out and "consonnes" written in the margin. Jean le Rond d'Alembert, for his part, equated music with a language without vowels in "De la liberté de la musique" (1758); see d'Alembert *Oeuvres*, 5 vols. (Paris: Belin, 1821–1822), 1:544.

30. "Toute symphonie qui ne dit rien à l'âme est à peu près comme un discours allemand prononcé devant quelqu'un qui n'entendroit que le français." Jean le Rond d'Alembert, "Fragment sur l'opéra" (ca. 1752), in *Oeuvres et correspondances inédites de d'Alembert*, ed. with notes and appendix by Charles Henry (Paris: Perrin, 1887), 155.

is in those [arts] above all that imitation best resembles the objects that are represented, and speaks most directly to the senses."[31] Architecture follows as the third in this category. D'Alembert then moves on to poetry, which "only employs imitation by means of words," using arbitrary rather than natural signs to evoke its objects. The taxonomy concludes, however, with a problem posed by music:

> Finally music, which speaks at the same time to the imagination and to the senses, holds the last place in the order of imitation; not that its imitations are less perfect in the objects that it seeks to represent, but because until now it seems to have been limited to a small number of images. . . . It will not be useless to make some reflections on this. Music was perhaps in its origin reserved for representing noise. It has become, little by little, a sort of discourse or even language, with which one expresses the different sentiments of the soul, or rather the different passions. . . . All music that does not paint something is only noise, and without the habituation that changes everything it would create hardly more pleasure than a collection of harmonious and sonorous words stripped of order and connection. It is true that a musician attempting to paint everything would present us, in many circumstances, with scenes of harmony that would do nothing for the common senses; but all that one may conclude is that after having created an art of learning music one should also create an art of listening to it.[32]

31. Jean le Rond d'Alembert, "Discours préliminaire," in *Encyclopédie ou dictionnaire raisonné des sciences, des arts et des métiers, par une société de gens de lettres*, ed. Denis Diderot and d'Alembert, vol. 1 (Paris: Briasson et Le Breton, 1751), xi–xii. "Parce que ce sont celles de toutes où l'imitation approche le plus des objets qu'elle représente, & parle le plus directement aux sens."

32. "Enfin la Musique, qui parle à la fois à l'imagination & aux sens, tient le dernier rang dans l'ordre de l'imitation; non que son imitation soit moins parfaite dans les objets qu'elle se propose de représenter, mais parce qu'elle semble bornée jusqu'ici à un plus petit nombre d'images . . . il ne sera pas inutile de faire sur cela quelques réflexions. La Musique, qui dans son origine n'étoit peut-être destinée à représenter que du bruit, est devenue peu-à-peu une espece de discours ou même de langue, par laquelle on exprime les différens sentimens de l'ame, ou plûtôt ses différentes passions. . . . Toute Musique qui ne peint rien n'est que du bruit; & sans l'habitude qui dénature tout, elle ne feroit guere plus de plaisir qu'une suite de mots harmonieux & sonores dénués d'ordre & de liaison. Il est vrai qu'un Musicien attentif à tout peindre, nous présenteroit dans plusieurs circonstances des tableaux d'harmonie qui ne seroient point faits pour des sens vulgaires; mais tout ce qu'on en doit conclurre, c'est qu'après avoir fait un art d'apprendre la Musique, on devroit bien en faire un de l'écouter." D'Alembert, "Discours préliminaire," xii.

The entire taxonomy of the system of human knowledge ends here, with these wandering remarks on an art form that evidently flummoxed d'Alembert. This disquisition implies that a transformation in both musical practice and musical knowledge is under way. Something has gone on that has created a new kind of musical art that will also require a new "art of listening to it." In d'Alembert's miniature history, music began as an art of natural signs, strictly imitating only what its medium allowed: sounds. But slowly, music has been transformed into something that resembles an arbitrary sign. It depends, like language, on a sort of habituation or convention, without which it is simply (as other period commentators had it) a collection of sonorous but incomprehensible words, "stripped of order and connection." Still, it seems to d'Alembert that the transformation has not been fully successful, since "the common senses" might not grasp the images of a musician "attempting to paint everything." We need, therefore, a new way of understanding what music is communicating, a new art of listening.

Despite d'Alembert's frustration, there had been a slowly growing body of theory that was attempting to explain music, and listening, anew. Over the course of the eighteenth century, a small number of critics had suggested a nonmimetic aesthetic framework for music. The consensus in this vein of criticism was that music, instead of imitating, could somehow bypass the traditional structure of representation through its physical reality as sound; it was said to vibrate the nerves of the listener and thereby arouse an affective response. This was a theory of affective attunement, an entirely new theory of affect crafted specifically for music—and, regrettably, one that is usually ignored in the typical historiography of the *Affektenlehre*.

Drawing on the *musica humana* tradition, in which the body and its parts are thought of as a finely tuned instrument, theorists postulated a sympathetic resonance between the physical sounds of music and the inner workings of the human. As Christian Gottfried Krause explained, "The soul is like a stringed instrument that sounds sympathetically whenever a tone is given that corresponds to one of its strings, even though the string itself was not touched."[33] This view attracted adherents from all sides of critical opinion—from Denis Diderot, a materialist champion of Italian opera buffa, to Élie-Catherine Fréron, a staunchly conservative detractor of the musical revolution sweeping

33. "Die Seele ist, wie ein besaites Instrument, welches mitklingt, wenn man einen Ton angiebt, den eine von dessen Saiten hat, obgleich die Saite selbst nicht berühret worden." Christian Gottfried Krause, *Von der musikalischen Poesie* (Berlin: Johann Friedrich Voß, 1752), 79. For a more detailed reading of Krause, see chapter 4.

Europe. Although it was not a majority opinion and it could not be easily squared with the prevailing explanatory paradigm in aesthetic theory, its attractions were many. It solved the problem of explaining how music managed to evoke affect in a way that none of the other arts did, and it accounted for the mediation of affect through a phenomenon — sympathetic resonance — that was empirically verifiable and a known fact of physics.[34]

Theories of affective attunement were not simply adaptations of aesthetic theory meant to accommodate music. Instead they were entirely new theoretical models for affect that construed its basic operation in sonic terms. These theories shifted the discourse away from the specific qualities of musical objects and directed focus toward the reverberating interior of listeners. Antonio Planelli, a late eighteenth-century scientist and opera critic, described in detail how sympathetic vibrations of the "diathetic nerves" could engender distinct affective states.[35] "It seems beyond obvious that our nerves, like so many strings of an instrument, have a determined pitch. . . . Because of the correspondence between the movement of [the nerves] and the passions of the soul, their oscillations will arouse that passion that corresponds to the given motion produced in them."[36] The arousal of affect in his account was an autonomic, physiological response to sound vibration. By the end of the century, Johann Nikolaus Forkel could speak of a "completely unmediated [ganz unmittelbare]" relation between musical sound and human emotion.[37] Theorists began to strike music from the list of imitative arts. As the famous literary critic M. H. Abrams explained, "Music, by its nature the weak spot in the theory of imitation, as this theory was usually interpreted in the eighteenth century, was thus the first of the arts to be severed from the mimetic principle by a critical nexus."[38] The theory of affective attunement had displaced earlier mimetic theories and provided a corporeal, immediate, nondiscursive expla-

34. This transition, from the aesthetics of mimesis to a new view of affective attunement, bears some resemblance to what Joseph Roach describes as a shift from mechanism to sensibility in the realm of theater. See Roach, Player's Passion, esp. "Vitalism and the Crisis of Sensibility," 93–115. Nevertheless, the theoretical issues are significantly different, since acting was more easily accommodated within the prevailing aesthetic doctrine of imitation.

35. Antonio Planelli, Dell' opera in musica (Naples: Donato Campo, 1772), 106.

36. "Sembra in oltre manifesto, che i nostri nervi, come altrettante corde d'uno stromento, abbiano un tuono determinato. . . . E per quella corrispondenza, che passa tra il movimento di questi e le passioni dell'animo, il loro oscillamento ne desterà quella passione, che corrisponde a quel dato moto prodotto in essi." Planelli, Dell' opera in musica, 109–110.

37. Johann Nikolaus Forkel, Allgemeine Geschichte der Musik, vol. 1 (Leipzig: Schwickertschen Verlage, 1788), 3.

38. M. H. Abrams, The Mirror and the Lamp: Romantic Theory and the Critical Tradition (Oxford: Oxford University Press, 1953), 92.

nation of music's affective power. Any aesthetic specificity once accorded to musical objects had been collapsed into their vibrational mode of transmission to the listening subject. This was a new stage in theories of musical affect: the attunement *Affektenlehre*.[39]

The attunement *Affektenlehre* is the largest missing piece in the vital history of musical affect theories, and it most closely corresponds to twenty-first-century theories of affect. Within it are theories that are so allergic to representation—indeed they were built to avoid a problem in the theory of representation—that they are grounded in something wholly nonconceptual, namely, the physical materiality of sound vibrations. These theories attempt to account for a modification of the body that is not mediated by discourse or, rather, that explains something that discourse fails to explain.

If all of this materialism and corporeality sounds familiar to you, the reason is that peculiar attunements are back. Once again theorists and commentators on the arts have sought out ways of talking about affect that deemphasize its (long-held) relationships with representation, theories of the sign, and discourse. Once again it has become productive to offer up materialist accounts of the body's inner workings in order to bolster arguments about art. While this most recent posture is the result of a need to find new methodologies in the wake of the linguistic turn, the theory of affective attunement was the result of a crisis in aesthetic theory that arose when theorists sought out a nonmimetic account of musical sound.

Affect without Representation

Although the genealogy of affect theory is unbroken from the early modern era through to the present day, its popularity has been far from uniform. After the late eighteenth-century heyday of affective attunement, the discourse on musical immediacy went on to become a central component of early nineteenth-century romanticism in the writings of Johann Wolfgang von Goethe, Ludwig Tieck, Wilhelm Heinrich Wackenroder, and E. T. A. Hoff-

39. A recent growth of scholarship on attunement—particularly in its German manifestation as *Stimmung*—has placed emphasis on the post-Kantian developments of this figure. In chapters 2 and 4 of this book, I seek to uncover an earlier history of attunement that stretches further back in eighteenth-century aesthetic debates concerning music, mimesis, and affect. On *Stimmung*, see in particular David Wellbery, "Stimmung," in *Historisches Wörterbuch Ästhetischer Grundbegriffe*, ed. Karlheinz Barck et al., vol. 5 (Stuttgart: Metzler, 2003) 5:703–733; Hans Ulrich Gumbrecht, *Atmosphere, Mood*, Stimmung: *On a Hidden Potential of Literature*, trans. H. Erik Butler (Stanford, CA: Stanford University Press, 2012); and Erik Wallrup, *Being Musically Attuned: The Act of Listening to Music* (Farnham, UK: Ashgate, 2015).

mann.[40] Affect theory on the whole, however, became less central to aesthetics and instead had its center of gravity shifted, at the dawn of the new century, to the field of physiology; important contributions came from the anatomist Charles Bell and, later in the century, from Charles Darwin.[41] Since the mid-twentieth century, a new interest in affect has slowly radiated outward from the physiological and psychological sciences, taking firm hold within the critically oriented humanities and — once again — in theories of the arts. As we shall see, this return to aesthetic questions has brought with it dilemmas once rehearsed within the domain of music theory.

One of the most important immediate sources for contemporary affect theory is the work of the midcentury psychologist Silvan S. Tomkins, whose landmark multivolume *Affect, Imagery, Consciousness* (1962–1992) served as a major source of inspiration both within and beyond psychology.[42] In a recent compelling study on affect theory since the 1960s, Ruth Leys has described in detail the ongoing debate within emotions research to which Tomkins's work contributed. Tomkins and his followers, inspired by William James among others, espoused a noncognitive, nonintentional theory of the affects emphasizing corporeal processes and contrasting affect with meaning. The opposing camp, represented by cognitivists such as Richard Lazarus and philosophers such as Martha Nussbaum, Anthony Kenny, and Robert Solomon, has concentrated on the object orientation of the emotions and stressed their intentionality.[43] One crucial nuance of Tomkins's reaction to the cognitivist

40. See, for instance, Goethe's letter to Zelter of May 2, 1820: "Die reinste und höchste Malerei in der Musik ist die, welche du auch ausübst, es kommt darauf an, den Hörer in die Stimmung zu versetzen, welche das Gedicht angibt, in der Einbildungskraft bilden sich alsdann die Gestalten nach Anlaß des Textes, sie weiß nicht wie sie dazu kommt." Johann Wolfgang Goethe to C. F. Zelter, Carlsbad, May 2, 1820, in *Johann Wolfgang Goethe zwischen Weimar und Jena*, vol. 2, vols. 8–9 of *Sämtliche Werke: Briefe, Tagebücher und Gespräche* (Frankfurt am Main: Deutscher Klassiker Verlag, 1999), 47; or Wilhelm Heinrich Wackenroder, in his letter to Ludwig Tieck of May 2, 1792: "Es ist sonderbar, daß ich, in diese Stimmung versetzt, auch am beßten über Musik als Aesthetiker nachdenken kann, wenn ich Musik höre: es scheint, als rissen sich da von den Empfindungen die das Tonstück einflößt, allgemeine Ideen los, die sich mir dann schnell u[nd] deutlich vor die Seele stellen." Wackenroder to Tieck, May 5, 1792, in *Sämtliche Werke und Briefe*, ed. Silvio Vietta and Richard Littlejohns, vol. 2 (Heidelberg: Carl Winter Universitätsverlag, 1991), 29; see the genealogy traced in Wellbery, "Stimmung."

41. Charles Bell, *Essays on the Anatomy and Philosophy of Expression*, 2nd ed. (London: John Murray, 1824); Charles Darwin, *The Expression of the Emotions in Man and Animals* (New York: D. Appleton, 1886); and see also chapter 4 of this book.

42. Silvan S. Tomkins, *Affect, Imagery, Consciousness: The Complete Edition*, 2 vols. (New York: Springer, 2008).

43. Ruth Leys, "Introduction: Setting the Stage," in *Ascent of Affect*, 1–25. Leys's compelling and extremely well-documented critique is important for me because of her brilliant ability to summarize and render legible the state of psychological and philosophical scholarship on the

position has become extremely important in his subsequent reception: for Tomkins, affects are inherently objectless. As Leys writes, "for Tomkins the affects are non-intentional states."[44] In this model, affective experiences are defined as independent of objects.[45]

The definitional turn away from objects in Tomkins's thought was not — as eighteenth-century music theory can remind us — a novel swerve for theories of affect. But its impact on recent scholarship is hard to overestimate. This aspect of Tomkins's thinking went on to influence subsequent developments in the noncognitivist camp of emotions research within psychology, becoming a cornerstone of what Leys calls the "Tomkins-Ekman 'affect program theory' or Basic Emotion Theory."[46] It also found its way into the affect theories of Eve Sedgwick and Adam Frank, who brought Tomkins's work to the attention of scholars across the humanities and social sciences during the last decade of the twentieth century.[47]

Like Tomkins, Sedgwick and her followers were also looking for a powerful alternative to status quo thinking, although in a different intellectual context. If representation and discourse were the watchwords of critical thought during the middle decades of the twentieth century, the late 1990s and the early 2000s saw a turn toward the body, its autonomic processes, and those experiences for which language is seen as an inadequate tool. Theorists from across the humanities began a slow but decisive shift away from discourse and signification and toward materiality, away from epistemology and toward ontology. The effect on theory has been long lasting. In this critical context, Tomkins's nonintentional, corporeal, objectless theory of affect had and continues to have tremendous appeal.

Perhaps it is unsurprising, then, how frequently the Tomkins position has

---

emotions from the middle decades of the twentieth century to the present day. Leys and I also share a fundamental skepticism about affect theories that leave no room for affecting objects. But unlike Leys, I am uninterested in the scientific validity of contemporary affect theorists' claims (just as I am uninterested in the scientific validity of eighteenth-century affect theorists' claims) and want instead to draw attention to repeating patterns of thought within a longer history of affect theory.

44. Leys, *Ascent of Affect*, 32.

45. As Leys writes, "Tomkins then went on to argue that because the emotions are not tied to any one object but can be contingently attached to a vast range of objects, *they are intrinsically independent of all objects*. He therefore claimed that the multiplicity of objects of the affects means that the emotions are in principle objectless, and hence can be satisfied without the means-end logic of the drives." Leys, *Ascent of Affect*, 31 (emphasis in original).

46. Leys, *Ascent of Affect*, 3.

47. Sedgwick and Frank, "Shame in the Cybernetic Fold," 495–522; and Sedgwick and Frank, eds., *Shame and Its Sisters: A Silvan S. Tomkins Reader* (Durham, NC: Duke University Press, 1995).

been made to harmonize with that of another prominent follower of William James, Gilles Deleuze. Explicitly acknowledging his debt to the American philosopher, Deleuze describes the basic paradigm for affective experience in the following manner: "(1) the perception of a situation, (2) the modification of the body, a reinforcement or a weakening, (3) the emotion of consciousness or the mind."[48] There is a clear echo of Spinoza here, particularly with the inclusion of the increase or decrease in the body's power, but what is now missing is any mention at all of the objects in the world, much less their specific qualities or properties, that trigger affective responses in the first place. Also important in this context is the distinction between affect—which is the first, corporeal transformation—and emotion, the subsequent cognitive assessment thereof. Affect, for these twentieth-century theorists, is both something that happens to the body and something that can be read on the body. It concerns the subject, not the object. There is still a role for images in this system of thought, though they are now symptoms or markers of affect rather than their cause. Michael Hardt summarizes this new understanding clearly in his forward to the edited collection *The Affective Turn*: "Affects require us, as the term suggests, to enter the realm of causality, but they offer a complex view of causality because the affects belong simultaneously to both sides of the causal relationship. They illuminate, in other words, both our power to affect the world around us and our power to be affected by it, along with the relationship between these two powers."[49] Hardt endeavors to explain two sides of a causal relationship, though his active-passive polarity remains centered on the subject of affect. Indeed, the subject's body is found on both sides of this polarity: it occupies the site of inception as well as the site of reception. In this sense, contemporary affect theory continues a tradition of theorizing affective mediation, though it now concentrates on the transmission of affect between individuals.[50] Even when—in exceptional cases—contemporary affect theorists do consider an affecting object or its nature, they rarely venture to stipulate anything concrete in their description of it.[51]

48. Deleuze, "Shame and the Glory," 123.

49. Michael Hardt, "Foreword: What Affects Are Good For," in *The Affective Turn: Theorizing the Social*, ed. Patricia Clough with Jean Halley (Durham, NC: Duke University Press, 2007), ix.

50. As in Theresa Brennan's aptly titled *The Transmission of Affect* (Ithaca, NY: Cornell University Press, 2004).

51. See for instance Sara Ahmed, "Happy Objects," in *The Affect Theory Reader*, ed. Melissa Gregg and Gregory J. Seigworth (Durham NC: Duke University Press, 2010), 29–51. There are, of course, some significant exceptions. Jane Bennett, for instance, suggests a theory that admits of a wide variety of affective transfers among human and nonhuman actors, "a kind of geo-affect or material vitality," as she puts it. This essentially renders affect, for Bennett, equivalent

The most fascinating aspect of our current situation is that we have returned to affect theory in studies of the arts while nevertheless maintaining an
avoidance of discussing an affective object's qualities — a theoretical situation
not witnessed since the dilemmas of the eighteenth-century musical *Affektenlehre*. While eighteenth-century theorists had trouble construing musical objects as either natural or arbitrary signs, twenty-first-century theorists attempt
to avoid discussions of signification altogether in their assessments of art objects. The commitment, generally held among affect theorists of the past two
decades, is to concentrate on the immediate, precognitive aspects of aesthetic
experience and to elaborate the corporeal and material conditions of their
operation. Signification, in these theories, is understood as a subsequent cognitive assessment of that visceral immediacy; it is not discussed as something
emanating from the properties of objects themselves. This is what gives Simon
O'Sullivan license to claim, "Affects can be described as extra-discursive and
extra-textual. Affects are moments of *intensity*, a reaction in/on the body at the
level of matter. . . . They occur on a different, *asignifying* register. In fact this
is what differentiates art from language."[52] This sort of binary thinking, which
opposes the signifying power of language with the numinous domain of art,
is precisely what Lawrence Kramer has critiqued as a "logic of alterity."[53] Discourse, text, signification, and language are here all conflated and construed
as affect's others. They are, unsurprisingly, the buzzwords of the intellectual
moment that directly preceded the recent affective turn.

While eighteenth-century theories of affective attunement responded
to a crisis within the theory of mimesis precipitated by music, twenty-first-
century affect theories respond to a desire for alternatives to linguistic-turn-era
thought. Frustrated with the (then) widely held dogma contending that discourse shapes and underpins every human activity, theorists at the turn of

---

to all material force. Bennett, *Vibrant Matter: A Political Ecology of Things* (Durham, NC:
Duke University Press, 2010), 61. As Ruth Leys writes, "For Bennett, debate over ideology is
irrelevant. Her fantasy is rather of a language of nature that isn't itself a representation because
it consists of material vibrations or neural currents by which the affects are inevitably passed on,
though not exactly understood." Leys, *Ascent of Affect*, 349. For two alternative models with sub-
stantive discussions of objects — though not as invested in sharp distinctions between affect and
emotion — see in particular Jonathan Flatley, *Affective Mapping: Melancholia and the Politics
of Modernism* (Cambridge, MA: Harvard University Press, 2008); and Ngai, particularly in *Our
Aesthetic Categories*.

    52. Simon O'Sullivan, "The Aesthetics of Affect: Thinking Art beyond Representation," *An-
gelaki* 6, no. 3 (2001): 126.

    53. Lawrence Kramer, *Classical Music and Postmodern Knowledge* (Berkeley: University of
California Press, 1996), 34–40.

the twenty-first century felt as though their accounts were incomplete. They struck out to identify and describe those autonomic processes for which cognition comes "too late."[54] In so doing, they initiated a new strand of affect theory or, indeed, an entire "affective turn" that shares much with eighteenth-century theories of affective attunement. Both are committed to deciphering aesthetic experience but attempt (for rather different reasons) to avoid the attribution of aesthetic power to the signification of aesthetic objects. They draw, therefore, on similar resources. These theories emphasize the role of the body, concentrate on the physical and material properties of aesthetic experience, and make use of what the science of their day can explain about transference, mediation, and the mind-body relationship. They champion the immediate, the drastic, the automatic, the indescribable aspects of art.

This may be the reason why contemporary theories of affect sound so musical. Resonance and attunement remain powerful models of mediation, possessed of physical, observable corollaries in the natural world, and they have therefore retained a prominent place in the figurative language of affect theory. We still describe individuals as high-strung, low-key, or bad-tempered, referring to their temperament or tuning — phrasing derived from the *musica humana* tradition and disseminated through music theory. As Rei Terada notes, "The discourse of emotion is curiously saturated with musical metaphors, instruments figuring selves and music figuring feeling."[55] It was, perhaps, the persistence of this tradition that enticed Nam June Paik and Charlotte Moorman to insert a short "human cello" action into their performance of John Cage's *26'1.1499" for a String Player* (pictured on the cover); in it, a shirtless Paik knelt between Moorman's legs, pulling taut a single amplified cello string, which Moorman bowed, effectively transforming Paik into a resonant human instrument.[56]

But the musical correspondence is not only figurative for contemporary affect theorists. Several of the authors in this tradition use music and sound in paradigmatic or explanatory ways. Gregory Seigworth and Melissa Gregg, for instance, locate affect in "those resonances that circulate about, between,

54. Following Leys, "What the new affect theorists and the neuroscientists share is a commitment to the idea that there is a gap between the subject's affects and its cognition or appraisal of the affective situation or object, such that cognition or thinking comes 'too late' for reasons, beliefs, intentions, and meanings to play the role in action and behavior usually accorded to them." Leys, *Ascent of Affect*, 315.

55. Terada, *Feeling in Theory*, 92.

56. For more on this aspect of Moorman and Paik's performance, see especially Joan Rothfuss, *Topless Cellist: The Improbable Life of Charlotte Moorman* (Cambridge, MA: MIT Press, 2014), 113–114.

and sometimes stick to bodies and worlds."[57] For Lauren Berlant, "The transmission of noise performs political attachment as a sustaining intimate relation."[58] These theorists find a productive mediating force at work in raw noise or resonance, availing themselves of the burgeoning intellectual enthusiasm for sound in recent decades.[59]

Like the authors writing in the eighteenth-century tradition of affective attunement, contemporary affect theorists frequently concentrate their attention on the reverberating body of the affected subject. Affect itself, when they venture to describe it, is often rendered an abstract vibrational force or energy coming from an unspecified exterior. Thus Brian Massumi draws affect into comparison with intensity, relating both to "nonlinear processes: resonation and feedback which momentarily suspend the linear progress of the narrative present from past to future."[60] He goes on, in this formulation of affect, to stipulate, "It is not exactly passivity, because it is filled with motion, vibratory motion, resonation. . . . It resonates to the exact degree to which it is in excess of any narrative or functional line."[61] Massumi here employs a rhetorical strategy distinctive to contemporary affect theory, in which the definition of affect is quickly followed by concepts that it is defined against.[62] These most typically involve rational containment: category, narrative, sign, representation, and so forth. In contrast to these, affect for Massumi is an uncontainable force that reaches the subject by resonant, vibrational means.

Contemporary affect theorists differ from their eighteenth-century antecedents in that they frequently and explicitly posit a mind-body union. But in describing affect through sympathetic corporeal resonance, they nevertheless frequently wind up creating an inadvertent dualism between the body's sensation and the subject's mind. This is a phenomenon that Amy Cimini has called "cryptodualism," and it is a tendency toward which theorists of both

57. Gregory J. Seigworth and Melissa Gregg, "An Inventory of Shimmers," in *The Affect Theory Reader*, ed. Seigworth and Gregg (Durham, NC: Duke University Press, 2010), 1.

58. Lauren Berlant, *Cruel Optimism* (Durham, NC: Duke University Press, 2011), 224.

59. For prominent examples, see Brian Kane, *Sound Unseen: Acousmatic Sound in Theory and Practice* (Oxford: Oxford University Press, 2014); Jonathan Sterne, ed., *The Sound Studies Reader* (New York: Routledge, 2012); Trevor Pinch and Karin Bijsterveld, eds., *The Oxford Handbook of Sound Studies* (Oxford: Oxford University Press, 2012); and Jonathan Sterne, *The Audible Past: Cultural Origins of Sound Reproduction* (Durham, NC: Duke University Press, 2003).

60. Brian Massumi, *Parables for the Virtual: Movement, Affect, Sensation* (Durham, NC: Duke University Press, 2002), 26.

61. Massumi, *Parables of the Virtual*, 26.

62. On this point, see Eugenie Brinkema's incisive criticism in *The Forms of the Affects* (Durham, NC: Duke University Press, 2014), xiv.

time periods are tempted.[63] It is, therefore, an important component of this book's investigation. For my own theoretical purposes, I will use the term "subject" to indicate a mind-body union, though in my discussions of source material, I will endeavor to make clear the claims of authors in relation to mind, body, dualism, and cryptodualism.

On the whole, though, contemporary affect theorists often write prose that would nearly find itself at home in a work of eighteenth-century music theory, especially as they wax poetic about sound vibration. Consider in this light William Connolly's rebuttal of Ruth Leys's *Critical Inquiry* article "The Turn to Affect: A Critique," in which Connolly seeks further to delineate his object of study and the method of its operation. "Media mixtures of noise, rhythm, image, concept, and music touch the infrasensible register as they also convey conscious judgments. That register, again, precedes, augments, or intensifies the others in *something* like the way the subaudible vibrations of organ music infuse the composition of moods without themselves being felt."[64] The content of this passage could well have come directly from an eighteenth-century attunement materialist like Diderot, though Connolly's awareness of the intellectual legacy is less interesting than the renewed relevance of music, noise, sound vibration, and sympathetic resonance as explanatory mechanisms for affect in the present day.

Twenty-first-century affect theory, with its focus on the affected subject and avoidance of the distinctive aesthetic properties of affecting objects, finds a ready and reliable resource in affective attunement — the outgrowth of and the forgotten chapter from the eighteenth-century *Affektenlehre*. Like its historical antecedent, this manifestation of affect without representation uses the sounding vibrations of attunement as a form of mediation for free, because affective attunement provides a way of accounting for aesthetic impact without having to stipulate anything specific about the nature of its initiating object. Both the late eighteenth century and the twenty-first are attracted to this model, and both find within it a happy solution for avoiding representation. For thinkers in the eighteenth century, it provided a solution to the long-standing misfit of musical sound with the theory of imitation; for thinkers in our own century, it provides an alternative to the now-unfashionable reliance on text, discourse, and signification that characterized critical thought

---

63. Amy Cimini, "How to Do Things with Dualism: The Political Expedience of the Musical Mind-Body Problem," in "Baruch Spinoza and the Matter of Music: Toward a New Practice of Theorizing Musical Bodies" (PhD diss., New York University, 2011), 21–84.

64. William E. Connolly, "Critical Response I: The Complexity of Intention," *Critical Inquiry* 37, no. 4 (2011): 795.

at the end of the twentieth. In both cases, the initiating objects of affect are missing — they have been dissolved into the processes of their transmission and into the bodies of subjects that receive them.

There are plenty of reasons to be worried about this development within the humanities: the way, first of all, that it seems to grasp for a solid hold on the real, as though vibration and materiality had some extra purchase on existence that ideas and significations do not; or perhaps the way that this kind of affect theory reinscribes dualisms in its celebration of the body, the immediate, and the sensorium and in its concomitant denigration of thought; or even the way that this line of thinking, especially in its more romantic incarnations, hints toward an older notion of musical transcendence that has not been part of the discourse on music and feeling since the mid-twentieth century.[65]

These developments are potentially worrying, though what motivates them is what we have not yet understood: the structure of events in intellectual history that created these parallel historical turns away from representation and toward affect. The reason we have not yet fully understood the repeating return to affect is that we have not yet understood affect dialectically.

Dialectics of Affect

At the opening of Dubos's celebrated *Réflexions critiques sur la poésie et sur la peinture* (1719), the author sets his task. We all know of the pleasure that arises from art, he asserts, "but it is difficult to explain what this pleasure consists in."[66] Dubos's charge, then, will be nothing short of "instructing others of the manner in which their own sentiments arise in them." "I therefore cannot hope for the reader's approval," he continues, "if I do not succeed in making known to him that which passes within himself; that is, in short, the most intimate movements of his heart."[67] Dubos, standing at the opening of eighteenth-century affective aesthetics, has committed himself to an impossible task. He will settle for nothing less than explaining to his readers the innermost states of feeling that even they themselves cannot understand.

Dubos's introduction rehearses a typical paradox: affect, on its own, is an

---

65. For one recent and notable exception, see Pieter Van den Toorn, *Music, Politics, and the Academy* (Berkeley: University of California Press, 1995).

66. "Mais il n'est pas moins difficile d'expliquer en quoi consiste ce plaisir." Dubos, *Réflexions*, 1.

67. "C'est vouloir instruire les autres de la maniere dont leurs propres sentimens naissent en eux. Ainsi je ne sçaurois esperer d'être approuvé si je ne parviens point à fair connoitre au Lecteur dans mon livre ce qui se passe en lui-même, en un mot les mouvemens les plus intimes de son cœur." Dubos, *Réflexions*, 3.

elusive experience that resists the capture of description. It is said to be a nearly indescribable state of being, for which our tools of rationality are inadequate. And so as a result, we use the supreme instruments of rationality, especially the taxonomy, to capture it. Affect therefore emerges as a concrete entity only when it has been doubled through a kind of estrangement or opposition in the form of theory; the two make each other possible. The supposed indescribability of affect—its nondiscursiveness, its immediacy—only fuels our attempts to describe it. But despite our best efforts, our theories of affect always appear to be lacking something. They might seem somehow incomplete or inadequate, or they might not match up with other scholars' accounts of the same phenomenon (recall Buelow's criticism of the *Affektenlehre*, or think of the ever-proliferating and often-conflicting definitions of affect in recent decades). As even the arch-taxonomist Johann Mattheson wrote of affects early in the eighteenth century, "the more one aspires to determine something positive about them, the more contradictions one may find, since the opinions about this material are almost numberless."[68] And so affect theory, through its attempts and its contradictions, therefore bolsters the notion that affect is indescribable and uncapturable, and the entire process is in position to repeat. The opposition between affect's drastic immediacy and affect theory's calculated Gnosticism is mutually reinforcing.[69]

The shape of this opposition bears a resemblance to the central duality of the historical period at the heart of this study: the Enlightenment conflict—first diagnosed by Hegel—between faith and pure insight. Faith, like affect, is pure content with no method for or desire to determine the truth. Pure insight, like the instruments of reason that attempt to understand affect, will tolerate nothing that does not measure up to its standard of self-evidence, even while it is completely devoid of any content itself. These twin eighteenth-century impulses are mutually dependent; the existence of the one reinforces the practice of the other. The historiography of Hegel's account of faith and pure insight in the *Phenomenology of Spirit* has influenced this study, as has the dialectical understanding of these foundational Enlightenment impulses.[70]

---

68. "Allein je mehr man sich bestreben wolte, etwas positives davon zu statuiren, je mehr contradicentes würden sich vielleicht finden, sintemahl die Meinungen in dieser Materie fast unzehlig sind." Johann Mattheson, *Das neu-eröffnete Orchestre* (Hamburg: Mattheson and Benjamin Schillers Witwe, 1713), 252.

69. Carolyn Abbate, "Music—Drastic or Gnostic?," *Critical Inquiry* 30, no. 3 (2004): 505–536.

70. G. W. F. Hegel, *Phenomenology of Spirit*, trans. A. V. Miller (Oxford: Oxford University Press, 1977), §§ 527–529, pp. 321–324. On this particular aspect of the *Phenomenology of Spirit*,

The conflict between faith and pure insight is also the basis for what Max Horkheimer and Theodor Adorno identified as the "dialectic of Enlightenment," the structure of which has also inspired the methodology of this investigation. It is not incidental that one of the central examples in their text, the story of Odysseus and the Sirens, concerns affect and music. There could be no better allegory for the inscription of affect theory. Like Odysseus, we seek to give ourselves over to the affects in the writing of affect theory, but in so doing, we must alienate ourselves from them in the form of rationality and in the bounded constraints of scholarship. As Horkheimer and Adorno point out, "the estrangement from nature that [Odysseus] brings about is realized in the process of the abandonment to nature."[71] There is cryptodualism at work here too; Odysseus allows himself to hear and experience the Sirens' music because his body is constrained. This cryptodualist abandonment to and estrangement from the affective power of music finds expression just as much in Odysseus's tethers as it does in the taxonomic instruments of affect theory. Both would appear to have constrained the auditor with a form of bondage, but through that bondage, they permit access to what would otherwise be overwhelming.

So there is something about the nature of affect itself that requires dialectical thinking — something that we attempt to capture but that refuses to be captured. But this is not just a synchronic duality nestled within the concept of affect theory; it is also the structure of a diachronic unfolding within the history of ideas. First, affect is said to provide an important explanatory tool for theories of representation in art; affect is a component of the rational explanation for art's power and takes account of the objects that stir the affects in subjects; affect explains the power of the sign. But as affect theory evolves and the challenges of capturing affect are played out, theorists begin to contrast affect with rationality, with language, and even with all of signification. Affect theory begins to focus on the affected states of subjects and to avoid engaging the specific properties of the objects that engender them. Affect becomes nondiscursive, purely corporeal, precognitive, or opposed to language and the sign. Affect is said, again, to be ungraspable, even while we continue to try to grasp it.

It is the contention of this book that the dialectics endemic to theorizing affect have also shaped periods of its history. That is, something about the form or structure of affect theory has produced similar intellectual dilemmas

see Jean Hyppolite, *Genesis and Structure of Hegel's "Phenomenology of Spirit,"* trans. Samuel Cherniak and John Heckman (Evanston, IL: Northwestern University Press, 1974), 426–447.

71. Max Horkheimer and Theodor W. Adorno, *Dialectic of Enlightenment*, trans. John Cumming (New York: Continuum, 1989), 48.

at two different historical moments. The synchronic dialectics of affect theory are part of its diachronic unfolding. With sustained attention to the eighteenth century, and particularly to the *Affektenlehre*, this book explains one way in which the dilemmas of twenty-first-century affect theory were historically prefigured. It also demonstrates the special relevance of music for these problems, since music shares with affect contested relationships to signification and language.

Like Horkheimer and Adorno's study, this book locates its central concept in disparate historical periods, even while there is one period — the eighteenth century — that proves most crucial. There is therefore no single, stable term — *Affekt* or *passio*, for example — that maps consistently from this earlier period to our own. Different theorists in different periods use various terms to describe the same phenomenon. The endeavor made here is to abstract from terminology (not making much of word identities or nonidentities) and to inspect the workings of each of the theories in a formal manner in order to identify their dynamics, drawing their conceptual structures into comparison.[72] That is why contemporary theoretical terminology will often gloss historical concepts in this book. Neither, it should be said, is there a single definition or description of affect that remains exactly consistent from theorist to theorist — indeed, the nuances are a major component of the investigation. Instead the comparison is drawn on the basis of the phenomenon we now call affect, and the effort is to understand its precursors, its elaboration, and its evolution during two distinct historical periods. It is this comparative method that reveals a dynamic much like the one Horkheimer and Adorno find in the *Dialectic of Enlightenment*. And so, because the terms have changed and the concepts have shifted, it is left to us to sort through the meaning of this tradition, to identify its dynamics, and to understand its history.

The Musical Antecedents of Contemporary Affect Theory

In order to understand contemporary affect theory, we must confront its musical antecedents. This is currently the most obscure aspect of affect theory's history, not only because contemporary affect theorists are reluctant to discuss it but also because musicologists have been slow to join the conversation. The documents of historical music theory that are pertinent to this history are

---

72. Scholars have previously noted the terminological difficulties that attend historical work in affect theory. See the discussions in Paola-Ludovika Coriando, *Affektenlehre und Phänomenologie der Stimmungen: Wege einer Ontologie und Ethik des Emotionalen* (Frankfurt: Vittorio Klostermann, 2002), 6–8; and Hultquist, "Introductory Essay," 274–275.

mostly untranslated or only partially translated. They require a great deal of interpretation in order to be made relevant to a wider audience since, until now, they have been read by only a handful of specialists. This book seeks to remedy these problems and to demonstrate the importance of this history for the intellectual concerns of the present day. It is, for that reason, a work in the history of music theory. But it asks historical music theory to do some heavy lifting to which it has not always been accustomed and to be responsible for the intellectual legacy of a widely used and broadly understood domain of critical theory. It asks historical music theory to explain its relevance to the humanities at large. This is why the examinations of music in this book will not involve or require notated musical examples or esoteric terminology; the substance of the investigation should be accessible to all who are interested in affect or in music.

The narrative traced in this book begins in the late seventeenth century, with the stabilization of musical conventions that took place in the opera theater. Chapter 1 concerns the aesthetics of early modern opera — the *dramma per musica* and the *tragédie en musique* — the dramatic spectacle that united poetry with stage action and music to create an integrated series of mimetic representations for its audiences. Music's affective power was clearly felt in this medium, though theorists around the turn of the century could only gesture toward its method of operation. Their efforts form the body of knowledge I call the mimetic *Affektenlehre*. Studying early modern opera and the affect theory that attempted to explain it provides us with a clear contrast to the affect theory of the present day, while also demonstrating some of the central pitfalls of taxonomic affect programs.

Chapter 2 focuses on comic opera, which emerged as a metatheatrical commentary on the conventions of serious opera. In its mockery of the mimetic doctrine, comic opera forced critics to articulate what was new about its musical style. It therefore precipitated a new wave in the *Affektenlehre* that severed music's affective power from the operations of mimesis and from the structure of signification as it was understood within aesthetic theory. Critics built on earlier claims concerning opera's appeal to the body and the senses in order to propose new resonance-based theories of affective attunement. The chapter concludes with an assessment of Diderot's experimental contribution to the new theory of affective attunement in *Le neveu de Rameau*.

Chapter 3 shifts the discussion to instrumental music, another problem area for eighteenth-century aesthetics. Since critics already questioned the ability of music to function as a sign and to move listeners within the multimedia spectacle of opera, they were even more dubious about instrumental music. Lacking any clear mimetic capacity, instrumental music seemed to make its appeal directly to and only to the body of the listener, providing a mere corporeal tickle. Even worse, composers of instrumental music were slowly adopting techniques from comic opera, showcasing their ability to hybridize styles. Most critics found the result disorderly, confusing, and lacking in content, equating instrumental music to a performing body without a soul. Nevertheless, a small group of thinkers began to propose an alternative, cryptodualist solution: they posited that it was specifically music's special material relationship with the body that made it so effective at moving the souls of its auditors to the affects.

The theoretical texts of the attunement *Affektenlehre* are the focus of chapter 4. In the wake of debates surrounding both comic opera and instrumental music, theorists felt the need to offer a new explanatory mechanism for musical affect. They turned, in this endeavor, to the empirical phenomenon of sympathetic resonance, postulating a mechanical operation whereby the vibration of musical sound could stimulate the nerves of the human body; the interior of the listener was then said to be attuned to the affect through this nonrepresentational, corporeal mode of transmission. Scrutinizing the details of these attunement theories, the chapter concludes with an early nineteenth-century critique made of sense-certainty.

Having thus traced the eighteenth-century *Affektenlehre* from its mimetic mode to its nonrepresentational, corporeal instantiation as affective attunement, we return to twenty-first-century theoretical questions. The coda finds in more recent theory a certain musicality and a tendency to rehearse dynamics that once played out within historical music theory. This final chapter closes with a call to restore diachronicity and movement to affect theory: to think affect historically and therefore to pay close attention to the movements between objects and subjects that have generated it.

What this study offers, then, is a historical, dialectical, musical reassessment of affect theory. It stems from the conviction that early modern affect theory and contemporary affect theory form parts of a tradition with definable contours and describable patterns. And it demonstrates that our twenty-first-century, objectless, nonrepresentational formulation of affect is not new and that it might be a temptation toward which — like music — affect theory is ineluctably drawn.

1
Eighteenth-Century Opera and the Mimetic *Affektenlehre*

The Powers of Music

Lully's *Armide*, which premiered at the Paris Opéra in 1686, tells a story of the eponymous Muslim warrior princess and her struggle against the Christian knight Renaud. The entire opera revolves around the interior feeling life of its protagonist. At its dramatic crux is a scene that so captivated the attention of critics that it became a prism through which eighteenth-century musical affect theory was refracted. The turbulent reception history of *Armide* demonstrates the assembly of a fragile network of ideas connecting music, signification, mimesis, and affect in the early modern era. It is this set of ideas that I call the mimetic *Affektenlehre*: an unstable consensus among theorists that music could employ formal conventions in order to act as a sign and evoke specific affects in audiences.

Armide begins in Damascus, which is decorated in celebration of the title character's recent victory over Christian Crusaders. Armide's confidants applaud her bravery, but Armide herself remains fixated on the single knight who managed to escape. Renaud, she admits, is haunting her dreams. The people of Damascus attempt to reassure Armide and mount a series of dances praising her beauty and her power. But the celebrations are interrupted when Armide's fears are realized and a messenger brings news that Renaud has single-handedly set the captive knights free.

Act 2 of the opera opens in the desert countryside, where Renaud has strayed from his fellow warriors. Armide and her uncle Hiradot, the king of Damascus, magically transform the landscape around Renaud into an irresistible oasis that lulls the Christian knight to sleep. Armide now has her chance, and she takes the stage to sing one of the most memorable and remarked-on passages of music in opera history, "Enfin, il est en ma puissance."

> Finally, he is in my power,
> This fatal enemy, this arrogant conqueror.
> The charm of sleep gives him over to my vengeance.
> I will pierce his invincible heart.
>
> Enfin, il est en ma puissance,
> Ce fatal ennemi, ce superbe vainqueur.
> Le charme du sommeil le livre à ma vengeance.
> Je vais percer son invincible cœur.[1]

As she approaches the sleeping Renaud, Armide begins an ascending melody in E minor that approximates the natural intervals of a trumpet signaling victory. "Finally he is in my power!" she exclaims, concluding on "puissance" with a triumphant trill. Armide begins to shift key as she calls Renaud her "fatal enemy," coming to a confident close in a new, certain key area of G major as she describes his emotional distance, his haughtiness as a warrior. Armide's music underscores Renaud's emotional wound to her, over and above his actions as a combatant in war.[2] As she describes his sleep, Armide's vocal line itself reposes, moving in smaller intervals as it declines on the staff. Then, with new insistence, Armide's singing confidently ascends, coming to a close in the home key of E minor as she intones her powerful vow to pierce Renaud's heart.[3]

> Because of him all of my captives have escaped their bonds
> Let him feel all of my rage . . .
>
> Par lui, tous mes captifs sont sortis d'esclavage.
> Qu'il éprouve toute ma rage . . .[4]

With these words, Armide hesitates for the first time. Somehow during the declaration of fury, her music has gone off course, bending away from the home key and on its way toward a harmonic destination not yet known.

---

1. Jean-Baptiste Lully, *Armide*, ed. Lois Rosow (Hildesheim: Georg Olms, 2003), 15.

2. Jean-Philippe Rameau, *Observations sur notre instinct pour la musique et sur son principe* (Paris: Prault fils, Lambert, Duchesne, 1754), 70. On Rameau's analysis, see Charles Dill, *Monstrous Opera: Rameau and the Tragic Tradition* (Princeton, NJ: Princeton University Press, 1998), 60–67; and also Cynthia Verba, *Music and the French Enlightenment: Rameau and the "Philosophes" in Dialogue*, 2nd ed. (Oxford: Oxford University Press, 2016), 23–33.

3. Rameau, *Observations*, 81–82.

4. Lully, *Armide*, 15.

Armide makes her attempt to strike the fatal blow but halts in action.[5] Both she and the accompanying orchestra fall silent. She is in the grip of a new affective state — one she cannot yet articulate to herself.

> What trouble seizes me! What makes me hesitate!
> What does pity want to say to me on his behalf?
> Let me strike . . . Heaven! What can be stopping me!
> Let me finish! I shudder! Let me avenge myself . . . I sigh!

> Quel trouble me saisit! qui me fait hésiter!
> Qu'est-ce qu'en sa faveur la pitié me veut dire?
> Frappons . . . Ciel! qui peut m'arrêter!
> Achevons . . . je frémis! Vengeons-nous . . . je soupire![6]

As Armide attempts introspection, she wanders harmonically, reaching temporary stopping points in G major, C major, and A minor. Her effort to understand her own internal transformation unsuccessful, she makes another break for action. "Frappons! Ciel!" she exhorts herself, returning to the home key of E minor and outlining the same victorious melody with which she entered.[7] This is her bid to remain in control and to use the force of reason against whatever other power has undermined it. But this effort to fulfill her original mission is thwarted again. She tells us that something is stopping her, even as she calls for herself to engage: "Achevons . . . Vengeons-nous." Harmonically, Armide is preparing the way for a different key area, and she finds it with a firm cadence in sweet G major as she tells us that she sighs.

> Is this how I must avenge myself today?
> My anger removes itself when I approach him.
> The more I look at him, the more my fury is in vain,
> My trembling arm refuses my hatred.
> Ah! What cruelty to rob him of life!
> To this young hero all on earth accede.
> Who could believe that he was made only for war?
> He seems to be made for love.

> Est-ce ainsi que je dois me venger aujourd'hui!
> Ma colère s'éteint quand j'approche de lui.

---

5. "Armide va pour frapper Renaud, et ne peut exécuter le dessein qu'elle a de lui ôter la vie." Lully, *Armide*, 16.

6. Lully, *Armide*, 16.

7. Rameau, *Observations*, 96–100.

Plus je le vois, plus ma fureur est vaine,
Mon bras tremblant se refuse à ma haine.
Ah ! quelle cruauté de lui ravir le jour!
À ce jeune héros tout cède sur la terre.
Qui croirait qu'il fût né seulement pour la guerre?
Il semble être fait pour l'amour.[8]

Armide has decided that her revenge will be sweeter if, rather than killing Renaud, she manages to seduce him and thereby humiliate the cool, distant soldier. This is a calculated choice: it is a decision to exert command over Renaud in precisely the way that the mere sight of his sleeping body has disordered Armide. At the opening of the scene, our protagonist appears to be in complete possession of herself. She imitates the utilitarian war signal of a brass instrument. She is focused on her target. But at the moment she instructs herself to strike, a new affective state overtakes her. At first she registers her inability to understand the transformation that has occurred ("What can be stopping me," she asks), but she soon realizes that she has recognized Renaud's humanity ("What cruelty to rob him of life!") and even his charm ("He seems to be made for love"). Now to kill him no longer seems satisfactory. Instead, Armide must control the way Renaud feels.

"Enfin, il est en ma puissance" represents the pinnacle of seventeenth-century French *tragédie en musique*. Within this tradition of sung tragedy, music was said to support and amplify the meaning of the libretto's poetry. As Jean-Baptiste Dubos later put it, music's primary ability was "to add new power to poetry and to set it in such a manner that it is able to make a greater impression upon us."[9] As in the general aesthetic framework for all early opera, music provided a distinct affective tincture for every moment in the drama — even those that were not sung — assisting in the work of mimesis.

This was, at least, the conceit that guided the extensive criticism surrounding "Enfin, il est en ma puissance" through the eighteenth century. Later thinkers remembered Lully's opera as a model of operatic practice, and Armide's dramatic act 2 scene eventually became a litmus test for the perceived success or failure of operatic aesthetics in general; its merits and its detriments

8. Lully, *Armide*, 16.

9. "Pour donner une nouvelle force à la Poësie & pour la mettre en état de faire sur nous une plus grande impression." Jean-Baptiste Dubos, *Réflexions critiques sur la poésie et sur la peinture*, vol. 1 (Paris: Jean Mariette, 1719), 634.

were continually debated through the century.[10] When Jean-Philippe Rameau looked back at "Enfin, il est en ma puissance" in his 1754 *Observations sur notre instinct pour la musique,* he saw not only Lully's work but also, somewhat anachronistically, the entire history of operatic convention stretching from Lully's day to his own. For Rameau, each musical detail, each melodic fragment, and choice of harmony held dramatic significance. "Lully thinks in grand terms," he wrote, praising the musical intuition of an artist whose careful choice of harmonies demonstrated "the great stroke of the Master."[11] In Rameau's reading, every last measure of Armide's music could be shown to augment and sensationalize the meaning of the operatic poetry. Lully's late seventeenth-century intentions aside, what Rameau saw in "Enfin" in the middle of the eighteenth century was a tradition he had inherited — a tradition in which musical gestures were systematically coordinated with dramatic meaning.

Seventeenth- and early eighteenth-century opera, with its predictable forms and plotlines, nurtured a budding set of musical codes and conventions that allowed the multimedia opera ensemble to create a mimetic artwork. Rhythm, meter, melodic shape, harmony, choice of key, and many other musical parameters all contributed to a system around which a new consensus had formed. Music was now a powerful component in opera's imitation of the natural and the supernatural. If Lully's "Enfin, il est en ma puissance" signaled the maturity of the late seventeenth-century version of this practice, for Rameau it marked the opening of a tradition he himself now led.

Early modern opera's conventionality gave rise to two developments that need to be understood in dialogue with each other: the first was an operatic poetics with a significant musical component, and the second was the mimetic *Affektenlehre,* a set of music theory documents that attempted to capture the technical basis of this poetics in musical terms. Early modern opera and the *Affektenlehre*: these two things need to be thought of as part of a single aesthetic movement. Composers, critics, operagoers, and theorists alike all knew that convention was taking shape and that they could — at least by the first decades of the eighteenth century — specify something definite about the way that it was happening in music. But there was a shade on this bright new adventure in meaning. Both in the world of operatic practice and

---

10. In particular, this portion of recitative becomes the focal point of one of the many quarrels between Rameau and Rousseau, discussed further under the subheading "The Powers of Music Lost" and also in greater detail in Verba, *Music and the French Enlightenment.*

11. Rameau, *Observations,* 78, 75.

in the world of theory, there was a sense that the entire system was flimsy and imperfect, indeed that it was merely a dull echo of something much more powerful known only to the ancient world and now lost forever. There was a melancholic, even nostalgic aspect to early serious opera, as there was also to the mimetic *Affektenlehre*. Both developments realized that they were nearly in the grasp of some new understanding just about to take shape but that even as they approached it, it somehow receded.

Read as a group, the documents in the mimetic *Affektenlehre* tradition do not provide evidence that any set of correspondences linking musical materials and affective states was ever generally agreed on. Quite the opposite: theorists in this tradition contradicted each other and even themselves both in content and method. But, more importantly, the growth of this discourse testifies to a general excitement that such correspondences between music and affect might exist and that they could be specified by studying the conventionality of widespread musical practices, particularly opera. This is why early modern opera and the mimetic *Affektenlehre* developed together, in mutual influence.

The Codes and Conventions of Early Modern Opera

At the opening of the eighteenth century, the art form of opera had already spread across western Europe. This practice of musicalized literary theater was cultivated not only in the courts — which were interested in its classicized portrayal of sovereignty — but also in the major city centers, in independent opera houses and in theaters that hosted bands of traveling opera performers. Opera captivated Europeans as a way of illuminating historical characters and dramas as well as portraying intricate fantasies of the supernatural. While the latter was more closely associated with the French *tragédie en musique* and the former with the Italian *dramma per musica*, the basic conceit was the same: new poetry on classical subjects was realized onstage with music, dance, elaborate sets and consumes, and in some cases with machinery for special effects. It was often dazzling and spectacular, which meant that critics were simultaneously enraptured and also somewhat worried about the excess of this relatively new art.[12]

12. On this period of the French *tragédie en musique* and the attempt to develop a distinctly French poetics of opera, see Catherine Kintzler, *Poétique de l'opéra français de Corneille à Rousseau* (Paris: Minerve, 1991); on the *drama per musica*, see Reinhard Strohm, "Introduction: The *Drama per Musica* in the Eighteenth Century," in *Dramma per Musica: Italian Opera Seria of the Eighteenth Century* (New Haven, CT: Yale University Press, 1997), 1–29; and Melania Bucciarelli, *Italian Opera and European Theatre, 1680–1720: Plots, Performers, Dramaturgies*

The important differences among the French and Italian practices and the more local traditions that blossomed in the English, German, and Spanish languages are united in the vital set of formal commonalities that run through them all. The serious genres (in contrast to some comic and parodic offshoots) were sung entirely through, alternating between recitative and aria. Although it is an exaggeration to say that all of the action of the opera took place in rec- itatives and that the subsequent emotional reflection on that action took place in the arias, it is nevertheless true that the structure of an opera was typically a dependable alternation between these two modes of performance. Characters were brought onto the stage to join the drama and rotated out after singing their aria. As Martha Feldman has put it, "the result was a series of stage pic- tures, shifting in density by graduated degrees before peaking at resolution."[13] Countless different narratives could be built out of this same formal plan.

In a recent and significant study, Emily Wilbourne has demonstrated how the Italian theatrical practices of the commedia dell'arte provided an import- ant precursor for early opera — especially the Italian *dramma per musica*. The commedia dell'arte did more than simply influence the later development of comic opera. Rather, its stock characters and formulaic plots created for all op- era the template of a dramatic logic grounded in repeated conventions.[14] The aria itself is one of these — a convention within which smaller-scale conven- tions were nurtured and solidified. Its traditional da capo form — an ABA struc- ture in which the return to A was often embellished with improvisation — lent itself to the portrayal of one or two contrasting affects. It is in the structured space of the aria that we come to know the depth of each operatic character and his or her relationships to events and others. As Pietro Metastasio tells us, arias could convey "characters, situations, affects, opinions, and reasonings."[15] As in oratory, arias employed figures and rhetorical devices to paint their sub- jects; this was as true for their poetry as it was for their musical design.

(Turnhout: Brepolis, 2000); on this period of opera in general, see Gary Tomlinson, "Early Mod- ern Opera," in *Metaphysical Song: An Essay on Opera* (Princeton, NJ: Princeton University Press, 1999), 34–67.

13. Martha Feldman, *Opera and Sovereignty: Transforming Myths in Eighteenth-Century Italy* (Chicago: University of Chicago Press, 2007), 47; on this point, see also Gregory J. Decker, "Pastorals, Passepieds, and Pendants: Interpreting Characterization through Aria Pairs in Han- del's *Rodelinda*," *Music Theory Online* 19, no. 4 (2013), http://mtosmt.org/issues/mto.13.19.4 /mto.13.19.4.decker.html.

14. Emily Wilbourne, *Seventeenth-Century Opera and the Sound of the Commedia dell'Arte* (Chicago: University of Chicago Press, 2016), 1–18.

15. "Caratteri, situazioni, affetti, senso, ragione." Quoted in Paolo Gallarati, *Musica e ma- schera: Il libretto italiano del setteccento* (Turin: EdT, 1984), 60.

Opera's formal conventionality was a resource for the art insofar as it afforded an iterability for its codes and therefore allowed them to become broadly intelligible. Similar processes occurred in other forms of sacred and secular texted music, but critics spilled the most ink on opera. As we shall see, opera's formal regularities also rendered it vulnerable to criticisms of predictability and structural rigidity. Nevertheless, it was through these dependable forms that composers began systematically to link musical gestures with signified meanings and thus that musical figures and patterns began to hold affective force for the audiences of operas.

Consider the lament. With its origins as a literary topic in Greek antiquity, the lament was primed for special treatment in opera. Already during the seventeenth century it had become a recurring element in operatic drama, and it quickly became coupled with a specific set of musical features: a slowly descending, repeated bass line (a "descending tetrachord" to be exact, in which the bass sinks four scale degrees before repeating), a cycling harmonic pattern that drives the repetition of that bass line, and frequently (though not always) the minor mode. Early vocal laments, such as Monteverdi's *Lamento della ninfa* (1638), prepared the way for the formalized lament opera aria, which spread beyond the Italian tradition even before the close of the seventeenth century.[16]

"When I Am Laid in Earth," Dido's lament from Purcell's *Dido and Aeneas* (1689), is one of the most famous lament arias, with an extensive reception history. Nahum Tate's libretto for the opera differs in many respects from the narrative in Virgil's *Aeneid*, but Dido's suicide and its motivation remain intact. When Dido hears that Aeneas plans to abandon her, no amount of his subsequent recanting will bring her comfort. "For 'tis enough, whate'er you now decree," she sings to Aeneas, "that you had once a thought of leaving me."[17] Dido's lament aria takes the place of any explicit description of suicide. We know of her intentions not only from what she sings but from the way she sings it.

When I am laid, am laid in earth,
May my wrongs create

---

16. The earliest seventeenth-century musical laments were not, in fact arias; the spontaneous outpouring of emotion that this gesture signifies was thought unfit for the contained space of that form. But by the end of the century, the convention had shifted, and the lament aria was a common type. See Ellen Rosand, "The Descending Tetrachord: An Emblem of Lament," *Musical Quarterly* 65, no. 3 (1979): 346–359; Rosand, "*Il lamento*: The Fusion of Music and Drama," in *Opera in Seventeenth-Century Venice* (Berkeley: University of California Press, 1990), 361–386; and Tomlinson, *Metaphysical Song*, 52–54.

17. Henry Purcell, *Dido and Aeneas*, ed. under the supervision of the Purcell Society by Margaret Laurie (Borough Green, UK: Novello, 1979), 90.

No trouble, no trouble in thy breast,
Remember me! Remember me! But ah! Forget my fate.
Remember me! But ah! Forget my fate.[18]

Dido's lament begins with a single line of music, and this line is the most important marker of the lament genre: a slowly descending bass. This particular G minor bass-line descent is chromatic, moving down by only half steps. A short figure completes the last few notes of the line, preparing for the repetition of the pattern. Dido's voice enters with the rest of the strings, which fill in the repeating harmonic sequence that will drive the pattern forward and instigate its return. The orchestral accompaniment is mimetic not only of the sounds of weeping—with the slowly falling bass—but also of fixation and obsession.[19] Purcell's treatment of Dido's vocal line against the repeating ostinato is distinctive. The accompaniment pattern ends in the middle of Dido's second line of text, on "create," beginning its next cycle on "No trouble," so that Dido's cadence on "thy breast" occurs in the interior of the pattern. This staggered arrangement then itself repeats, creating a second-order reiteration of the entire structure.

Dido begins the second half of the aria with a plaint on a single pitch, "Remember me! Remember me!" which she interjects over the ostinato, leaving space for the orchestra to shine through. Purcell sets her next line, "But ah! Forget my fate," in two different ways; the first iteration extends the "ah" on a figure that descends and then returns upward; the second takes the opposite shape, ascending on the "ah" syllable before descending to the cadence on "Forget my fate." This final sentiment marks the only alignment of Dido's melodic cadence with the closure of the accompaniment. Everything has fallen into place with this last request. After a further repetition of the entire structure from "Remember me," Purcell closes the aria with an orchestral postlude. This music is imitative, with each string instrument group echoing the next in a cascading series of falling lines that pull downward by half steps until the final close. The instrumental postlude is a troped lament topic, with its lament-like melodies crafted over the lament bass.

Not every lament aria was so uniform in its adherence to this formula. Slight differences in the treatment of the lament material could create a textured image, and da capo form arias could include a contrasting affect in the B section. Cleopatra's aria "Piangerò," from Handel's *Giulio Cesare* (1724) is an example of both of these. The aria takes place at the opening of the third act of the opera and marks Cleopatra's capture by Ptolemy. Unlike the suicidal

18. Purcell, *Dido and Aeneas*, 94–96.
19. Rosand, *"Il lamento,"* 370.

Dido, Cleopatra has not accepted any fate on her own terms, and her lament appropriately conveys a nuanced form of mourning mixed with resilient hope and, in the B section, extreme anger.[20]

I will weep, I will weep over my fate
So cruel and especially wicked
As long as I have life in my breast.

Piangerò, piangerò, la sorte mia,
sì crudele e tanto ria,
finchè vita in petto avrò.[21]

The aria begins with the characteristic, slowly descending bass line of a lament, though its key is E major. This creates an atmosphere of somber dignity — lamentation with the head held high. Cleopatra's opening vocal line on "Piangerò" does not imitate weeping; rather, Handel writes a small ascending interval for the melody. The orchestra echoes this motive as Cleopatra takes a moment to breathe. She sings the next "piangerò" to a still-larger ascending interval, and the orchestra responds with a full octave ascent. As Cleopatra closes the first phrase and the lament bass beneath her repeats, the violins in the orchestra take up the octave ascent motive at a higher pitch level, the second violins imitating the first. Cleopatra then enters as the third in the imitative sequence of octave ascents, describing the cruelty of her fate. In the following phrase, which begins with another orchestral echo of the same octave, Cleopatra sings a melody with even larger intervals, ascending the greatest distance yet on the word "vita." It is at this point that Handel has broken the lament bass pattern from its strict repetition. The rest of the A section uses a modified, abbreviated form of the lament bass to punctuate its phrases — it has left the straightforward lament paradigm behind. Here is a lament that expresses a complicated and resistant form of grief.

But after death
From all around, the tyrant
night and day,
I will, as a specter, agitate.

Mà poi morta
D'ogn'intorno il tiranno

20. For a slightly different topical reading of this aria, see Gregory J. Decker, "Colonizing Familiar Territory: Musical Topics, Stylistic Level and Handel's Cleopatra," *Opera Journal* 47, no. 2 (2014): 23–27.

21. George Frideric Handel, *Giulio Cesare*, ed. Walter Gieseler (Kassel: Bärenreiter, 1972), 207–208.

E note e giorno
Fatta spettro, agiterò.[22]

Handel makes clear the full complexity of Cleopatra's emotional situation in the contrasting B section of the aria. The key has changed from E major to the closely related C-sharp minor, and the meter has shifted from the moderate 3/8 to an energetic allegro in C (4/4). The orchestra opens the B section with uniform, vertical, declamatory chords that accompany Cleopatra's threat of action after her death. As she enters with "il tiranno," the orchestra bubbles over with energy; the cellos begin a compound melody with rapid sixteenth-note motion, adding a frenetic quality to the texture of exasperation in this portion of the aria. Cleopatra is not far behind. On the final syllable of "agiterò," she breaks into her own extensive, melismatic run in sixteenth notes. The entire scene is now one of rage. Cleopatra and the orchestra trade virtuosic performances of speed, creating a sonic specter of the agitation that the queen promises to deliver after her own death.

Handel's "Piangerò" illustrates the range of musical gestures that had become linked with signification in the early decades of the eighteenth century. In order for composers to depict the interior world of a character in an aria—and thereby create an affective response in the audience—they had to rely on convention and code. In this endeavor, they had at their disposal a huge collection of meters, rhythms, melodic devices, and harmonic choices; they could invoke dance types such as the minuet, the sarabande, the passepied, the contredanse, and many others; or they could refer to established topics such as the pastoral, the military, the hunt, or the lament. All of these are now integral components of a twenty-first-century scholarly activity that we call topic theory;[23] still, we have yet to do justice to the body of eighteenth-century theory that linked this practice of musical conventionality with affect.

Topical reference in early opera was specific enough that it could even include ideas such as a musical characterization of sleep. Known as a *sommeil* or "sleep scene," the convention was typical in the French *tragédie en musique*.[24]

22. Handel, *Giulio Cesare*, 208–210.

23. It also bears noting that analyses within topic theory focus, for the most part, on the music of the second half of the eighteenth century. See especially Leonard Ratner, *Classic Music: Expression, Form, and Style* (New York: Schirmer Books, 1980); Wye Jamison Allanbrook, *Rhythmic Gesture in Mozart: "Le nozze di Figaro" and "Don Giovanni"* (Chicago: University of Chicago Press, 1983); and Danuta Mirka, ed., *The Oxford Handbook of Topic Theory* (Oxford: Oxford University Press, 2014).

24. Caroline Wood, "Orchestra and Spectacle in the 'Tragédie en Musique,' 1673–1715: Oracle, 'Sommeil' and 'Tempête,'" *Proceedings of the Royal Musical Association* 108 (1981–1982): 25–46.

In fact, it is this device that allows Lully's character Armide to burst into action in "Enfin, il est en ma puissance" with Renaud slumbering at her mercy. In the scene previous, she has put him to sleep under a magic spell with musical accompaniment that is representative of the *sommeil*: recorders and muted violins play a slow G minor melody that oscillates by small intervals. They are joined by the lower strings, also muted, which each imitate the opening melody at staggered entrances. Renaud remarks that he is entranced by his beautiful surroundings and lies down, "hardly able to defend [himself] from the charms of sleep."[25]

By the early eighteenth century, music could be said to hold the power to assist in mimesis. It could paint individual words, it could invoke general images or moods — which would in turn create affects in listeners — or it could imitate the affects themselves. The early eighteenth-century critic Jean Terrasson put it this way: "With its very slow and very fast tempos and its transposed keys, it is able to imitate whatever one wants, not only the sound of the wind or the murmur of the water but also joy, sadness, and all the passions that are distinguished by accents or characteristic inflections of the voice."[26] Music, it turned out, was an excellent resource for an art that attempted to put the supernatural on display. "Musicians often compose *symphonies* [instrumental interludes in opera] to express sounds that we have never heard and that perhaps never existed in nature," Dubos explained, "such as the roar of the earth when Pluto leaves the underworld, the whistling of the wind when Apollo inspires the Pythia, the noise made by a ghost upon leaving his tomb, and the trembling of the foliage from the oaks of Dodona."[27] The singers and

---

25. "Des charmes du sommeil j'ai peine à me défendre." Lully, *Armide*, 15.

26. "D'un autre côté pourtant, comme elle a des mouvemens fort lents ou fort vîtes, & des modes transposés; elle est propre à imiter quand on veut, non seulement le bruit des vents ou le murmure des eaux, mais encore la joye, la tristesse & toutes les passions qui se distinguent par des accens ou des inflexions de voix caracterisées." Abbé Jean Terrasson, *Dissertation critique sur l'Iliade d'Homère*, vol. 1 (Paris: François Fournier and Antoine-Urbain Coustelier, 1715), 224. On Terrasson's contributions to the early eighteenth-century debates on opera, see especially Downing Thomas, *Aesthetics of Opera in the Ancien Régime, 1647–1785* (Cambridge: Cambridge University Press, 2002), 40–52. While Thomas sees in Terrasson's optimistic remarks a view of music as an aesthetic medium already independently capable of mimesis, I understand that transformation in aesthetic theory to occur later, during the middle decades of the eighteenth century (in sources covered in chapter 2 of this book).

27. "Les Musiciens composent souvent des symphonies pour exprimer des bruits que nous n'avons jamais entendus, & qui peut-estre ne furent jamais dans la nature. Tels sont le mugissement de la terre quand Pluton sort des Enfers, le siflement des airs quand Apollon inspire la Pythie, le bruit que fait un Ombre en sortant de son tombeau, & le frémissement du feuillage des chênes de Dodone." Dubos, *Réflexions*, 653.

musicians of opera were thought capable of providing a live soundtrack for a series of real and surreal representations in the poetry of the operatic librettos.

Nevertheless, critics looked on the state of music, around the turn of the eighteenth century, as a faded and imperfect realization of a much greater, much more powerful, and more morally improving art that existed in antiquity. Whether the craft, its practitioners, or its audiences were to blame was in question, but many eighteenth-century critics insisted that there was something lacking in the power of music. In the ancient world, as they understood it, music could actually perform in reality the kind of magical transformations that it now only farced on the opera stage. The *sommeil* could really have induced a magical sleep. "Perhaps," Dubos ventured, "the muted violins in *Armide*, and many other *symphonies* of the same author, would have produced these effects—which to us seem fabulous in the texts of the ancients authors—if they were listened to by men of a nature as lively as the Athenians."[28] It could be that the character of the audience was lacking in some way that detracted from the music's potency.

Others were less generous. Several Italian critics launched a full-scale attack on modern opera composition, claiming not only that it failed to measure up to the force and nobility of ancient music but also that its current state of degradation posed a real threat to the integrity of its audiences.[29] Related in some ways to the more general quarrel of the ancients and moderns, this strand of criticism nevertheless cannot be reduced to it. In a strategy dissimilar to other period proponents of ancient art and culture, the authors in this tradition insisted that ancient music was the only type that really had the ability to evoke the affects and achieve catharsis for listeners.[30] As Ludovico Antonio Muratori explained, "Music itself, without doubt, possesses the power to move the passions. Ancient history tells us of several miracles relating to this virtue. But ordinarily, our operas do not produce this remarkable effect, because of both their own deficiencies and those of the singers themselves. These days, no one either studies or uses the kind of music that can stir the affects; it is possible that we have lost the science of it, since we now only know the names of the [ancient] modes, such as Phrygian, Lydian, Aeolian, Dorian, Hypo-

---

28. "Peut estre . . . les sourdines d'Armide & plusieurs autres symphonies du même Auteur auroient produit de ces effets qui nous paroissent fabuleux dans le recit des Auteurs anciens, si l'on les avoit fait entendre à des hommes d'un naturel aussi vif que des Atheniens." Dubos, *Réflexions*, 647–648.

29. For a summary of these criticisms, see Strohm, "Introduction," 23–29.

30. On the forward-looking character of the proponents of ancient culture in the "Quarrel of the Ancients and Moderns," see Dan Edelstein, *The Enlightenment: A Genealogy* (Chicago: University of Chicago Press, 2010), 37–43.

phrygian, and so forth."[31] For Muratori, ancient music was not only forgotten but also probably irrecoverable by means of study. But holding this position curiously allowed Muratori and the other period detractors of opera to believe fervently in musical affect. "We have lost ancient music," Gian Vincenzo Gravina tells us unequivocally, "which so animated and regulated natural expression and which so effectively penetrated the human heart and — according to the testimony of many, and particularly Plato — excited and sedated the passions, cured diseases, and changed habits."[32] Precisely because ancient music was lost forever, these critics could claim for it a universal, supreme, and incredibly transformational affective power that was morally improving and in accordance with the highest standards for art.

This was one important critical response to the musical codes and conventions of opera: allow that music can move its auditors to the affects but deny that modern music has that ability;[33] claim instead, as these same authors did, that the form and medium through which opera attempted to signify are suspect; draw attention to opera's embarrassing, fleshy materiality; and hold that its only appeal is to those of a base nature. "Nowadays," Gravina continued, "theaters . . . extol the harmony that stirs those diluted, dissonant, and lacerated souls and damages those whose senses are guided by reason, because instead of expressing and imitating, it extinguishes and removes all semblance of truth."[34] Convinced that modern musical composition could not be the

---

31. "La musica, non v'ha dubbio, è possente per se stessa a muovere le passioni; e l'antica Storia narra alcuni miracoli di questa tal virtù. . . . Ma ordinariamente ne' Drammi la Musica non produce questo riguardevole effetto, sì per suo mancamento, come per quello de' Cantanti medesimi. O non istudiasi, o non si usa oggidì quella Musica, la quale sa muovere gli affetti; e forse ancor la scienza se n'è perduta, non conoscendosi più se non i soli nomi de' Modi, o Tuoni Frigio, Lidio, Eolico, Dorico, Ipofrigio, e simili." Ludovico Antonio Muratori, *Della perfetta poesia italiana*, vol. 2 (Modena: Bartolomeo Soliani, 1706), 46.

32. "Perduta l'antica musica, la quale animava, e regolava tanto l'espressione naturale, e con tanta efficacia ne i cuori umani penetrava, che, per testimonianza di molti, e particolarmente di Platone, eccitava, e sedava le passioni, curava i morbi, e cangiava i costumi." Gian Vincenzo Gravina, *Della tragedia*, vol. 1 (Naples, 1715), 70.

33. This notion is the beginning of a tradition that runs through the century, most notably in writings by Rousseau, including the *Lettre sur la musique françoise* (Paris, 1753) and the *Essai sur l'origine des langues*, published posthumously in *Œuvres completes de J. J. Rousseau, citoyen de Genève*, vol. 8 (Geneva, 1782), 137–231. For more on this tradition, see chapter 2.

34. "Per gli teatri, a dì nostri, una musica sterile di tali effetti, e perciò da quella assai difforme, e si esalta, per lo più, quell' armonìa, la quale, quanto alletta gli animi stemperati, e dissonanti, tanto lacera coloro, che danno a guidare il senso alla ragione: perchè in cambio di esprimere, ed imitare, suol più tosto estinguere, e cancellare ogni sembianza di verità." Gravina, *Della tragedia*, 70.

stuff of ancient power, Gravina saw instead an appeal to the lowest elements of life. Music alone could not express or imitate anything at all, and therefore it must just distract us from matters of importance.

For Muratori, the threat was more directly related to a gendered understanding of opera's corporeality. "These [operas] do not leave the spectators full of serious or noble affects but only with a feminine tenderness," he explained.[35] Opera had lost the entire point of drama, flipping its priorities from the poetry of the libretto to the sensuousness of the music. This rendered opera a "counterfeit" (*contraffare*) of good verisimilitude.[36] Here was drama that had been clothed in superficial musical drag. Music distracted and drew attention away from the edifying lessons and moving experiences of the poetry. "The aim of true tragedy, which is to move and to purge the passions of humanity, is frustrated."[37] And it was modern music, outgrowing its supportive role with its bold attempt to signify, which was to blame.

When critics were not as reactionary about the perils of musical effeminacy, they critiqued the form, or formulaic nature, of opera. This afforded writers the chance to cut in two directions at once with their criticisms. On the one hand, the relatively new art of opera — with just over a century of practice in its history — seemed unworthy of anything resembling a set of aesthetic rules. Opera was not a real art, just a haphazard hodgepodge of performances. But on the other hand, critics were slowly becoming aware of the codes and conventions that opera composers had adopted and were ready to use the transparency and easy recognizability of those devices against them.

Pier Jacopo Martello's entertaining satire *Della tragedia antica e moderna* (1715) channels the voice of Aristotle himself in making this tension apparent. Asked to create a poetics of opera, the character of Aristotle in Martello's satire responds, "Since you want me to give you some rules for a sort of composition that, in order to please, is intentionally dissolute [*sregolato*], I will give you some founded on observation and experience rather than reason."[38] Aristotle

35. "Da questi non si partono giammai gli Spettatori pieni di gravità, o di nobili affetti; ma solamente di una femminil tenerezza." Muratori, *Della perfetta poesia italiana*, 38.

36. Muratori, *Della perfetta poesia italiana*, 48.

37. "Ecco adunque in mezzo a tanti difetti de' Drammi perduto il fine della vera Tragedia, che è quello di muovere, e di purgar le passioni dell' uomo." Muratori, *Della perfetta poesia italiana*, 49.

38. "Allora Aristotile: Giacchè tu vuoi, ch'io ti dia qualche regola per un componimento, che per piacere vuol' essere sregolato, te ne dirò qualcheduna più tosto fondata su l'osservazione, e su la sperienza, che su la ragione." Pier Jacopo Martello, *Della tragedia antica e moderna* (Rome: Francesco Gonzaga, 1715), 172–173. Melania Bucciarelli provides what appears to be a nonsatiric, straightforward interpretation of Martello's document in *Italian Opera and European Theatre*,

goes on to mock opera's dependence on a formal plan and its appeal to the
senses. "Exit arias," he says, "must close every scene, and a musician cannot
leave without a warbling canzonetta. Whether or not this satisfies verisimilitude amounts to little. It is so stirring to hear the scene ended with spiritedness
and vitality."[39] Martello's Aristotle implies that the construction of an opera is
a simple affair, in which composers adopt recycled formal frames and pour in
banal sentiments, hackneyed texts, and cheap musical tricks. "In the arias,"
he relates, "I urge you to imitate some little butterflies, little boats, little birds,
and little streams, . . . and you will also observe that even in the worst operas, a musician carries distinguished applause when singing something . . .
in which gracefulness is added with diminutives."[40] Fans of the opera did not
respond to affective catharsis but rather to frivolous, repeatable musical designs and saccharine texts. Martello's exasperated Aristotle was echoed, on
this point, in Benedetto Marcello's polemic of 1720: "All canzonettas should
be made up of the same things, that is to say, *passages of extreme length, syn-
copations, half steps, alterations of syllables, meaningless repetitions of words
with no significance,* such as Amore Amore, Impero Impero, Europa Europa,
furori furori, orgoglio orgoglio, etc. etc. etc., but when composing an opera
out of these effects, the modern composer should always have before his eyes
a *note* or *inventory of all the above things,* without which he cannot end an
arietta."[41] If the trifling art of opera should deserve a poetics, it would seem

---

see especially 2–4; contrast this understanding of Martello with Piero Weiss's introduction to
"Pier Jacopo Martello on Opera (1715): An Annotated Translation," *Musical Quarterly* 66, no. 3
(1980): 378–381. On the difficulties of interpreting Martello's sincerity, see Robert S. Freeman,
Opera without Drama: Currents of Change in Italian Opera, 1675–1725 (Ann Arbor: UMI Research Press, 1981), 35–49.

39. "Gl'ingressi debbono chiudere ogni scena, e un musico non dee mai partire senza un
gorgheggiamento di canzonetta. Siasi, o non siasi verisimile poco importa. Troppo solletica quel
sentire la scena terminata con spirito, e con vivezza." Martello, *Della tragedia antica e moderna,*
181–182.

40. "Ti raccomando nelle arie qualche comparazione di farfalletta, di navicella, di augelletto,
o di ruscelletto, . . . ed avrai osservato anche ne' pessimi melodrammi, che il musico riporta dis-
tinto applauso, cantandone una di queste, nelle quali i diminutivi tanto odiosi alla lingua, e genio
franzese, aggiungono leggiadria." Martello, *Della tragedia antica e moderna,* 187.

41. "Dovranno formarsi tutte le Canzonette delle medesime cose, cioè di *Passaggi lung-
hissimi,* di *Sincope,* di *Semituoni, d'alerazioni di Sillabe,* di *repliche di Parole nulla significanti*
v. g. *Amore Amore, Impero Impero, Europa Europa, furori furori, orgoglio orgoglio, &c. &c. &c.*
che però dovrà il Compositore *moderno* per *tal effetto,* quando compone l'Opera, aver sempre
dinanzi agl' occhi una *Nota,* o *Inventario delle sopradette cose tutte,* senza alcuna delle quali
non terminerà mai Arietta veruna." Benedetto Marcello, *Il teatro alla moda* . . . (Venice, 1720;
facsimile edition, Milan: Ricordi, 1883), 18–19.

as though its elaboration would not be a difficult affair at all, since the features out of which opera composers made meaning were so reliably — and
regrettably — clear.

The criticism of early eighteenth-century opera as formulaic and predictable managed to stick and found a way of repeating in twentieth-century
scholarship. Joseph Kerman, in his influential *Opera as Drama* (1954), referred to this period in opera history as "The Dark Ages," describing Italian
opera in particular as "impassive and highly predictable. Each scene runs its
appointed course to the 'exit aria,' each act balances its scenes, each opera
shuffles the standard contrasts."[42] He thought of these operas as, at best, "a
catalogue of 'affects' spaced off and displayed by means of recitative."[43] Even
twenty-first-century accounts refer to this corpus as predictable and describe
the arias as "frozen."[44] In many ways, the early modern criticisms of these
operas are still with us.

But if the opera composers of the late seventeenth and early eighteenth
centuries were not quite so innovative with the formal designs of their works, it
was because they were conducting a much grander experiment in music, signification, and affect. The outwardly formulaic nature of the operas allowed
composers to set the conventions and codes that gradually linked musical gestures with meaning, producing affective responses in audiences. The anxiety
of the negative critical responses speaks to the success of this grand experiment. Critics were tempted to imagine almost too much about music's power
and were therefore suspicious of the operas of their day. Some writers, like
Gravina, wanted to believe in a music that could universally move audiences
to affective responses on its own — without any text, without the poetry of the
libretto — but they could not reconcile this belief with the necessarily varied
reactions of contemporary audiences. For Gravina, then, the only music imaginable that could have worked this way was ancient music, now lost forever.
Others, like Muratori, Martello, and Marcello, were clearly so fascinated with
musical composition that they were repelled by it; as a new object of attention,
it did not earn their aesthetic approbation but only their disqualification as a
strange, dangerous, and misgendered appeal to the senses.

In these critics' censorious remarks on opera, they helped to define what
was now becoming legible to everyone: opera was a multimedia system of

---

42. Joseph Kerman, *Opera as Drama* (1956; repr., Berkeley: University of California Press,
1988), 49.

43. Kerman, *Opera as Drama*, 49.

44. Carolyn Abbate and Roger Parker, *A History of Opera: The Last Four Hundred Years*
(London: Allen Lane, 2012), 77.

mimesis. Uniting poetry, stage action, and often extravagant appeals to all of the senses, it employed musical sounds in its effort to convey significations and stir the affects of its rapt spectators. The only question was what to think of it.

The Powers of Music Captured

While Gravina, Muratori, Martello, and Marcello dismissed the aesthetic functions of musical sounds, other writers were at work attempting to better understand them. These authors were not anxious about music's material reality as sound, nor were they interested in denigrating the formal conventions of opera or doubting its ability to move audiences to the affects. Instead they ventured—however haphazardly—to understand all of these things as part of a grand system of affective signification. The result was as experimental as opera itself. It was a new sort of affect theory that we have come to know as the *Affektenlehre*: a broad, multilingual, European intellectual movement that drew together aesthetics, natural and ancient philosophy, compositional craft, and taxonomic structure.

History has not been kind to the *Affektenlehre*. We owe the discursive formulation of this movement qua movement to early twentieth-century German musicology, which created a distorted view of the *Affektenlehre* as a German phenomenon with a fairly coherent set of principles.[45] American musicology of the mid-twentieth century picked up and developed this errant notion but in a pejorative fashion; Manfred Bukofzer, for example, wrote that the *Affektenlehre* "set stringent rules" for composers who sought the "rigid" maintenance of a single affect in each composition.[46] This understanding parallels that of the mid-twentieth century's appraisal of eighteenth-century opera. Both came under scrutiny for their supposed enforcement of unbending procedure. The recent musicological reactions to these views have been on the one hand to rehabilitate the operas—finding nuances and dramatic resources in their repeating patterns—but to dismiss the *Affektenlehre* as ever having existed at all. In the 1984 article "Johann Mattheson and the Invention of the *Affektenlehre*," George Buelow critiques the mid-twentieth-century understanding of the movement as having been universal and inflexible in application. His conclusion, however, is that the *Affektenlehre* is merely a historical casualty of

45. See, for example, Hermann Kretzschmar, "Allgemeines und Besonderes zur Affektenlehre," *Jahrbuch der Musikbibliothek Peters* 18 (1911): 63–77; 19 (1912): 65–78.

46. Manfred F. Bukofzer, *Music in the Baroque Era: From Monteverdi to Bach* (New York: Norton, 1947), 388–389.

twentieth-century scholarship and that scholars would be better off abandoning both the term and the notion that this movement ever took place.[47] Even while more recent work in musicology has become newly interested in the role of affect in eighteenth-century music, there has been scant work on the *Affektenlehre* since Buelow's pronouncement.[48]

The *Affektenlehre* needs a rehabilitation. While it is true that the term itself was bequeathed to us by German musicologists of the early twentieth century — and that it has occasionally brought with it some heavy and problematic baggage — it is nevertheless common enough musicological currency that it ought to do better work. The *Affektenlehre* should describe the broad, messy, and contradictory developments in eighteenth-century intellectual history surrounding music and affect. This movement involved many different types of texts: works of prescriptive music theory (with all of their frightening normativities), descriptive tracts that combine music theory with natural philosophy, speculative works of aesthetic theory, writings in the vein of music criticism, performance manuals, and many other types of documents. Some fraction of these texts consists, indeed, in sets of suggestions or guidelines for composition or performance. But the fact that no coherent or universal system emerged from these attempts is less important than the intellectual foment that they generated.

I call the first stage of this intellectual tradition the mimetic *Affektenlehre* because of the general theoretical consensus that music evoked specific affects through the power of imitation. When eighteenth-century thinkers set out to theorize the relationships between musical patterns and affects, they were building on a time-honored, if somewhat obscure, tradition of thinking along these lines. Several speculative tracts of the previous two centuries had

---

47. George J. Buelow, "Johann Mattheson and the Invention of the *Affektenlehre*," in *New Mattheson Studies*, ed. Buelow and Hans Joachim Marx (Cambridge: Cambridge University Press, 1983), 393–407.

48. Danuta Mirka, for example, can write, "Undoubtedly, the basic premise of eighteenth-century music aesthetics was the connection between music and affects," but then, the "attempt to explain the affective power of music" is "frequently — if improperly — called the doctrine of affections (*Affektenlehre*)." Mirka, introduction to *Oxford Handbook of Topic Theory*, 10; Wye J. Allanbrook's dismissal is more direct when she writes of "the *Affektenlehre*, that mythical mother lode of baroque affective devices that scholars have assumed must exist somewhere in the ether." Allanbrook, *The Secular Commedia: Comic Mimesis in Late Eighteenth-Century Music* (Berkeley: University of California Press, 2014), 91. One notable exception, also critical of Buelow, is found in Isabella van Elferen, "Affective Discourse in German Baroque Text-Based Music," *Tijdschrift voor muziektheorie* 9, no. 3 (2004): 217–233.

combined Galenic humoral theory with the music theoretical science of ratio in order suggest a link between musical material and affective response. The general consensus in this vein was that of a correspondence between the proportions of the humoral vapors and the proportions of various musical properties; these differed according to each author but included melodic intervals, harmonic intervals, rhythms, and the qualities of complete scales. Gioseffo Zarlino, in *Le istitutioni harmoniche* (1558), attributed this force to ancient music when he wrote, "the same proportions of qualities that cause anger or fear or other passions are also found in [ancient] harmonies, and cause them to excite similar effects."[49] Both Marin Mersenne, in *Harmonie universelle* (1636), and Athanasius Kircher, in *Musurgia universalis* (1650), described this power as obtaining to the music of their own day. While Mersenne wrote at length on the physics of sound and Kircher emphasized the work of the humoral vapors, both authors generated novel theories of affect that correlated musical motions with corporeal motions. Thus, for Mersenne, musicians manipulate sound vibrations with "artificial intervals that musicians have established, namely, the semitones, tones, thirds, etc. through which we explain the movements and the passions of our souls."[50] Likewise, for Kircher, "height and lowness of pitch, tension and relaxation, acceleration and slowness of the sound's speed, softness and hardness, by their proportion and temperament accordingly alter the spirit, and this in turn alters the soul."[51] Kircher's substantial theoretical explanation, frequently cited in later texts, also included a neoplatonic description of the soul as a stringed instrument—an idea that

49. "La onde potemo dire che quelle istesse proportioni, che si ritrovano nella cagione dell'Ira, o del Timore, o di altra paßione nelle sopradette qualità; quelle isteße si ritrovino anco nell'Harmonie, che sono cagioni di concitare simili effetti." Gioseffo Zarlino, *Le istitutioni harmoniche* (Venice: Francesco de i Franceschi Senese, 1558), 73. A similar assertion is found in Pierre Maillart's *Les tons ov discovrs svr les modes de mvsique, et les tons de l'eglise, et la distinction entre iceux* (Tournay: Charles Martin, 1610), 157–158. I thank Giulio Minniti for bringing this passage of Maillart to my attention.

50. In Mersenne's "Traitéz de la voix et des chants: Livre II Des chants," Proposition II reads, "L'air est un mouvement, une conduite, ou saillie des sons, ou de la voix par les intervalles artificiels que les Musiciens ont estably, à sçavoir par les Demitons, le Tons, les Tierces, &c. dont nous expliquons les mouvements & les paßions de nostre ame, ou celles du sujet de la lettre." Marin Mersenne, *Harmonie universelle* (Paris: Sébastien Cramoisy, 1636–1637), "Traitéz de la voix et des chants: Livre II Des chants," Prop. II, 1:92.

51. "Acumen itaque & gravitas, intensio & remissio, celeritas & tarditas sonori motus, quas mollities & durities consequuntur, qua porportione & temperamento spiritum alterant, hoc eodem & animam alterabunt." Athanasius Kircher, *Musurgia universalis* (Rome: Eredi di Francesco Corbelletti, 1650), 566.

was eventually to become central to the next stage of affect theory during the later eighteenth century.[52]

Early eighteenth-century texts retained some of the speculative flavor from their predecessors, but their emphasis shifted toward the practical in response to the changing musical situation before them. As the codes, conventions, and topics of musical composition became more apparent and more legible to these authors, so too did the desire to codify them. The result of their efforts was the full blossoming of the mimetic *Affektenlehre*, which took place in the early decades of the eighteenth century. Johann Heinichen's *Der General-Bass in der Composition* (1728) contains one of the best known and most widely discussed texts in this tradition. Heinichen's major foray into the musical affects is found in the introduction to this treatise, and its principal concern is opera composition. It should probably come as no surprise that some of the most sophisticated and detailed examinations of operatic practice came from outsiders attempting to learn, to reproduce, and to excel within the Italian operatic style. Heinichen, a German composer of Italian opera seria, provides us with a supreme example.[53]

Heinichen finds his way into a lengthy disquisition on the musical affects through a remark on rhetoric. When a composer is given the task of setting an affectively ambiguous opera aria text, he must look to the surrounding language for guidance in creating its musical setting. "In the case of the most unfruitful materials," he tells us, "one can just examine the three *fontes principales*, namely, *antecedentia, concomitantia,* and *consequentia textus* according to the *locus topicus*."[54] That is, one need only look at the material that precedes the aria, the text in the other sections of the aria, or the material that follows the aria; these will help to clarify the meaning of the "uninspired" words and help the composer to decide on an appropriate setting. Heinichen's

---

52. At the turn of the eighteenth century, the ideas of Zarlino and Kircher were summarized in Zaccaria Tevo's *Il musico testore* (Venice: Antonio Bortoli, 1706), 99–106. For more on the musical affect theories of Zarlino, Mersenne, Kircher, and their contemporaries, see Claude Palisca, "Moving the Affections through Music: Pre-Cartesian Psycho-Physiological Theories," in *Number to Sound: The Musical Way to the Scientific Revolution*, ed. Paolo Gozza (Dordrecht: Kluwer, 2000), 289–308.

53. Johann David Heinichen, *Der General-Bass in der Composition* (Dresden: Heinichen, 1728), 30–92. A Dresden composer schooled in Leipzig, Heinichen wrote *Der General-Bass in der Composition* after a six-year stay in Italy.

54. "Man mag auch bey denen allerunfruchtbahresten Materien nur 3 *fontes principales*, nehmlich *Antecedentia, Concomitantia, & Conseqventia Texuts* nach denen *Locis Topicis* examiniren." Heinichen, *Der General-Bass in der Composition*, 30.

lengthy taxonomy of the musical affects — richly illustrated with sixteen generous musical examples — unfolds from this cue. Its unwritten premise is that
musical composition can and should help to clarify the meaning of an otherwise vague text. Heinichen begins with words to a hilariously ambiguous aria:

> It is not unique, it is not strange
> the cause, it is true;
> I do not doubt, no.
> The truth
> Is often better discovered by itself. (Da Capo)

> Non è sola è straniera
> la causa, chè vera;
> non dubito nò.
> scoprire si sà
> spesso meglio de se la verità. D.C.[55]

"But what should a composer make of this?" he jests. "For not once in the
whole aria . . . is there even a single word available that gives the slightest
opportunity to express one of the affects."[56] This text could, indeed, be made
to mean almost anything.

What follows are numerous ways of composing an aria to the banal text
such that it seems furious or bold or quarrelsome and so forth. Heinichen
motivates his taxonomy as a specifically rhetorical problem: the text to be set
is flat and imprecise in feeling, and the composer therefore needs to take account of the surrounding drama in order to know what sort of music to write.
This is an inventive and even playful way of tackling the grand problem of
the musical affects. What Heinichen presents as a question concerning the
rhetorical interpretation of texts is really a remarkable quandary concerning
the power of music to signify. It almost seems as though he deflects the enormity of the endeavor with levity; his proposed task is to rescue an operatic
poem that is absolutely pitiful — a charge often brought against the texts of the
dramma per musica tradition. Heinichen both anticipates this criticism and
combats it with the skill he displays in making the various meanings of the text
absolutely vivid in the different musical settings he composes for it.

Imagine, as Heinichen invites us to do, that his sample text is sung by

---

55. Heinichen, *Der General-Bass in der Composition*, 31.
56. "Was soll aber ein *Componiste* hieraus machen . . . weil nicht einmahl in der ganzen
Aria . . . kein einziges Wort vorhanden, welches zu *exprimirung einiges Affectes* die geringste
Gelegenheit gebe." Heinichen, *Der General-Bass in der Composition*, 31.

a character who is heroically resolute in a pompous manner. The example he creates for this scenario, in the key of B-flat major and meter of C (4/4), opens with a strong, unison accompanimental gesture.[57] With the marking "Vivace," it begins with an octave leap and outlines a tonic triad in a manner that calls to mind a trumpet voluntary; this bellicose topic is somewhat akin to the opening of Lully's "Enfin, il est en ma puissance." By the third measure of the example, Heinichen's accompaniment picks up in pace, tinting toward the brilliant style with a fast compound melody in the upper register. When our pompous character enters with "Non è sola, no è straniera," her vocal line clings to the contours of the B-flat major triad, the stressed syllables of the line's square rhythms falling on the downbeats of the measure. There can be no doubt about her resolve. The compound melody of the accompaniment follows our singer, adding energy to her determination. Heinichen pens some ornamental passagework for her on "vera" and concludes the example with a return to the unison trumpet voluntary with which it had begun.

Contrast this with Heinichen's example for "volatile or raging fortune."[58] At this point in the discussion, Heinichen has shifted to a different ambiguous text:

He who has fortune as an enemy
Will always see himself struggle.

Chi hà nemica la fortuna
si vedrà sempre penar.[59]

The problem with these words, according to Heinichen, is that we do not know the content of fortune itself. One might wish to express its contrariness, the sorrow that it brings, or, as in the case of the example at hand, its fleeting intensity. Heinichen's music for this vignette is also in B-flat major and C (4/4) meter, but this excerpt is marked "Furioso." The pace immediately signals the brilliant style, with the bass moving in eighth notes and the treble ripping upward through the B-flat major scale in sixteenth notes. The stepwise accompanimental opening is constantly changing direction, and the bass voice continually rearticulates octave leaps. In all of this activity, there is something resembling the fire of the B section from Handel's "Piangerò," though the major mode of this example and the constant changes of direction seem to

57. Heinichen, *Der General-Bass in der Composition*, 39–41.
58. "Das flüchtige oder rasende Glück." Heinichen, *Der General-Bass in der Composition*, 43–45.
59. Heinichen, *Der General-Bass in der Composition*, 41.

signal an intense restlessness rather than rage. Our singer enters with a melody that is almost a vocal exercise in leaps, each larger than the next. When she finally reaches a held note — a duration long enough to savor — it is on a pitch (D-flat) that moves us away from the home key. Her music now makes its way through B-flat minor to a new key, F, at the close of this wandering excerpt.

Heinichen's other examples include topics that are frequently found in the operas of his day, such as a pastoral siciliana in 12/8 meter, an aria full of sighing gestures, and a playful love tune in 3/8 with sixteenth-note triplets. With the intention of demonstrating how many different ways there are available to set an aria text, he has built a taxonomy of musical significations. "If an experienced master should be wagered, he could oblige himself to compose any aria, and therefore an entire opera, five or six times differently according to the opportunities of the text, without any of the arias having the slightest in common with each other."[60] Heinichen has absorbed the operatic practice of his day and distilled it using the reasoned tool of taxonomy.

From the vantage point of an outsider looking in, Heinichen was able to capture the dynamic interior to Italian *dramma per musica*, in which composers consistently associated certain musical patterns and gestures with specific meanings. These meanings were, in turn, intended to create affective responses in listeners and to support, in this way, the communication of their operatic poetry. Although the style of *Der General-Bass in der Composition* is decidedly practical — Heinichen's introduction does not propose to solve the problem of how music does its affective work — it nevertheless amounted to a significant preliminary attempt to codify this system of musical codes. The taxonomy was, for Heinichen, a device for better accomplishing the primary goal of the composer: to write music that amplified the mimetic work of the text.

Other documents in the mimetic *Affektenlehre* tradition were less reserved in speculation. When Johann Mattheson ventured a taxonomy of the musical affects in *Der vollkommene Capellmeister* (1739), it was not in the context of a guide for opera composition but instead in the speculative portion of his treatise, in a chapter concerning "sound in itself, and the natural theory of music."[61] Mattheson begins this chapter, which contains the first nonintro-

60. "Auff diese Arth ein *exercirt*er Meister sich gar wohl *obligir*en könte, eine jedwede *Aria*, und folgbahr eine ganze *Opera*, wenn es eine Wette gelten solte, 5, 6, und mehr mahl nach Gelegenheit des *Text*es anders zu componieren, ohne daß eine einzige *Aria* der vorigen *Composition* in geringsten ähnlich sey." Heinichen, *Der General-Bass in der Composition*, 88.

61. "Vom Klange an sich selbst, und von der musicalischen Natur-Lehre." Johann Mattheson, *Der vollkommene Capellmeister* (Hamburg: Christian Herold, 1739), 9.

ductory material in the entire book, with a gesture that distances his work from the tradition of *musica theorica*. There will be no science of numerical ratios here but instead, he proudly announces, an account of sound and hearing. Citing Aristoxenus with approval and dissociating himself from Aristotle and Boethius, Mattheson describes the material properties of sound vibrations, the transmission of sound, and the characteristics of sounding bodies. The account includes sympathetic vibration, though he understands the effects of this physical phenomenon only as potentially medicinal qualities of music. Since sound "works strongly on the nerves [*Spann-Adern*] of the human body, . . . all diaphoretic medicines and dances or movements do not measure up without music to what they do with music."[62] Mattheson's preamble on the nature of sound has prepared us to think of music as an art grounded in the material properties of sound vibrations with all of their corporeal ramifications.

The last of these to be described in the chapter are the emotions and passions of the soul ("Gemüths-Bewegungen und Leidenschafften der Seele"). Mattheson's taxonomy of the affects in music is brief in comparison to Heinichen's, and it lacks musical illustrations. Rather than describing established musical codes and conventions of meaning, as Heinichen does, Mattheson begins with the assumption that some inherent relation exists between the properties of musical sounds and the affective responses of listeners. For Mattheson, this relation itself is mimetic. "So for example because joy is felt through an expansion of our soul," we learn, "it follows reasonably and naturally that I could best express this affect through wide and expanding intervals."[63] Composers express sadness, by contrast, with the smallest of intervals. Although Mattheson provides scant musical details for the fifteen affects listed in this taxonomy, the relation is consistently one of direct correspondence: whatever movement naturally occurs within the human body experiencing an affect can be achieved, musically, with some imitation of that movement.

There are other elements in Mattheson's taxonomy that suggest an awareness of and reliance on the growing systematicity of operatic code and conven-

62. "Weil der Klang auf die Spann-Adern des menschlichen Leibes starck arbeitet, gar artig erweist, daß, z. B. alle Schweiß-treibende Arzeneien und Tänze oder Bewegungen ohne Music lange das nicht ausrichten, was sie mit der Music thun." Mattheson, *Der vollkommene Capellmeister*, 15.

63. "Da z. B die Freude durch Ausbreitung unsrer Lebens-Geister empfunden wird, so folget vernünfftiger und natürlicher Weise, daß ich diesen Affect am besten durch weite und erweiterte Intervalle ausdrücken könne." Mattheson, *Der vollkommene Capellmeister*, 16.

tion.[64] Pride and arrogance, for instance, are expressed in ascending musical lines; but then the composer "draws, for the most part, on a bold, inflated character. One has the opportunity to bring on all sorts of grand, euphonious figures that require a special seriousness and grandiloquent motion."[65] This seems reasonable enough—we might think of the trumpet voluntary that opens Heinichen's example for heroic resolution or again of the opening intervals to Lully's "Enfin, il est en ma puissance." But Mattheson does not illustrate any of these gestures for us directly. Instead, his abstract reference to the existence of such "grand figures" indicates the expectation of a shared, tacit knowledge concerning them. Mattheson's taxonomy was made possible by the growing systematicity of the musical culture surrounding it.

If there were any doubt about the purpose of evoking affects in listeners through music, Mattheson's framing comments make it quite clear: "it is the proper nature of music that it is above all a teacher of propriety [*Zucht-Lehre*]."[66] Music mimetically reproduces the affects of a text or a dramatic context, further amplifying the multimedia mimesis of an edifying idea or a morally improving sentiment. "One should seek out a good, truly good poetic work in which nature is vividly painted, and strive to distinguish precisely the passions contained therein," Mattheson instructs.[67] Doubling poetry's imitation of the natural world, music regrounded the affects portrayed in the material of nature through sound vibration.

Mattheson's taxonomy is unusual in that it frames its endeavor squarely around affective arousal; oddly this has rendered it the principal list recalled in connection with the *Affektenlehre*, despite its uncharacteristic nature.[68] A third type of taxonomy, resembling neither of the two just inspected, is tucked into the interior of a great many eighteenth-century music treatises. This sort finds itself amid detailed descriptions of specific musical parameters or de-

64. Mattheson was himself an opera composer residing in Hamburg, a major center for opera in the early eighteenth century. He also favorably cites Heinichen's *General-Bass in der Composition*. Mattheson, *Der vollkommene Capellmeister*, 16–17.

65. "Meistentheils auf ein kühnes, aufgeblasenes Wesen beziehet. Man bekömt dadurch Gelegenheit, allerhand prächtig klingende Figuren anzubringen, die eine besondre Ernsthafftigkeit und hochtrabende Bewegung erfordern." Mattheson, *Der vollkommene Capellmeister*, 18.

66. "Denn das ist die rechte Eigenschafft der Music, daß sie eine Zucht-Lehre vor andern sey." Mattheson, *Der vollkommene Capellmeister*, 15.

67. "Man suche sich eine oder andre gute, recht gute poetische Arbeit aus, in welcher die Natur lebhafft abgemahlet ist, und trachte die darin enthaltene Leidenschafften genau zu unterscheiden." Mattheson, *Der vollkommene Capellmeister*, 19.

68. See, for example, Bruce Haynes and Geoffrey Burgess, *The Pathetick Musician: Moving an Audience in the Age of Eloquence* (Oxford: Oxford University Press, 2016), 55–57; Bukofzer, *Music in the Baroque Era*, 388–389; and Buelow, "Johann Mattheson."

signs, such as chord types, varieties of meter, types of dances, and so forth. Indeed, deeper into the pages of Mattheson's *Der vollkommene Capellmeister*, we learn that the gavotte's true affect is joy, while the passepied evokes frivolity.[69] These sorts of casual associations between musical materials and affects were just as indicative of the growing consensus connecting music with signification, even if theorists typically gave over less space to concerns of how and why these associations existed.

Take, for another example, the correlations observed in Rameau's 1722 *Traité de l'harmonie*, which one arrives on in the unassuming chapter "On the Properties of Chords."[70] "It is certain," Rameau asserts, "that harmony can move the different passions within us in accordance with the chords that one uses. There are chords that are sad, languishing, tender, agreeable, gay, and surprising."[71] This taxonomy is succinct but highly specific in some aspects, making distinctions between prepared dissonances (evocative of "sweetness and tenderness") and unprepared dissonances ("despair").[72] Contrast Rameau's compact list with another French example from slightly later in the century, found in Antoine Vion's *La musique pratique et theorique* (1742). Vion provides a richly illustrated chart of the meter signatures and the affects they afford, occupying ten pages with seventy different examples — fully one-eighth of the entire treatise. The examples draw heavily on older repertoire to make their point, especially on the operas of Lully and instrumental works from Corelli, Couperin, and others.[73] Here again a tacit understanding of the performance and composition conventions support the work of the mimetic *Affektenlehre* taxonomy while the taxonomy itself aims to codify its codes and conventions. The two developments must be understood together — not in any relationship of direct linkage or fidelity but rather as nodes in a network of mutual reinforcement.

Vion's taxonomy of meters as they relate to affects is one of legions of its type. Through the eighteenth century, theorists struggled to come to terms with the proliferation of options for notating the meter of music, and they spent a considerable amount of energy and ink on the relationship between

69. Mattheson, *Der vollkommene Capellmeister*, 225, 229.

70. "De la proprieté des Accords." Jean-Philippe Rameau, *Traité de l'harmonie* (Paris: Jean-Baptiste-Christophe Ballard, 1722), 141.

71. "Il est certain que l'Harmonie peut émouvoir en nous, differentes passions, à proportion des Accords qu'on y employe. Il y a des Accords tristes, languissans, tendres, agréables, gais, & surprenans." Rameau, *Traité de l'harmonie*, 141.

72. Rameau, *Traité de l'harmonie*, 141.

73. Charles Antoine Vion, *La musique pratique et theorique* (Paris: Jean-Baptiste-Christophe Ballard, 1742), 21–32.

meter and affect.[74] But mimetic *Affektenlehre* taxonomies popped up in less likely places as well. Even Johann Joseph Fux's *Gradus ad Parnassum* (1725), the treatise best known for codifying the principles of sixteenth-century counterpoint, includes a short passage on the affects in the context of recitative composition. Here again the relationship is one of direct mimesis, in which the composer is encouraged to musically copy the characteristic motions and gestures of the affects in order to evoke them in listeners.[75] This attitude persisted well into the late eighteenth century and across the continent. As the Glaswegian theorist John Holden put it in *An Essay towards a Rational System of Music* of 1770, "Sorrow, humility, and reverence, require a slow movement, with gentle, easy inflexions of the voice; but joy, thanksgiving, and triumph, ought to be distinguished by a quicker movement, with bolder inflexions, and more distant leaps, from one sound to another."[76] Comparing Holden's observations on joy to Mattheson's, for example, it is evident that no uniform catalogue of correspondences was ever agreed on. But the powerful notion that such correspondences might exist, and that they could have something to do with the waxing conventionality of the day's musical practices, was the underlying principle for the mimetic strand of the *Affektenlehre* tradition.

The Powers of Music Lost

When Rameau wrote in painstaking detail on Lully's "Enfin, il est en ma puissance" in his *Observations sur notre instinct pour la musique* of 1754, it was very much in the vein of the mimetic *Affektenlehre*. Each change of chord, every melodic outline, each feint toward a new key, every rhythm — they all held dramatic significance to Rameau's ears. No matter that Lully, composing in the late seventeenth century, would not have had access to the explosion of *Affektenlehre* discourse produced in the decades intervening; for Rameau, every gesture had the power to move audiences to different affects. This piece of musical drama set the gold standard for opera composition. It was the task of the best composers to emulate it and the job of the best theorists to explain it as a reflection of some deeper set of musical principles.

Just what those principles were, though, is not at all clear from Rameau's

---

74. For further documentation of this phenomenon, see Roger Mathew Grant, *Beating Time and Measuring Music in the Early Modern Era* (New York: Oxford University Press, 2014), especially 134–146.

75. Johann Joseph Fux, *Gradus ad Parnassum* (Vienna: Peter van Ghelen, 1725), 276–279.

76. John Holden, *An Essay towards a Rational System of Music* (Glasgow: Robert Urie, 1770), 36.

close examination of "Enfin." In certain remarks, he seems to operate with a set of assumptions akin to Mattheson's doctrine, in which musical motion is mimetically related to the motions of the affects. This is particularly true when he links Armide's changing emotional states to changes of harmony. But at other times, he writes in a manner that closer approximates Heinichen's method only in reverse; he is finding in Lully's 1686 "Enfin" the codes and conventions of opera that had become all the more clear during the early decades of the eighteenth century. Of the opening melody and the following trill on "puissance," for instance, Rameau tells us, "Armide applauds herself here for having Renaud in her power, and to express her triumph one could not imagine anything better than the trill she uses: a trill precisely resembling those of trumpets in victory songs."[77] Here the tie to the intended affect exists only through received tradition rather than through a duplication of affective motion through music.

Such were the confusions of the mimetic *Affektenlehre* tradition that contradictions were the fabric of its existence during the eighteenth century. Not only did the *Affektenlehre* taxonomies fail to match each other in content, but the very basis of their supposed operation was internally inconsistent even in the writings of a single author. The flourishing of this tradition, then, does not bear witness to a sudden rigidity in operatic practice or a new music theoretical protocol with strict dicta for composition or performance. To be certain, none of these theorists agreed. Instead, this intellectual foment testifies to a heightened sense that something definite could be codified about music's ability to signify and therefore to arouse the affects. The new awareness concerning the regularity of opera's codes and conventions — particularly in places where Italian opera was appreciated but not native — emboldened theorists in their efforts to capture music's affective powers. The result was a mimetic *Affektenlehre* doctrine that mixed speculation with observation, offering no clear systematicity but only a glimmer that there was some system to be observed at all.

The consequences of these contradictions could, therefore, unfold directly on the surface of any piece of music, as they did in the case of "Enfin." Rameau's detailed reading of the scene was not a simple matter of his enthusiasm for Lully; it was in fact a response to Rousseau's cutting criticism of the same scene in his incendiary *Lettre sur la musique françoise* (1753), an attack on the

---

77. "Armide s'applaudit ici d'avoir Renaud en sa puissance, & pour y exprimer son triomphe, rien n'est mieux imaginé que le *Tril* qu'elle y employe: *Tril* justement semblable à celui des Trompettes dans les Chants de Victoire." Rameau, *Observations*, 70.

French operatic style.[78] Where Rameau heard profound significance in the smallest details of the harmonic setting in "Enfin," Rousseau heard vacant banality. Lully had done nothing, in his opinion, to express the dramatic content of the text.

> The reticences, the interruptions, the intellectual transitions which the poet has offered to the musician were not a single time seized on by him. The heroine finishes by loving him whose throat she wanted to slit at the beginning; the musician finishes in E minor as he had begun, without having left for an instant the chords most closely related to the home key, without having for a single time put the slightest exceptional inflection in the declamation of the actress that would faithfully render the agitation of her soul, without having given the slightest expression to the harmony. And I defy him who would assign the music alone — whether the key, the melody, the declamation, or the accompaniment — any sensible difference between the beginning and the end of this scene by which the spectator may judge the prodigious change that has occurred in Armide's heart.[79]

For Rousseau, the fact that "Enfin" remained — for the most part — in the home key of E minor without any drastic change of style betrayed an absolute failure of expression. Armide undergoes a huge internal upheaval in this scene, but at its close she still sings similar phrases in the same key. What was worse, for Rousseau, was that Lully had festooned the music with extraneous trills and ornaments. For him, this celebrated scene was paramount proof that the French operatic style was inferior to the Italian. Italian opera's open vowels, simple melodies, and thin accompaniments were closer echoes of the impassioned cries of primitive humanity. And since music's power was derived from its ability to approximate that lost original human expression, in which

---

78. Here we enter into the territory of the *querelle des bouffons*, which is treated in greater detail in chapter 2.

79. "Les réticences, les interruptions, les transitions intellectuelles que le Poëte offroit au Musicien n'ont pas été une seule fois saisies par celui-ci. L'Héroïne finit par adorer celui qu'elle vouloit égorger au commencement; le Musicien finit en E *si mi* comme il avoit commené, sans avoir quité un instant les cordes les plus analogues au ton principal, sans avoir mis une seule fois dans la déclamation de l'Actrice la moindre inflexion extraordinaire qui fît foi de l'agitation de son ame, sans avoir donné la moindre expression à l'harmonie : & je défie qui que ce soit d'assigner par la Musique seule, soit dans le ton, soit dans la mélodie, soit dans la déclamation, soit dans l'accompagnement, aucune différence sensible entre le commencement & la fin de cette scéne, par où le Spectateur puisse juger du changement prodigieux qui s'est fait dans le cœur d'Armide." Rousseau, *Lettre sur la musique françoise*, 80–81.

speech and song were one, the music of the French *tragédie en musique* was not really even music at all.[80]

Here we encounter the considerable difficulties of theorizing music's capacity for meaning. Although critics were slowly beginning to understand that musical sound might have some ability to signify (and to augment the poetry of the libretto), it was completely unclear to them which sorts of music qualified and how this function operated. The same sounds — those in Lully's "Enfin, il est en ma puissance," for instance — could for two different authors provide proof of opposite opinions. Somehow this music accommodated the different views that these two thinkers projected onto it. When Rameau originally singled out Lully's recitative for praise, it was to demonstrate a principle of harmony; in the *Nouveau système de musique théorique* of 1726, Rameau described how musicians should match their harmonic plans with the meanings of the text to be set, and Lully's "Enfin" served as his prime example. But further on in his technical explanation of this operation, Rameau was forced to encounter the enormity of his project. "If it is not absolutely impossible to determine the melodies and the modulations that would best suit the most marked expressions, it is moreover an enterprise that would demand more than the lifetime of a single individual."[81] The system of signification that would tie musical sounds to words was simply too complex or enormous for Rameau to elaborate himself. It was far easier to point to an excellent example of opera composition by an old master like Lully. The fundamental problem was that not everyone could hear it in the way that Rameau did.

So neither opera itself nor the mimetic *Affektenlehre* taxonomies could do the work of capturing what many people thought that they knew, which was that sounds had the ability to act as signs and thus to move their audiences to the affects. Music's power was so difficult to contain. Some critics looked to the past, to an imagined singing at the dawn of humanity suffused with passion (Rousseau) or to an ancient Greek art that morally improved and edified its listeners (Muratori and Gravina). This nostalgia for a lost but more perfect music was contrasted with the ambition of other critics who struggled to capture the power of sounds through music theory. In radically different

---

80. Rousseau's criticism of "Enfin" occupies the entire conclusion of the *Lettre sur la musique françoise*, 79–92; his thoughts on the earliest passionate human utterances are further developed in the *Essai sur l'origine des langues*.

81. "S'il n'est pas absolument impossible de déterminer les Chants, & les *Modulations* en consequence, qui conviendroient le mieux aux expressions les plus marquées, c'est d'ailleurs une entreprise qui demanderoit peut-être plus que la vie d'un seul homme." Jean-Philippe Rameau, *Nouveau système de musique théorique* (Paris: Jean-Baptiste-Christophe Ballard, 1726), 43.

ways, and with divergent results, this position was held by thinkers such as Rameau, Heinichen, Mattheson, Vion, and their later exponents. But in their texts, too, there is a melancholy pall cast over the project. When these authors encounter the enormity and impossibility of their task, they shrink from it, acknowledging the limitations of the printed word. Rameau, for one, imagined that his undertaking would outlast his lifetime. "Consider," Mattheson wrote at the conclusion of his own taxonomy, "that it is with the affects, especially, as it is with a bottomless sea: however much effort one might take to write something comprehensive about it, still only the least bit of significance could be used, and endless more unsaid would remain."[82] Elsewhere, in an earlier effort at a taxonomy of the musical affects, Mattheson admitted, "The more one aspires to state something positive thereon, the more contradictions one will probably find, since the opinions about this material are almost numberless."[83] Numberless indeed; this melancholic acknowledgment of impossibility and infinitude was the engine that proliferated the taxonomies of the mimetic *Affektenlehre* tradition.

This first period in the eighteenth-century musical *Affektenlehre* set into motion a principal dynamic that has retained significance for twenty-first-century affect theory. Although its content might be unfamiliar to modern eyes and ears, its form is important to us. Music, and particularly opera, functioned in this earlier period as a contested zone in which conflicts concerning affect and aesthetics were staged. Critics claimed incredible power for music; then they found reasons that it could not be captured. This power really only existed long ago or far away. Or, they claimed, this power could be harnessed with the supreme tools of reason — it could be measured and explained with science. But along the way to so doing, these same thinkers admitted that this nearly impossible task would always overspill the limits of the page, outlast the lifetime of the author, or flummox the precision of the method. What this early period in the history of musical affect theory amounts to, then, is a consistent invocation of music's affective power linked with a refusal to pronounce any codification of it complete.

---

82. "Anerwogen es mit den Affecten insonderheit eben die Bewandniß hat, als mit einem unergründlichen Meer, so daß, wie viel Mühe man sich auch nehmen mögte, etwas vollständiges hierüber auszufertigen, doch nur das wenigste zu Buche gebracht, unendlich viel aber ungesagt bleiben . . . anheimgestellet werden dürffte." Mattheson, *Der vollkommene Capellmeister*, 19.

83. "Allein je mehr man sich bestreben wolte, etwas *positives* davon zu statuiren, je mehr *contradicentes* würden sich vielleicht finden, sintemahl die Meinungen in dieser *Materie* fast unzehlig sind." Johann Mattheson, *Das neu-eröffnete Orchestre* (Hamburg: Mattheson and Benjamin Schillers Witwe, 1713), 252.

2
Comic Opera: Mimesis Exploded

"They're laughing at the opera, they're splitting their sides with laughter!"[1] Or at least so claimed Paul H. D. d'Holbach, whose words would have been no small matter when they were penned in 1752. The Paris Opéra had been "profaned," he satirically wrote, by "senseless laughter and indecent gaiety."[2] As the home of sung French tragedy, or *tragédie en musique*, the Paris Opéra was a most unusual place for comedy.[3] A space for gods and heroes, for love and death and classical ideals, the opera treasured there was nothing to laugh about. But that summer a small traveling group of Italian opera buffa performers took up residency at the Opéra, bringing to Paris for the first time a new form of comic opera that was slowly spreading across Europe from its origins in Neapolitan theaters. This new form of comic opera lampooned the traditions of its tragic counterpart. Its stories concerned aspirational servants and hapless old misers, bumbling, pretentious losers and the tricksters who could hoodwink them with outrageous disguises. Though smaller in cast and

---

1. "On rit à l'Opera, on y rit à gorge déployée!" Paul H. D. d'Holbach, *Lettre a une dame d'un certain age, sur l'état présent de l'opéra* (Paris, 1752), in *La querelle des bouffons: Texte des pamphlets*, ed. Denise Launay, vol. 1 (Geneva: Minkoff, 1973), 122.

2. "Nous avons vû, à la honte de la Nation & de notre siècle, le Théâtre *auguste* de l'Opera profané par d'indignes Bâteleurs. Oui, Madame, ce spectacle si grave, si vénérable . . . avoir pris soin d'écarter les ris insensés & la gayeté indécente." d'Holbach, *Lettre a une dame*, 2; *La querelle des bouffons*, 122.

3. The one notable exception that directly anticipated Italian comic opera's new popularity was Jean-Philippe Rameau's *Platée*, first performed in 1745. See Downing A. Thomas, "Rameau's *Platée* Returns: A Case of Double Identity in the *Querelle des bouffons*," *Cambridge Opera Journal* 18, no. 1 (2006): 1–19.

in duration, it specialized in the overblown. Everything about it was exaggerated: the stage action and gesture, the inappropriate sentiments, the antics of the plot, and, most of all, the music.

Comic opera presented a challenge to the aesthetic doctrine of mimesis. Until the mid-eighteenth century, critics had seen opera as a union of poetry with music on the stage. Each moment in the drama employed these forces together to create a coherent image and action, using stock musical codes and conventions to amplify the intended affect of the drama. Especially in the case of French criticism, music was understood to be subservient to the poetry of the libretto; even in passages without singing, the music of the opera was tied to the expression of its text.[4] Using these procedures, opera fell into accord with the neoclassical doctrine of mimesis, in which the goal of art was the imitation of the natural world.

Comic opera originated, in part, as a parodic, metatheatrical critique of this operatic aesthetic.[5] Composers of comic opera adopted several new mimetic techniques that mocked the predictable musical procedures of serious opera and, further, the mimetic doctrine itself. These composers employed mimesis in exaggerated, excessive, and rapidly changing forms; they also began to use poetry and music as autonomous signifying systems, engaging in musical mimesis to suggest something other than what was expressed in the opera's poetry and thereby subverting the meaning of the text. These practices bolstered the relatively new notion that music had the power to act as a sign independent of poetry.

The growing awareness of comic opera's peculiar use of mimesis and of its distinctive musical style facilitated a transformation in operatic aesthetics. Curiously, instead of creating a more expansive mimetic theory to accommodate the new Italian style and its significations, critics explicitly turned away from this doctrine in favor of a new view in which music, independently, was said to attune its audience to an affective state in a material fashion. In the domain of aesthetic theory, then, the extreme mimesis in this music was no longer mimetic — it was instead directly affective. This transformation marked the beginnings of a new attunement *Affektenlehre*.

Precisely because the historiography of comic opera is tightly associated with the aesthetics of mimesis, the important role that this musical idiom played in catalyzing a reassessment of the mimetic doctrine has not always

4. See Catherine Kintzler, *Poétique de l'opéra français de Corneille à Rousseau* (Paris: Minerve, 1991), esp. 365.

5. See Keith James Johnston, "È caso da intermedio! Comic Theory, Comic Style, and the Early Intermezzo" (PhD diss., University of Toronto, 2011), esp. 178–223.

been apparent. Instead, historians and theorists of this repertoire have traditionally emphasized its contributions to the development of mimetic techniques in music.[6] But one result of the critical quarrel on comic opera was the theoretical displacement of mimetic representation with affective attunement. Seen from this perspective, the twenty-first century's turn to affect is only the most recent motion of a dialectic concerning affect and signification that has been in place at least since early modernity.

The new attunement *Affektenlehre* arose as a response to a myriad set of intellectual problems, of which comic opera's capers were only one. I place special emphasis on comic opera in this chapter because of the intensity of the period's critical debates surrounding that art form.[7] Crucially, the domain of affect theory itself was in constant flux during the middle decades of the eighteenth century, with some of its basic principles of operation as yet undetermined by any sort of theoretical consensus. This goes some way toward explaining how it was that music theory — grappling with problems of signification and mimesis — and affect theory became entangled with each other during their mutual development, deeply associating affect with music, sympathetic resonance, and sound vibration.

Three Comic Operas

To be sure, there was something immediately appealing, new, and funny about Italian opera buffa for Parisian audiences. Recalling Giuseppe Maria Orlandini's *Il marito giocatore* (which had its Paris premier in August of that infamous 1752 summer), the conservative critic Élie-Catherine Fréron noted with some disdain that the opera provoked "convulsions" and "extravagant movements" in the *parterre*. "It couldn't better resemble the sort of delirium that always follows the excessive exaggeration caused by strong alcohol."[8] But

6. Notable examples include Wye Jamison Allanbrook, *The Secular Commedia: Comic Mimesis in Late Eighteenth-Century Music* (Berkeley: University of California Press, 2014); Mary Hunter, "Topics and Opera Buffa," in *The Oxford Handbook of Topic Theory*, ed. Danuta Mirka (Oxford: Oxford University Press, 2014), 61–89; and Daniel Heartz, *From Garrick to Gluck: Essays on Opera in the Age of Enlightenment*, ed. John A. Rice (Hillsdale, NY: Pendragon, 2004), esp. 11–51.

7. Chapter 3 offers an alternative, focusing on debates about instrumental music.

8. "C'est le jouer d'*Orlandini*, ouvrage dans son genre même assez médiocre, qui causa dans le Parterre François de mouvemens extravagans qui ressembloient à des convulsions, des applaudissemens qui tenoient du transport, une joye excessive qui avoit l'air de la folie. . . . Rien n'a mieux ressemblé peut-être à cette sorte de délire qui suit toujours les excès outrés des liqueurs fortes." Elie-Catherine Fréron, "Les spectacles de Paris, ou Calendrier historique et

what Fréron describes as immoderate behavior in the audience could also
have aptly characterized the action onstage in any one of the works that the
troupe of *bouffons* brought to Paris. Part of what made this type of comic opera so fresh and so controversial was the way in which it used music to mock
serious opera, creating the hyperbolic exploits that Fréron describes.

Perhaps the best known of the works performed during the *bouffons*' three-
year tenure in Paris is Pergolesi's *La serva padrona,* an opera about a plucky
servant, Serpina, who convinces her employer, Uberto, to marry her. The
life of a housemaid does not suit her; she wants to be "revered like a mistress.
Arch-mistress! Mega-mistress!"[9] In order to pull off this stunt, she disguises
her fellow servant Vespone as her new potential husband: a mean-spirited
ruffian soldier she calls Captain Tempesta. In a brilliantly manipulative aria,
"A Serpina penserete," she asks Uberto to think of her from time to time when
she is gone and to remember how good she was to him. Of course, she reasons,
Uberto will marry her to avoid losing her and also to avoid the dowry he would
have to pay Tempesta.

"A Serpina penserete" explodes the mimetic conventions of the serious
opera aria with an overload of mimesis. The aria begins in a stately, slow
tempo with a corresponding 4/4 meter; Serpina's lines of entreaty are smooth
and sweet, and on their own, they could even sound earnestly saccharine. But
accompanying them we hear a passage of quickly repeated, detached, staccato
pitches in the orchestra that undercuts the sincerity of her text. This orchestral commentary begins just before Serpina sings her lines directed toward
Uberto, and it returns as she is finishing them. It mimetically depicts agitation
using the orchestra in order to deliver more information than is offered in
the text of the aria, suggesting an anxiety in Serpina's bluffing performance
within the performance. Suddenly, just as soon as she concludes her words
to Uberto, Serpina launches into her own solipsistic world, singing to herself
and the audience in a brisk allegro tempo and in 3/8, a meter associated with
peasant dances and frivolity. The effect is a dramatic, unprepared change of

---

chronologique des théâtres," in *L'Année littéraire, ou Suite des lettres sur quelques écrits de ce
temps,* vol. 1 (Amsterdam: Lambert, 1756), 159–167, esp. 161–162. For a skeptical view on the issue
of audience laughter in the Paris Opéra, see Dominique Quéro, "Rire et comique à l'Académie
royale de musique: La querelle du 'bouffon'?," in *La "Querelle des Bouffons" dans la vie culturelle
française du XVIIIe siècle,* ed. Andrea Fabiano (Paris: CNRS Éditions, 2005), 57–72; but for a
contrasting account, see David Charlton, *Opera in the Age of Rousseau* (Cambridge: Cambridge
University Press, 2012), 257–264.

9. "Voglio esser rispettata, voglio esser riverita, come fossi padrona, arci padrona, padro-
nissima." Giovanni Battista Pergolesi, *La serva padrona,* in *Opera omnia di Giovanni Battista
Pergolesi,* ed. Francesco Caffarelli, vol. 3 (Rome: Gli Amici della Musica da Camera, 1941), 10.

character. "It seems to me that he's already slowly beginning to soften!" she exclaims.[10] Then the slow tempo and the 4/4 meter return just as abruptly as they had left, and Serpina repeats her original entreaty, again directed toward Uberto and again agitated by the staccato figure in the orchestra. Twice more the aria rapidly changes character, with Serpina asking Uberto to please forget any of her bad behavior and remarking, again to herself, that the squeeze of his hand is a sign that her plot is working.

The entire scene is exaggeration, with Serpina's insincere serenade accompanied by the anxious violins and placed directly back-to-back with her joyous and energetic interior monologue. Serpina effectively listens to herself perform the aria — the music she sings as an aside comments on the song she directs to Uberto. Although eighteenth-century arias often contained a single contrasting emotion expressed in the interior of their form, the many abrupt changes in meter, tempo, and character of "A Serpina penserete" were far more drastic than what was typically heard in the Paris Opéra.[11] This aria attempted to outdo mimesis with emotional portrayal that was simultaneously more exacting — altering the entire musical fabric with each rapidly encountered emotion — and also more formally complex, with each different affective disposition commenting metatheatrically on those around it. The result was a style of performance that was aware of itself as performance in its formal shifts of perspective.

La serva padrona was not the only one of Pergolesi's works to arrive in Paris with the bouffons. The less well-known but equally adventurous Livietta e Tracollo had its Paris premier in May 1753. This is another work that doubles mimetic procedures through performances within performances; the opera begins with every character in disguise. Livietta, dressed as a French country boy, and her friend Fulvia, wearing false jewels, are attempting to seek revenge against the thief Tracollo, who is himself disguised as an old Polish woman (the disguise is musically complete with an entrance aria that sounds like a traditional Polish mazurka dance in 3/8 meter with emphases on the second beat of each measure). After a tussle in which both parties pretend to be incompetent in the Italian language, Livietta reveals her identity and calls for Tracollo's imprisonment. The second act begins with Tracollo in a new disguise. This time he has dressed himself up as an old, insane astronomer in

---

10. "Ei mi par che già pian piano s'incomincia a intenerir." Pergolesi, *La serva padrona*, 37–38.

11. In Charlton's words, "A total shift of sensibility was at stake, away from the aria or set-piece as musicalised poetry towards set-piece as musicalised emotion. Italy presented a simulacrum of sentiments expressed in 'real time.'" Charlton, *Opera in the Age of Rousseau*, 258.

a bid to win Livietta over. Here again, Pergolesi's score clothes the character in appropriate costume. The libretto indicates that Tracollo should gesticulate and "laugh indecently [*sconciamente ride*]," and we hear the orchestra perform this task for him.[12] Just before his first lines, the violins rip upward in two iterations of a rapidly ascending scale, descending from their height at half the pace in staccato pulses. The result is something that sounds like an arching of the back and filling of the chest followed by a bursting cackle in a high register. "I seem to be doing this well," Tracollo says of his newfound character. "But in pretending, I really don't want to go, as they say, off my rocker."[13] The orchestra concludes each of his lines with more instrumental laughter.

Tracollo is constantly transforming. A character that is always playing a character, his troped mimetic representations destabilize traditional mimetic technique. In this scene, his exaggerated peculiarity is emphasized in the orchestral cackling, which lends the otherwise inconsistent and elastic Tracollo a temporary mechanical rigidity.[14] Later in the opera, as he watches what he thinks is Livietta's death (she is faking it), he is overtaken by her body's flailing, dying motions and begins to act them out with his own body while punctuating each one with a sung "ha."[15] Tracollo, like many comic opera characters, is an empty vessel ready to receive any distinct persona or action.[16] He is in some ways like the malleable sounds of music itself, adaptable to the presentation of a broad palette of affects.

Parisians heard many kinds of orchestral laughter during the tenure of the *bouffons*. Rinaldo di Capua's *La zingara*, which received its premiere at the Paris Opéra in June 1753, contains several experimental scenes that employ

---

12. Pergolesi, *Livietta e Tracollo*, trans. and ed. Charles C. Russell, in *Complete Works/Opere Complete*, ed. Gordana Lazarevich, vol. 6 (Stuyvesant, NY: Pendragon, 1991), 47–52.

13. "Par che ci pigli gusto. Non vorrei che, fingendo, fingendo da vero poi, siccome dir si suole, avessi a dar di volta alle carriole." Pergolesi, *Livietta e Tracollo*, 11 (my translation modified from Russell's).

14. In this sense, Tracollo embodies the tension between human life and mechanized action that Henri Bergson identified as a hallmark of comedy; see Bergson, *Laughter: An Essay on the Meaning of the Comic*, trans. Cloudesley Brereton and Fred Rothwell (New York: Macmillan, 1914).

15. In an interesting twist, he seems not to believe her when he sings "Ah, Livietta, now you're exaggerating. When are . . . ? Either hurry up and die or get up and live." But he returns to miming her movements with the next utterance: "It looks like I've got the convulsions too." Pergolesi, *Livietta e Tracollo*, 14. So contagious is the mimicry of mimicry.

16. This is what connects Tracollo—and many other comic opera characters—to the commedia dell'arte figure of the *zanni*. See in particular Sianne Ngai, "The Zany Science," in *Our Aesthetic Categories: Zany, Cute, Interesting* (Cambridge, MA: Harvard University Press, 2012), 174–232.

this effect. Nisa, the female protagonist, has contrived to simultaneously rob and also marry the elderly miser Calcante. She enlists the help of her brother, Tagliaborsi, who is disguised as a bear. The opera begins with the two siblings onstage, and Tagliaborsi complains in his first aria that Nisa is laughing at him in the bear suit while he suffers its constraints. Immediately after he sings "you laugh" (that is, "you're laughing at me"), Tagliaborsi halts for a moment, and we hear the orchestra perform a high, rapid, descending figure in the violins — just long enough for a short chuckle.[17] This device — which is straightforwardly mimetic of laughter, using orchestral sound during a break in Tagliaborsi's singing — is repeated fourteen times in the short aria to solidify its effect.

Later, Nisa convinces Calcante that the bear in her company is in fact a famous and talented animal, and she sells it to him for twenty ducats. Calcante is quite pleased with his purchase, imagining that this famous bear will fetch more than a thousand when he offers it for sale. While he is celebrating his good fortune, Tagliaborsi quickly slips away. Calcante, now shocked and horrified, laments his financial ruin in an accompanied recitative that is particularly innovative. He begins to sing haltingly — "Where, where could the bear have gone?" — and the orchestra fills in his pauses with high, rapid turning figures reminiscent of the orchestral chuckles in Tagliaborsi's aria.[18] The music settles for a moment in G major, and its quick, light giddiness taunts Calcante as he searches hopelessly for the bear. "My poor ducats! They've gone to hell!" he exclaims.[19] Any seriousness with which we could possibly take this old scrooge is undercut by the lighthearted orchestral accompaniment.[20]

In Rinaldo's ingenious writing, we hear one sentiment expressed in the text with a contrasting feeling provided in the musical design. The opera's music gives us a way to regard comically what is otherwise expressed in serious words. This method of using music against the text is typically associated with opera composition of the late eighteenth century onward, but it is present already in these early comic operas.[21] To midcentury Parisian audiences attempting

17. "Anzi ridi a mio dispetto, ridi, a mio dispetto!" Rinaldo di Capua, *La zingara*, ed. Eva Riccioli Orecchia (Florence: Edizioni Musicali Otos, 1969), 6.

18. "E dove, dove l'orso n'andò?" Rinaldo, *La zingara*, 43.

19. "Poveri miei ducati! Alla malora se ne sono andati!" (More precisely: "To hell if they've been lost!"). Rinaldo, *La zingara*, 44–45.

20. Although the music eventually moves to E minor before the onset of Calcante's upcoming aria, the giddy turn figure is developed throughout.

21. Scholars have generally overlooked the early manifestations of this innovation in early opera buffa, associating it instead with opera composition in the final decades of the century. See, for instance, Gary Tomlinson, *Metaphysical Song: An Essay on Opera* (Princeton, NJ: Prince-

to make sense of the new Italian style, it would have been unprecedented. Music, it seemed, was being employed as an independent aesthetic force, not limited to the expression or enhancement of the opera's poetry.

It was bad enough that people in the *parterre* were laughing indecently, but Pergolesi and Rinaldo put laughter, impropriety, and bad behavior on center stage, using orchestral devices to inflate, surpass, and comment on the text. In so doing, they parodied the very notion of mimesis, ridiculing the formulaic ceremony of serious opera in which sung tragedy used stock musical gestures to support its poetry. Serious opera worked to depict a unified image in each scene, while comic opera changed out gestures even more frequently than its casts changed disguises. The characters we meet in these early comic operas are the prototypes for those more famous comic opera characters from the late eighteenth century, like Mozart's Leporello (from *Don Giovanni*, an Italian opera buffa) or the Queen of the Night (from *Die Zauberflöte*, a German *Singspiel*). Leporello runs his mouth on an unbelievable list at breakneck speed, and the Queen (who has no proper name; she is pure role) sings an aria requiring robotic pyrotechnics with popped high notes in the stratosphere of the soprano range. Their depictions are at once evocative of "*something mechanical encrusted upon the living*" — Bergson's famous formula for the comic — but also metatheatrically critical of the typical mimetic conventions of the opera.[22] The unexpected consequence was that this excess of mimesis destabilized the entire discourse surrounding music, an art whose purchase on mimesis was already tenuous.

Critical Quarrel

With performances like these, it was no wonder that everyone was talking about the opera. The arrival of the *bouffons* in Paris provoked a massive pamphlet war on the nature of opera and on musical aesthetics more generally. More than sixty pamphlets on the topic were printed and exchanged between 1752 and 1754, as defenders and detractors alike attempted to formulate what, exactly, was so thrilling or so objectionable about the comic Italian music.[23] Now known as the *querelle des bouffons*, the debate reignited the issues of

ton University Press, 1999), 55–61; and the examples collected in Hunter, "Topics and Opera Buffa," 83–87.

22. Bergson, *Laughter*, 37.

23. The collected pamphlets are available in facsimile in Denise Launay, ed., *La querelle des bouffons: Texte des pamphlets*, 3 vols. (Geneva: Minkoff, 1973).

an older French controversy: a musical version of the early modern quarrel between the ancients and the moderns, which had already included within it an interrogation of the limits of music's capacity to express outside of or beyond the operatic text.[24] The new quarrel placed increasing pressure on this question in particular.

There has been an understandable tendency in studies of the *querelle des bouffons* to see a polarization of opinions divided sharply between the supporters of serious, French opera (the *coin du roi*, or king's corner) and supporters of comic, Italian opera (the *coin de la reine*, or queen's corner). Typically, those who were in favor of the new Italian style are seen as the forward-thinking progressives; this group includes the Parisian encyclopedists Rousseau, d'Alembert, and Diderot, among others. The supporters of French opera are seen, by contrast, as a conservative group clinging to an older notion of operatic propriety; the members of this group are less well-known, as are their writings.[25]

Apart from the clear duality organized around the two different repertoires, there was in fact a great deal of consensus among critics in the quarrel. Contributors agreed that something very different was at work in the music of the comic Italian operas—whether they enjoyed it or reviled it—and that this musical difference required new theoretical tools or language for musical style itself. In this sense, both sides of the debate worked to stabilize the notion that music was an aesthetic force independent of language.[26] Up until this point, writers on music and aesthetics had generally understood musical sounds to convey and supplement the meaning of a text. Music without words was considered something of a form without a content, like random splashes of paint thrown against a canvas (as Charles Batteux had it)[27] or, in the words of Noël-Antoine Pluche, like "a fine suit separated from a body and hung from

---

24. In this sense, the larger eighteenth-century debate on musical aesthetics can likewise be seen as an aspect of the Enlightenment's ongoing ancients and moderns quarrel; see Dan Edelstein, *The Enlightenment: A Genealogy* (Chicago: University of Chicago Press, 2010).

25. Classic accounts of the quarrel can be found in Alfred Richard Oliver, *The Encyclopedists as Critics of Music* (New York: Columbia University Press, 1947); and Heartz, *From Garrick to Gluck*, 213–254. More recent work includes the essays collected in Fabiano, *La "Querelle des Bouffons"*; Thomas, "Rameau's *Platée* Returns"; Jed Wentz, "Gaps, Pauses and Expressive Arms: Reconstructing the Link between Stage Gesture and Musical Timing at the Académie Royale de Musique," *Journal for Eighteenth-Century Studies* 32, no. 4 (2009): 607–623; and Charlton, *Opera in the Age of Rousseau*.

26. On the stabilization of the new aesthetic category of music—as something distinct from song—see Tomlinson, "Early Modern Opera," in *Metaphysical Song*, 34–72.

27. See Charles Batteux, *Les beaux arts réduits à un même principe* (Paris: Durand, 1746), 280.

a peg."[28] Music without a text lacked a certain essence. It was the costume without the actor. It failed to communicate anything with specificity.

Because critics felt compelled to account for the musical differences between the French and Italian styles, they stumbled onto a new set of questions about music's capacity for mimesis. Since art was supposed to be mimetic, the question had to be asked: What, if anything, was the basis of music's mimetic power — what was it that the sound of music itself displayed? If music could be said to work mimetically, was it successful in its task? Answers to these questions were far from uniform along party lines in the debate, with both sides drawing on different aspects of the history of aesthetics in order to account for the new and provocative situation before them. While some authors insisted on grounding their account of the new style in mimetic theory, others doubted that this was even possible.

Among those who theorized the new Italian style along mimetic lines was a critic writing under the name Rousselet, who pointed out that in Italian opera's reproductions of the world, it had managed to depict all of the "little things" of mundane existence. The objects of its comic depiction were always "the petty and the low." French opera, by contrast, "does not debase itself to these puerilities."[29] Another, anonymous critic voiced the same objection in the context of a tongue-in-cheek pamphlet titled *Lettre ecrite de l'autre monde*. This piece pits an ostensible enthusiast of the new Italian style against a conservative Lullyst — a supporter of traditional French opera and its seventeenth-century master, Jean-Baptiste Lully.

> Paintings! Replied the [pro-Italian] musician, eh! This is where we
> shine. What richness! What profusions in our Italian opera! Every-
> thing is painted from tears, to laughter, to sneezes. . . . Your Lully
> had only one color for each image, which was sometimes tinged but
> basically dominant throughout. He never knew the science of details.
> We have varied designs for almost every modulation of the phrase;
> one also sometimes sees a single syllable artistically decorated and

---

28. "C'est un bel habit séparé du corps & pendu à une cheville." Noël-Antoine Pluche, *Le Spectacle de la nature, ou entretiens sur les particularités de l'histoire naturelle, qui ont paru les plus propres à rendre les Jeunes-Gens curieux, & à leur former l'esprit*, vol. 7 (Paris: Veuve Estienne et Fils, 1747), 115.

29. "Dans le genre Italien ne nous a peint que de petites choses. . . . Elles sont presque toujours dans le petit & dans le bas. . . . La Musique Françoise ne s'abaisse point à toutes ces puérilités." Rousselet (Jean-Baptiste-Claude Meunier, or possibly a pseudonym for Élie Catherine Fréron), *Lettres sur la musique françoise en réponse a celle de Jean-Jacques Rousseau* (Geneva, 1754), in Launay, *La querelle des bouffons*, 1:787–788.

delicately fluttered over one or two octaves presenting four different images at the same time.

Eh! It is this piling up of designs, replied the Lullyst, it is this clever decorating which is a hundred thousand miles from nature.[30]

In this exchange, the varied and exaggerated use of music as a mimetic medium was actually seen to detract from the often-repeated goal of the eighteenth-century mimetic doctrine: the imitation of the beautiful in nature. Rather than working to supplement the clear images of the text, the music of the Italians was all distraction, filigree, and falseness, attempting to depict far more than it was able.

Jean-Baptiste Jourdan was even more skeptical, wondering how it was that musical sounds could really depict anything substantial. He equated the folly of the Italian opera's comic characters with the semantic imprecision of music as a medium, wondering what on earth something like a musical flourish could possibly represent. Discussing the musical decoration at the conclusion of a melodic line (a cadenza), Jourdan wrote, "I would very much like for your philosophers of the *Coin de la Reine*, . . . who have read in Aristotle that the arts are an imitation of nature, to tell me honestly what one paints with a cadenza. Would it not be a drunk who, weak in the legs, wavers, beats the walls, comes, goes, slides to the ground, gets up, and finally falls to be applauded?"[31] Turning a musical figure into a comic opera character—a clumsy lush— Jourdan reversed comic opera's mimicry. Rather than using musical sounds for ridicule, instead he ridiculed musical sounds by drawing them into an

---

30. "Des tableaux! reprit le musicien, eh! c'est où nous brillons; quelle richesse! quelle profusion dans nos Opéra Italiens! tout y est peint, jusqu'aux pleurs, aux ris, aux éternuemens; & que ne peindroient-ils pas? Votre Lulli n'avoit qu'un coloris pour chaque image, qu'il nuançoit quelquefois, mais qui y dominoit toujours; il ne connut jamais la science des détails: nous autres, nous avons des desseins variés presqu'à chaque phrase de modulation; on voit même quelquefois une seule sillabe artistement *guillochée*, & voltigeant legérement sur une ou deux octaves, offrir à la fois quatre images différentes. Eh! c'est cet entassement de desseins, repliqua le Lulliste, c'est ce *guillochage* savant qui est à cent mille lieues de la nature." *Lettre ecrite de l'autre monde* (1753), in Launay, *La querelle des bouffons*, 1:367. On this letter, its authorship, and its perspective, see Elisabeth Cook, "Challenging the *Ancien Régime*: The Hidden Politics of the 'Querelle des Bouffons,'" in Fabiano, *La "Querelle des Bouffons*," 154–155.

31. "Mais à propos, je voudrois bien que vos Philosophes du Coin de la Reine (car c'est à eux à qui j'en veux principalement) eux qui ont lû dans Aristote que les Arts sont une imitation de la Nature, qu'ils me dissent de bonne foi ce qu'on veut peindre par un point d'Orgue. Ne seroit-ce pas un yvrogne qui, foible sur ses jambes, vacile, bat les murs, va, vient, glisse jusqu'à terre, se releve, & tombe enfin pour être applaudi." Jean-Baptiste Jourdan, *Le correcteur des bouffons a l'ecolier de Prague* (1753), in Launay, *La querelle des bouffons*, 1:200–201.

equation with sloppy bodily gestures, making an embarrassment of their materiality. Just as some subjects were deemed unfit for depiction on the stage,
Jourdan intended a disqualification of music from the power of signification.

In his disdainful evocation of undisciplined corporeality, Jourdan brought
the question of musical mimesis into conversation with another of the *querelle*'s central obsessions: the listening body. From the opening of the pamphlet war, both sides wondered not only at the other's judgment but also at
what physical constitution could have predisposed them to such musical par-
tialities in the first place. One early critic indicated that Italian fans of the
opera buffa might have "numb organs," for instance;[32] while d'Holbach, by
contrast, wrote with sarcasm of the French "good citizens" with "respectable
wigs," whose longtime patronage of the *tragédie en musique* had supplied
them not only with experience but also with a "vivacity of their organs."[33] And
indeed, as the debate drew on, it became clear that conservative proponents
of the *coin du roi* believed their bodies to be in better accord than those who
appreciated the sound of the Italians. Because, as the author of the searing
Epître aux bouffonistes tells us, "art penetrates the body," there is, in those who
appreciate it, "an instinct that cannot be learned."[34] In a fantastically biting
couplet, he reduces this capacity to the corporeality of listeners: "En un mot,
pour juger de la belle harmonie / Il faut avoir l'organe, & non pas le génie."[35]
It was the body's organs, and not the mind's genius, that provided the ability
to judge beautiful harmony.

This extreme position, taken by some of the defenders of serious French
opera, was simply a transformation of the belief that in order for music to
affect listeners, it had to penetrate their interior. This was a notion held on
both sides of the debate and reinforced by the huge amount of discourse produced in the volley of opinions. Friedrich Melchoir Grimm, whose *Lettre sur
Omphale* is said to have instigated the entire *querelle*, wrote of Italian music,
"[It] touches me and . . . pierces my soul."[36] Marc-Antoine Laugier, an apol-

---

32. *Remarques au sujet de la letter de M. Grimm sur Omphale* (Paris, 1752), in Launay, *La
querelle des bouffons*, 1:63.

33. "Les bon Citoyens . . . Ces vieillards à perruques respectables, que leur longue expérience
& la vivacité de leur organe ont mis en droit de juger depuis soixante ans." d'Holbach, *Lettre a
une dame*, 122–123.

34. "L'art pénétre le corps; le goût seul voit l'esprit: / C'est dans l'homme un instinct qui jamais ne s'apprit." *Epître aux bouffonnistes* (Paris, 1752), in Launay, *La querelle des bouffons*, 1:399.

35. *Epître aux bouffonnistes*, 1:399.

36. "Leurs plaintes, leurs malheurs me touchent &, si le Musicien le veut ou le peut, ils me
percent l'ame." Friedrich Melchoir Grimm, *Lettre de M. Grimm sur Omphale, Tragédie lyrique*
(Paris, 1752), in Launay, *La querelle des bouffons*, 1:26.

ogist for serious French opera, explained how Lully's music "penetrates the soul without violence, producing a pleasant reverie, a delightful languor."[37] Advocates of both types of opera were said to have had their deepest interiors suffused with musical sound.

This belief was so widespread within the discourse on opera that it was easily parodied. In the dialogue staged within *Lettre ecrite de l'autre monde*, two musicians enter into a hyperbolic dispute over music's mimetic capabilities. Just after the supporter of the Italian style has insulted Lully's music, his sparring partner comes to the defense of the old French master: "Lully was penetrated by the sentiments that he wished to paint, and he would seek in the movements of his heart the truest expression of his sensibility. It was not by dwelling on insignificant details . . . that he was able to create those grand pieces that have been admired in [his operas] *Armide, Roland, Atis*, &c. He would engage, he would shake the entrails."[38] Lully is seen here as having missed the mark slightly, and instead of penetrating the soul, his music agitates the bowels. In a critical exchange so closely inspecting the merits and detriments of an artistic practice that was parodic in its essence, it should be no surprise that some of this technique seeped into the language of criticism itself.

Among the most outspoken of the Italian opera's champions was Rousseau, whose scathing *Lettre sur la musique françoise* was a thoroughgoing condemnation of the French operatic style. For Rousseau, the advantage of Italian opera in musical mimesis was clear. The Italian language, with its sonorous, bright vowels, was more suited to song, and Italian composers were more adept at choosing the precise moments for modulations of the harmony and changes of meter. Most of all, though, Italian opera was primarily structured around its melodies. Its accompaniments, sometimes thin, existed only to support the voice and to reinforce what Rousseau called the "unity of melody" (a concept with classical roots).[39] Melody, Rousseau believed, possessed the power to imitate humanity's natural, passionate utter-

37. "Elle pénétre l'ame sans violence, pour y produire une aimable rêverie, une délicieuse langueur." Marc-Antoine Laugier, *Apologie de la musique françoise, contre m. Rousseau* (Paris, 1754), in Launay, *La querelle des bouffons*, 2:1175.

38. "*Lulli* se pénétroit des sentimens qu'il vouloit peindre, & il cherchoit dans les mouvemens de son cœur l'expression la plus vraie de sa sensibilité. Ce n'est pas en s'appesantissant sur des détails peu essentiels & qui écrasent toujours l'image principale, qu'il auroit fait ces grand morceaux qu'on a admirés dans *Armide, Roland, Atis*, &c. Il intéressoit, il remuoit les entrailles." *Lettre ecrite de l'autre monde*, 1:367–368.

39. See Jacqueline Waeber, "Jean-Jacques Rousseau's 'Unité de Mélodie,'" *Journal of the American Musicological Society* 62, no. 1 (2009): 79–143.

ances. It was an echo of the antediluvian cries of primitive man, which were simultaneously speech and song. "Italian melody," he explained, "finds in every movement the expressions for every character and paintings for every object."[40] Through the power of the voice, Italian opera was supreme in musical mimesis.

Rousseau's assessment draws on a long history of theorizing musical mimesis with reference to the voice. Especially in French neoclassical criticism — precisely of the variety typically used to uphold the values of serious French opera — the power of musical mimesis belonged to song. As Jean-Baptiste Dubos had put it as early as 1719, "Just as the painter imitates the features and colors of nature, so too the musician imitates the tones, accents, sighs, inflections of the voice, and, in short, all of those sounds with which nature exudes the sentiments and passions. These, as we have already seen, hold a marvelous power to move us, because they are the signs of the passions instituted by nature, whence they receive their energy."[41] Traditionally taken as a component of the conservative view that would have subordinated the power of musical sounds to that of the text they expressed, Rousseau repurposed this understanding of musical mimesis such that it supported a kind of music that did no such thing. With attention to the ways in which critics interpreted and employed various understandings of mimesis to their own ends, it becomes clear that the debate over comic opera only intensified the need for clarification on how, exactly, music was a mimetic art.

It was not long after Rousseau issued his missive that Fréron responded with a lengthy, multipart defense of French opera.[42] Point by point, he took on Rousseau's provocations. Quoting a passage in which Rousseau extols the ability of the Italian style to depict "all characters imaginable," Fréron had occasion to instruct Rousseau on music's mimetic capabilities. Music, Fréron insisted, appeals to the ear. Therefore, it can only imitate things that are themselves sounds or that produce sounds. Fréron anticipated the objections; if

40. "Mais la mélodie Italienne trouve dans chaque mouvement des expressions pour tous les caractéres, des tableaux pour tous les objets." Jean-Jacques Rousseau, *Lettre sur la musique françoise* (Paris, 1753), in Launay, *La querelle des bouffons*, 1:740.

41. "Ainsi que le Peintre imite les traits & les couleurs de la nature, de même le Musicien imite les tons, les accens, les soûpirs, les inflexions de voix, enfin tous ces sons à l'aide desquels la nature même exprime ses sentiments & ses passions. Tous ces sons, commme nous l'avons déja exposé, ont une force merveilleuse pour nous émouvoir, parce qu'ils sont les signes des passions instituez par la nature dont ils ont reçû leur énergie." Jean-Baptiste Dubos, *Réflexions critiques sur la poésie et sur la peinture*, vol. 1 (Paris: Jean Mariette, 1719), 634–635.

42. Élie-Catherine Fréron, *Suite des lettres sur la musique françoise: En réponse à celle de Jean-Jacques Rousseau* (Geneva, 1754), in Launay, *La querelle des bouffons*, 2:1009–1039.

music can only imitate things that are themselves sounded, it would seem to be a very limited art. How, then, ought we to account for the fact that music moves us? In response, Fréron elaborated an alternative way of thinking through the problem:

> Experience demonstrates that music inspires sentiments and passions, but it neither expresses them nor paints them. Please do not lose sight of this distinction. In order to make myself understood, I am obliged to enter into a mechanical examination of the effects of music on the human body. It is a proven experience that if you pluck one of two strings tuned in unison, the other will experience a very sensible vibration and will create a sound. The human body contains a multitude of nerves of different lengths and of different thicknesses, stretched to differing degrees. It is through them, as you know, that the soul receives its impressions. The chords of harmony that the musician passes over find themselves — regardless of the key — in unison with a more or less large number of nerves; these are then made to sound, they feel the vibrations and, by the inviolable laws of nature, allow the soul to experience sensations that, always more or less strong, are relative to the number of respective unisons.[43]

Operating neither mimetically nor expressively, music in Fréron's view attuned its audience to various sensations through its physical vibrations. Musicians were not simply supplying the live soundtrack to a series of representations — in his model, they were said to generate affect itself, directly. Fréron removed the problematic responsibility of mimetic depiction from music altogether, replacing it instead with an affective attunement predicated on the basis of music's material reality as sound vibrations. To be sure, his account of music's affective force was a limited one; the chief goal of music, he went on to say, is

43. "Cependant l'expérience nous prouve que la Musique inspire les sentimens & les passions . . . mais elle ne les exprime ni ne les peint. Je vous prie de vouloir bien ne pas perdre de vûe cette distinction. Je suis obligé, pour me faire entendre, d'entrer dans un examen méchanique des effets de la Musique sur le corps humain. C'est une expérience reconnue que si de deux cordes montées à l'unisson vous pincez l'une, l'autre éprouvera un frémissement très-sensible, & rendra du son. Le corps humain contient une multitude de nerfs de différentes longueurs & de différentes grosseurs, tendus à différens dégrés. Vous sçavez que c'est par leur moyen que l'ame reçoit ses impressions. Les cordes d'harmonie que le Musicien parcourt soit dans un ton, soit dans un autre, se trouvant à l'unisson d'un nombre de nerfs plus ou moins considérable, leur font rendre ces sons, & leur font ressentir ces frémissemens, loix inviolables de la nature, & font éprouver par conséquent à l'ame des sensations quelconques, toujours plus ou moins fortes, relativement au nombre d'unissons respectifs." Fréron, *Suite des lettres sur la musique françoise*, 2:1027–1028.

to "render more sensible the situation that the poet describes."[44] Nevertheless, in his effort to defend serious French opera, he completely reoriented the traditional formula connecting music with affect.

The concept of mimesis — with its long intellectual heritage — is expansive enough to include Fréron's theory of attunement. But to understand it in this way is to miss the explicit rejection of the mimetic framework that he and other period critics proposed.[45] Fréron was instead attempting to displace mimesis altogether in favor of an explanatory framework that favored the corporeal and material dimensions of musical listening; in this way, he effectively discarded the terms of one of the *querelle*'s central preoccupations by substituting in the elements of another. But in so doing, Fréron elevated the debate's awkward fascination with the listening body by recasting it in the terms of the older neoplatonic notion of *musica humana*, in which the human body is described as an instrument and its parts tuned in harmonious ratios. *Musica humana* is a microcosmography of the harmony of the spheres — or *musica mundana* — and an analogue of human music making, *musica instrumentalis*. Transmitted through medieval music theory, the *musica humana* tradition had also found its way into theories of the affects by the eighteenth century. Shaftesbury, for instance, had equated the affective disposition of the human as a kind of attunement in his 1711 *Characteristics of Men, Manners, Opinions, Times*. "Upon the whole," he wrote, "it may be said properly to be

44. "Rendre plus sensibles les situations où le Poëte le conduit." Fréron, *Suite des lettres sur la musique françoise*, 2:1030.

45. There has been a trend in historical studies of mimesis to read these eighteenth-century texts as representative of a transformation within mimetic theory rather than a move away from mimesis and toward affect. Most notable and direct on this topic is Stephen Halliwell, *The Aesthetics of Mimesis: Ancient Texts and Modern Problems* (Princeton, NJ: Princeton University Press, 2002), esp. "An Inheritance Contested: Renaissance to Modernity," 344–381; but this interpretation is also represented to a certain degree in Gunter Gebauer and Christoph Wulf, *Mimesis: Culture–Art–Society*, trans. Don Reneau (Berkeley: University of California Press, 1995), esp. 151–216 (Gunter Gebauer and Christoph Wulf's coverage of the late eighteenth century is notably thin). Recent musicological accounts of this period in the history of aesthetics follow Halliwell's historiography, seeing a transformation — but basic continuity — in mimetic theory through the century. Notable examples include Allanbrook, *Secular Commedia*; and Emily I. Dolan, *The Orchestral Revolution: Haydn and the Technologies of Timbre* (Cambridge: Cambridge University Press, 2013). But what these scholars take to be a new theory of mimesis I understand as something different altogether. Drawing on the historiography first suggested in M. H. Abrams's *The Mirror and the Lamp: Romantic Theory and the Critical Tradition* (New York: Oxford University Press, 1953), I see these accounts as representatives of a new and growing theory of affective attunement that provides an important historical counterpoint for the twenty-first century's affective turn.

the same with the affections or passions in an animal constitution, as with the cords or strings of a musical instrument. . . . It might be agreeable, one would think, to inquire thus into the different tunings of the passions, the various mixtures and alloys by which men become so different from one another."[46] For Shaftesbury, affective dispositions were dictated by the tuning in which the instrument of the body was set.

Closer to the time of Fréron's writing, the French Jesuit philosopher Yves Marie André had attempted a materialist explanation for musical beauty grounded in the *musica humana* tradition. In his *Essai sur le beau* (1741), André set out to provide for music an objective definition of beauty through an examination of the physical properties of its sounds and vibrations. He built on Rameau's notion that harmonic principles are derived from the naturally occurring overtone series, which can be demonstrated and observed in many types of vibrating bodies: single vibrating strings, musical instruments, and even, as Rameau had it, "the fibers that line the base of the shell of the ear."[47] This was the principle that Rameau called the *corps sonore*, and it was through the vibrations of these fibers that the "sentiments of the sounds and harmonies" were carried to the soul.[48] André, further elaborating Rameau's theory, had occasion to remind his readers, "the structure of the human body is entirely harmonic."[49] It is not, he immediately modifies, that our bodies are structured like a lyre or that our nerves are stretched like strings over our bones but, rather, that our nerves are indeed solid masses — rather than empty tubes for the transport of the animal spirits, as had been previously thought — and therefore they must vibrate in sympathy with musical sounds.

> [The discipline of] anatomy demonstrates to us that the nerves that
> line the bottom of the ear, and that serve the organ of hearing, are

46. Anthony Ashley Cooper, *Characteristics of Men, Manners, Opinions, Times* (1711), ed. Lawrence E. Klein (Cambridge: Cambridge University Press, 1999), 199.

47. "Des Fibres qui tapissent le fond de la Conque de l'Oreille." Jean-Philippe Rameau, *Génération harmonique, ou traité de musique théorique et pratique* (Paris: Prault fils, 1737), 7.

48. "D'où le sentiment des Sons & de l'Harmonie est porté jusqu'à l'Ame." Rameau, *Génération harmonique*, 7. For a detailed discussion of the *corps sonore*, see Thomas Christensen, "The *corps sonore*," in *Rameau and Musical Thought in the Enlightenment* (Cambridge: Cambridge University Press, 1993), 133–168; for an exegesis of this particular passage, relating it to Rameau's larger philosophical project and to the problem of dualism more generally, see Maryam Moshaver, "Rameau, the Subjective Body, and the Forms of Theoretical Representation," *Theoria* 23 (2016): 113–128.

49. "On s'en étonnera moins encore, si l'on considère, que la structure du corps humain est toute harmonique." Yves Marie André, *Essai sur le beau* (Paris: Hippolyte-Louis Geurin and Jacques Guerin, 1741), 255.

divided into an infinity of delicate fibers. These fibers extend from the eardrum and the [bony] labyrinth, and they expand to all parts; some to the brain, which is the seat of the mind and the imagination; others to the base of the mouth, which is the organ of the voice; others to the heart, which is the foundation of the affects and the sentiments; and still others finally to the lower viscera. All of these fibers have a great degree of mobility, a very prompt resilience, and under suitable tension can be shaken at the first movement of the acoustic membrane, almost as the strings of a harpsichord respond to the first movement of the keys. . . . How many sensible marks of a harmonic design, and of a harmony so touching and poignant![50]

Here André vacillates between the medieval notion of *musica humana* — in which the body's design is said to be harmonious and its parts ordered according to harmony — and a newer materialist variation thereon, in which the body is an instrument that is played by musical sounds.

The *musica humana* tradition had, by the middle of the eighteenth century, brought together both the theory of the affects and vibrational explanations of musical listening. Fréron had only to arrange these elements in the correct sequence in order to construct an alternative to the theory of musical mimesis. In so doing, he may also have been in an oblique dialogue with some of the most recent thinking in associationist philosophy. During the middle decades of the eighteenth century, associationist thinkers built on Lockean empiricism, holding that the simultaneous occurrence or enchainment of feelings and ideas was the primary source of all human meaning.[51] Only a few years before the start of the *querelle*, the English physician David Hartley had ventured the first synthesis of associationist philosophy with Newtonian

50. "L'Anatomie nous démontre, que les nerfs qui tapissent le fond de l'oreille, pour servir d'organe au sens de l'ouie, se divisent en une infinité de fibres délicates; que ces fibres au sortir du tambour & du labyrinthe, se vont répandre de toutes parts ; les unes dans le cerveau, qui est le siége des esprits & de l'imagination; les autres au fond de la bouche, où est l'organe de la voix; les autres dans le cœur, qui est le principe des affections & des sentimens; d'autres enfin dans les visceres inférieurs: que toutes ces fibres sont d'une très-grande mobilité, d'un ressort très-prompt, & dans la tension convenable pour être ébranlées au premier mouvement de la membrane acoustique, à peu-près comme les cordes d'un clavecin au premier branle des touches qui leur répondent. . . . Combien de marques sensibles d'un dessein d'harmonie, & d'une harmonie touchante & pathétique?" André, *Essai sur le beau*, 256–258.

51. Eric Mandelbaum, "Associationist Theories of Thought," in *The Stanford Encyclopedia of Philosophy* (Summer 2017 Edition), ed. Edward N. Zalta, accessed June 12, 2018, https://plato .stanford.edu/archives/sum2017/entries/associationist-thought.

physics in *Observations on Man* (1749).[52] His chief task, set out at the opening of the book, was to "establish and apply the Doctrines of *Vibrations* and *Association*."[53] While the first was taken from Newtonian physics, the second was from Locke, "concerning the Influence of *Association* over our Opinions and Affections."[54] Hartley described the solid matter composing the brain, the spinal marrow, and the nerves as "the immediate Instrument of Sensation and Motion."[55] In his view, external objects impressed themselves on this instrument through small vibrations. But if Hartley was a model for Fréron or for anyone else writing in this tradition, he was read quite selectively. Hartley goes on to describe specifically how vibrations disturb small particles in the nerves, traveling along them. "For that the Nerves themselves should vibrate like musical Strings, is highly absurd; nor was it ever asserted by Sir *Isaac Newton*."[56] Although Hartley's opinion was informed by the empirical science and anatomy of his day, it did not prevent critics from speculating endlessly to the contrary for decades following the publication of his treatise.

It is congruous, then, that Fréron's defense of serious French opera would build on ideas with an ancient pedigree that could be understood as aligning simultaneously with Rameau's harmonic theories, more recent commentaries thereupon (in the work of André), and also the day's empirical philosophy. That this was done in the service of one side of the debate is less important than its effectiveness at solving the quandaries of musical mimesis and the listening body in linking them up with each other. His contribution to the debate further solidified the growing consensus that musical sounds had the capacity for their own aesthetic force, which was a view Fréron in fact shared with Rousseau and with other proponents of the Italian style. What Fréron managed, knowingly or unknowingly, was to make possible an understanding of music as a nondiscursive, corporeal, and affective medium, which crystallized the period's twin goals of explaining how music could be an independent, efficacious art form and also how it managed to move

52. On Hartley's contributions, see Shelley Trower, *Senses of Vibration: A History of the Pleasure and Pain of Sound* (London: Continuum, 2012), 16–19; Carmel Raz, "'The Expressive Organ within Us': Ether, Ethereality, and Early Romantic Ideas about Music and the Nerves," *19th-Century Music* 38, no. 2 (2014): 115–144; and Joseph Roach, *The Player's Passion: Studies in the Science of Acting* (Ann Arbor: University of Michigan Press, 1993), 106–108.

53. David Hartley, *Observations on Man, His Frame, His Duty, and His Expectations* (London: S. Richardson, 1749), 5.

54. Hartley, *Observations on Man*, 5.

55. Hartley, *Observations on Man*, 7.

56. Hartley, *Observations on Man*, 11–12.

its audiences successfully without access to the mimetic capabilities of the other arts.[57]

Fréron's attuned, sympathetically affected musical listener was eventually to become the basis of a new attunement *Affektenlehre*. But before that process was thoroughly under way, the idea gained currency within the immediate context of the *querelle*. De Rochemont, a Swiss critic who later summarized the *querelle* in his *Réflexions d'un patriote sur l'opera françois, et sur l'opera italien* (1754), related the ability of arias to "move at once all the sensitive cords of the soul" and described again and again in his prose the ability of music to shake or rattle the deep interior of the listener.[58]

In fact, the clearest parallel to Fréron's account of affective attunement is not found in the pamphlets of his colleagues in the *coin du roi* but instead in the writings of Diderot, an enthusiast of the Italian style. An early translator of Shaftesbury, Diderot had already begun to sketch an account of musical attunement in his *Lettre sur les sourds et muets*, published just a year before the arrival of the *bouffons* in Paris.[59] One of the central considerations of the text is to distinguish the signifying systems of the various arts. To Diderot, music seems less precise than poetry in its ability to signify. Nevertheless, he observes, "even if sounds do not paint our thoughts as clearly as discourse, still they say something."[60] In an additional letter included in the volume, Diderot specifies the operation of music's affective power: "In music, the pleasure of sensation depends on a particular disposition not only of the ear but of the whole nervous system. If there are resonant heads, there are also bodies that I would gladly call harmonic: people whose fibers oscillate with so much swift-

57. Similar theories are elaborated later in the century. See James Usher, *Clio; or, A Discourse on Taste* (London: T. Davies, 1767); Michel Paul Guy de Chabanon, *Observations sur la musique, et principalement sur la metaphysique de l'art* (Paris: Pissot, 1779); and Johann Jakob Engel, *Ueber die musikalische Malerey* (Berlin: Christian Friedrich Voß und Sohn, 1780); among others.

58. "Remue à la fois toutes les cordes sensibles de l'ame." De Rochemont, *Réflexions d'un patriote sur l'opéra françois, et sur l'opéra Italien* (Lausanne, 1754), in Launay, *La querelle des bouffons*, 3:2163. Antoine-Alexandre Barbier attributes the authorship of this anonymously published document to "de Rochemont," as does Launay in the apparatus of the facsimile volume; I have not been able to determine a first name. See Barbier, *Dictionnaire des ouvrages anonymes* (Paris: Paul Daffis, 1879), 126.

59. See Denis Diderot, *Principes de la philosophie morale; ou Essai de M. S*** sur le mérite et la vertu, avec réflexions* (Amsterdam: Zacharie Chatelain, 1745). Another account that prefigures (and may have influenced) Fréron is found in Rémond de Saint-Mard, *Réflexions sur l'opéra* (The Hague: Neaulme, 1741), 10–11.

60. "Si on ne parle pas aussi distinctement avec un instrument qu'avec la bouche, & si les sons ne peignent pas aussi nettement la pensée que le discours, encore disent-ils quelque chose." Diderot, *Lettre sur les sourds et muets: À l'usage de ceux qui entendent & qui parlent* (1751), 55.

ness and vivacity that upon experiencing the violent movements that harmony provokes in them, they sense the possibility of movements even more violent and reach the idea of a sort of music that could make them die of pleasure."[61] Diderot develops Shaftesbury's theory on the different affective dispositions of individuals, figuring these differently tuned individuals as the subjects of music reception. Though not as detailed as Fréron's account, this scenario informed Diderot's fully elaborated response to the *querelle*: his celebrated work *Le neveu de Rameau*.

Comic Labor for Sale

It is a late afternoon in Paris, in the Café de la Régence — known for attracting the best chess players — when we meet the two central characters of Diderot's *Le neveu de Rameau*: Moi, the philosopher who would seem to approximate Diderot himself, and Lui, the ostensible nephew of the French opera composer and music theorist Rameau. The nephew is an excellent example of both a comic opera character and also a precarious laborer — roles that are thematized in Diderot's text. On their meeting, the philosopher describes the nephew as someone who is always appearing as different characters: on certain days, he is a hungry pauper in ragged clothing, while on others, he is stylish, plump, and debonair. He does not have a conventional job but supports himself through a number of informal arrangements such as teaching music lessons (really, gossiping with the mothers of his pupils) and attaching himself to wealthy patrons.

The dialogue that takes place between the philosopher and the nephew covers a great many topics, but the new Italian musical style runs consistently through it. In the words of Daniel Heartz, the *querelle des bouffons* is "the setting for [Diderot's] great satire."[62] If comic opera was often a mocking imitation of serious opera's mimetic doctrine, *Le neveu de Rameau* was a metamockery; borrowing the forms and procedures of comic opera for the dialogue, Diderot playfully repeated on that idiom the very same parody that

61. "En Musique, le plaisir de la sensation dépend d'une disposition particuliere non seulement de l'oreille, mais de tout le sistême des nerfs. S'il y a des têtes sonantes, il y a aussi des corps que j'appellerois volontiers harmoniques; des hommes, en qui toutes les fibres oscillent avec tant de promptitude & de vivacité, que sur l'expérience des mouvemens violens que l'Harmonie leur cause, ils sentent la possibilité de mouvemens plus violens encore & atteignent à l'idée d'une sort de Musique qui les feroit mourir de plaisir." Diderot, "Lettre a mademoiselle . . . ," in *Lettre sur les sourds et muets*, 299–300.

62. Daniel Heartz, "Locatelli and the Pantomime of the Violinist in *Le Neveu de Rameau*," *Diderot Studies* 27 (1998): 119.

it had performed on serious opera. In yet further doublings, the nephew both explicitly discusses the issues of the *querelle* and also performs them, enacting Diderot's theoretical contribution to the debate.

The nephew, despite being the descendant of an esteemed composer of traditional French opera, agrees with the philosopher that this older music is "rather flat."[63] The nephew's enthusiasm for the new Italian style manifests itself in a number of lengthy pantomime performances in which he shows off his musical abilities for the philosopher (hoping, perhaps, to win a student referral). He is not stopped by the fact that he has no instruments with him. Instead he plays air violin, sings all of the parts, and runs up and down imaginary keyboards, working up a sweat and attracting the attention of the entire café. These pantomimes are small performances within the drama in which the nephew takes on temporary roles — a formal conceit borrowed from comic opera. But the climax of the dialogue — and one of the most frequently quoted portions of the text — is a performance in which the nephew pushes his pantomime into overdrive, mixing together arias of the comic opera composers Giovanni Pergolesi and Egidio Duni with music in a wide variety of other styles.

> He piled up and mixed together thirty tunes, Italian, French, tragic, comic, with lots of different characters; at points, he would descend to the depths of the underworld in a low baritone, at others, he would go right up high in a glass-shattering fake falsetto, mimicking the different singing roles in the way he walked, held himself, and gestured; by turns furious, soothed, imperious, sneering. Now he's a young girl weeping, and he acts out her every simpering move; now he's a priest, he's a king, he's a tyrant, he threatens, he commands, he loses his temper; he's a slave, he obeys. He calms down, he is sorry, he complains, he laughs; never a false note, never out of time, always capturing the meaning of the words and the character of the music.[64]

Here the nephew is no longer emulating a single comic opera character; instead he has become an entire operatic cast in a single, zany metarole that folds various characters together.[65] Like the genre of comic opera, the

---

63. Diderot, *Denis Diderot's "Rameau's Nephew": A Multi-Media Edition*, trans. Kate E. Tunstall and Caroline Warman, ed. Marian Hobson (Cambridge, UK: Open Book, 2014), 66, www.openbookpublishers.com/product/216/ (hereafter cited as *RN*).

64. Diderot, *RN*, 68–69.

65. See, in this connection, Ngai's reading of both *Rameau's Nephew* and *The Cable Guy* (dir. Ben Stiller) in *Our Aesthetic Categories*, 189–191, 197–205.

nephew parodies styles by placing them in conversation with each other, rapidly adopting one and leaving it for the next. The scene continues:

> But you would have roared with laughter at the way he impersonated
> the different instruments. The horns and bassoons, he did puffing his
> cheeks up like balloons, and making hoarse, low sounds; he made a
> piercing, nasal noise for the oboes; his voice catapulting up and down
> at incredible speed, he did as close an imitation of the strings as he
> could; he whistled the piccolos and cooed the flutes; shouting, sing-
> ing, charging about like a madman, single-handedly doing the danc-
> ers, . . . a whole orchestra, a whole opera company, dividing himself
> between twenty different roles. . . . He was an unfortunate man, giving
> in to despair; he was a temple going up; birds falling silent at sunset;
> water burbling in a cool and solitary grove, or gushing forth in torrents
> from the mountain tops; a storm, a tempest, the cries of those about
> to perish, together with the howling of the wind and crashing of the
> thunder; he was night in all its darkness, he was shadow and silence,
> for even silence can be painted in sound.[66]

While opera uses orchestral instruments to aid in the depiction of character, this passage enacts a chiasmus in which the nephew portrays the characters of the various orchestral instruments. His whistling of the piccolos and cooing of the flutes is a demonstration of one way in which musical sounds constitute an aesthetic system on their own, outside of language. By the conclusion of the passage, the nephew has become affect itself. The philosopher shifts registers in his account of the nephew from concrete descriptions to abstract analogies — the nephew is no longer simply a character; now he is a state of darkness, a solitary grove, a tempest.[67]

The nephew's performance retraces the effect of Italian comic opera on musical discourse. He is the embodiment of the theory of affect that resulted from the *querelle des bouffons*: music has the power to offer up affective states directly to its audience.[68] Music does not have to rely on the opera's poetry in

66. Diderot, *RN*, 69–70.

67. As John T. Hamilton has put it, the "doctrines of mimesis are unworked" in Diderot's text. Hamilton, *Music, Madness, and the Unworking of Language* (New York: Columbia University Press, 2008), 55. Ultimately, for Hamilton, this draws music closer to nonmeaning and therefore to madness.

68. Just before the pantomime quoted in the text, the philosopher poses to the nephew a rather direct question on musical aesthetics: "All imitative arts have their model in nature. What model does the musician choose when he writes a song?" The nephew's answer is a parody of the intellectual indecision surrounding this issue during the *querelle*: "Song is the imitation of

order to render affects in its listeners. The nephew is the logical elaboration
of the new social roles scripted in this relationship, in which performers —
aware of themselves as performers within the performance — are said to be the
conduit of affective states rather than simply the creators of mimetic representations. Diderot uses the nephew to show us the human side of this new aesthetic system. The nephew is exceedingly malleable, virtuosic, and energetic,
but precisely because he is so amenable to so many roles, he is detached from
them all and committed to none; he is exacting, even mechanical, "never a
false note, never out of time."[69]

The social role scripted for the nephew within musical aesthetics extends
beyond the delimited area of the stage. The rest of his life is spent adopting
various temporary jobs and taking on countless functions without having any
of them stick to his person. He is a flatterer, seeking always to make others with
money and power feel good about themselves and, by extension, him. When
he works, he does not produce tangible products but rather uses a carefully
executed, perfectly harmonized science of feeling in order to put people in
affective states. His entire life proceeds according to an aesthetics of affective
attunement, in which he as a performer is aware of his own performances.
When the philosopher attempts to tell him that "deep down" he must "possess

---

a scale, either invented by art or inspired by nature, whichever you prefer, using either vocal or
instrumental sound to imitate either physical noises or emotional accents." Diderot, *RN*, 64,
65. The nephew almost manages to provide every position available in the debate in his list of
casually tossed-off options — every position, that is, except for Diderot's own theory of affective
attunement, of which he is the embodiment.

69. Diderot, *RN*, 69. In this sense, the nephew is the type of supreme actor that Diderot
describes in the *Paradoxe sur le comédien*. Indeed, Diderot uses musical harmony as the model
for carefully calculated affective portrayal in that text: "Dira-t-on, ces accents si plaintifs, si dou-
loureux, que cette mère arrache du fond de ses entrailles, et dont les miennes sont si violem-
ment secouées, ce n'est pas le sentiment actuel qui les produit, ce n'est pas le désespoir qui les
inspire? Nullement; et la preuve, c'est qu'ils sont mesurés; qu'ils font partie d'un système de
déclamation; que plus bas ou plus aigus de la vingtième partie d'un quart de ton, ils sont faux;
qu'ils sont soumis à une loi d'unité; qu'ils sont, comme dans l'harmonie, préparés et sauvés; qu'ils
ne satisfont à toutes les conditions requises que par une longue étude; qu'ils concourent à la
solution d'un problème proposé." (Tell me, what about those accents, so plaintive and dolorous,
that a mother draws from the bottom of her insides, and that shake her violently — is it not a real
feeling that produces them, and is it not despair that inspires them? Not at all. The proof is that
they are all measured; they form part of a system of declamation and that, raised or lowered by
a twentieth part of a quartertone, they ring false; they are subject to a law of unity; they are, as in
harmony, prepared and resolved; and that they can only satisfy all of these required conditions
after serious study.) Diderot, *Paradoxe sur le comédien* (1773), ed. Stéphane Lojkine (Paris: Armand Colin, 1992), 95. On Diderot's *Paradoxe sur le comédien*, see Roach, "Diderot," in *Player's
Passion*, 116–159.

a delicate soul," the nephew replies, "I'll be damned if I know what I am, deep down, . . . never false when it's in my interest to be true, never true when it's in my interest to be false."[70] Like the genre of comic opera, he parodies the baselessness of aristocratic convention. He is alienated from his labor in life as he is in art.

At least, this is what G. W. F. Hegel found so remarkable about the nephew and why he chose to feature Diderot's text so prominently in the *Phenomenology of Spirit*. As an individual whose life is completely governed by aesthetics to the exclusion of all else, the nephew illustrates for Hegel a crucial turning point in Enlightenment subjectivity.[71] The form by which he moves in and out of temporary attachments, momentary postures of flattery, and various affective dispositions does more than just render a caricature of comic opera. It also depicts a new social type: an individual thoroughly absorbed in virtuosic performances of the self who is nothing short of completely modern.

If eighteenth-century music was shaped by the emergence of the notional autonomy of art, it also provided for the history of subjectivity the model of a new aesthetic relationship. Comic opera's parody of serious opera had the effect of challenging the doctrine of mimesis, and musical aesthetics responded with fresh understandings of affect. In this exchange, the procedures of comic mimesis undermined mimetic theory, while at the same time criticism doubled art by absorbing its style. That a comic art form should have provoked this is fitting; comedy often trades in doublings in order to mobilize the incongruities that are foundational to its operation.[72] The consequences, however, precipitated a pivotal moment in the intellectual legacy of affect theory. As the Enlightenment doctrine of mimesis was fundamentally reoriented, both musical aesthetics and the modern subject were altered forever.

70. Diderot, *RN*, 48.

71. See G. W. F. Hegel, *Phenomenology of Spirit*, trans. A. V. Miller (Oxford: Oxford University Press, 1977), § 489, p. 298; on the nephew, esp. §§ 521–526, pp. 316–321. On this passage in Hegel, see Jean Hyppolite, *Genesis and Structure of Hegel's "Phenomenology of Spirit,"* trans. Samuel Cherniak and John Heckman (Evanston, IL: Northwestern University Press, 1974), 400–417.

72. On the incongruity theory of comedy and its intellectual precursors, see Michael Clark, "Humor and Incongruity," in *The Philosophy of Laughter and Humor*, ed. John Morreall (Albany: SUNY Press, 1987), 139–155. On incongruity theory and comic opera, see Johnston, "È caso da intermedio!," 224–279.

3

"Sonate, que me veux-tu?" and Other Dilemmas of Instrumental Music

Among the many characters the Parisian composer François Couperin animated at the keyboard, one was an amphibian. Published alongside several of his other short harpsichord portraits in the *Pièces de clavecin* of 1730, *L'Amphibie* is a musical shape-shifter. Like Rameau's nephew, the piece trades in dissimulation. While at one moment it appears proud and grand, by the next it has already begun to sound flippant and jocular, like a comic opera character rapidly cycling through scenes. The piece is a distillation of several dilemmas facing instrumental music in the eighteenth century: How can music without a text signify what it claims to depict? Does it have the power of mimesis like the other arts? In other words, can it show us anything? And if it cannot be said to convey an imitation of something—anything—with any regularity, can it nevertheless engender affects within us?

Couperin chose the musical form of the passacaglia for this six-minute piece. In this form, the fundamental structure of the bass register is meant to remain intact throughout, while the melodic ideas presented in the higher registers are always different and new. Nevertheless, even with respect to its adherence to this rule of constant change, the piece deviates from expectations: the original bass line is not strictly repeated (in some places it is only vaguely there), and at the end of the piece the beginning melody surprisingly returns.

The opening of *L'Amphibie* is confident and clear. The 3/4 meter and the rhythmic shape of the melody suggest the stylings of a sarabande dance, which was coded as both elevated and exotic (its origins said to be Spanish). Couperin provides the marking *"noblement,"* at the head of the piece, which—together with the meter and the characteristic rhythms—encourages a stately, moderate performance tempo. The musical elements collectively paint an aristocratic vision of foreign prestige. But as *L'Amphibie* gets under way, its high, confident style begins to sound garish. It is really all too much — the sarabande rhythms are emphasized with ornaments, and they are repeated nearly every measure. Perhaps this is not an image of nobility at all but a parody thereof. Nevertheless this single, puffed-up sarabande is the only character to which we have yet been introduced. Before the piece is over, we will meet six more.

At about two minutes into the piece, the rhythmic shape of the melody changes dramatically, and the texture thins out to become transparent. The sarabande is gone — now the melodic conceit is one in which the left and right hands are trading gestures at the keyboard. We seem to be listening in on some hidden dialogue thematizing proximity and pairing. The phrase written in this new style is repeated once but then altogether vanishes after about twenty seconds. We have come to yet another new section, marked "*gayment*," and the melodic groupings mean that Couperin has really switched the meter of the piece from the stately 3/4 to the playful 9/8 (although this is only implied and not notated). All of this brings forth a less formal and more energetic sound, a faster tempo and a new, upbeat enthusiasm. The left and right hands begin to play together to reinforce this new character. But this section lasts only two complete phrases, which take barely forty seconds to spin out.

A new phrase begins, darker and duller. We have plunged from the former major key into minor, and the pace of events slows considerably. The marking here is "*modérément*," reminding us of the weightiness of the opening 3/4 meter signature. After all of the previous gaiety, this new section sounds stuffy and tired. But that moderation only lasts thirty seconds. The piece then bounds into skipping rhythms with a leaping melody. We are still in minor, but here the marking is "*vivement*," fueling the up-tempo and newfound verve of the musical line. We run with this sprightly character for several phrases, but the rhythmic exuberance seems to drive forward to a moment of harmonic repose and is suddenly spent. The melody in the right hand climbs back up and begins a mawkish call and response with the left hand; the marking for this section is "*afectueusement*" and might be intended ironically.[1] Finally the music pulls itself upright into a more developed and more richly accompanied new section — the sixth different one yet — which Couperin labels "*marqué*." Correspondingly, the melody comes forward more distinctly, and

1. So suggest Jane Clark and Derek Connon, whose monograph study "*The Mirror of Human Life*" remains one of the most important studies of the *Pièces de clavecin*. See Clark and Connon, "*The Mirror of Human Life*": *Reflections on François Couperin's "Pièces de Clavecin*" (Huntingdon, UK: King's Music, 2002), 103.

the harmonies begin a return to the home key of A major. And then, at five minutes into the composition, the original sarabande dance returns in all of its exaggerated nobility.

L'Amphibie is one of the most complex in a large set of somewhat-mysterious character pieces that Couperin composed for the harpsichord. In a preface to the first book of these, published in 1713, he indicated that he "always had an object in composing all of these pieces; different occasions have furnished them."[2] Since Couperin's own day and continuing on into ours, there has been an effort to use the titles of these pieces together with their musical content in order to make some sort of determination about the characters Couperin intended them to depict.[3] Some, almost without doubt, paint specific individuals. The Pièces de clavecin of 1730 — the fourth book, which includes L'Amphibie — begins with a piece titled La princesse Marie; this piece is written in the style of a traditional Polish dance fitting for its likely target, Marie Leszczyńska, the Polish fiancée of Louis XV and one of Couper-in's students.[4] But many others among his pieces were most probably intended to depict character types or, more abstractly, states of feeling.

Take for example La boufonne, a skipping and playful piece in a light 6/8 meter marked "gaïllardement"; or L'Arlequine, written in the sprightly and unserious meter of 3/8 and full of jangling at the higher end of the keyboard's register, marked "grotesquement." Here we have stock characters common to the commedia dell'arte and the comic opera stage.[5] On the other side of the continuum, consider La bondissante (the bounding heart), which opens with a leap in the melody of the right hand echoed by the same leap in the imitating melody of the left. Whose bounding heart this might be is difficult, if

2. "J'ay toûjours eu un objet en composant toutes ces piéces: des occasions différentes me l'ont fourni." François Couperin, Pièces de clavecin . . . premier livre (Paris: Ballard, 1713), un-paginated preface.

3. For some recent examples and bibliography relating to this practice, see in particular Sara Gross Ceballos, "François Couperin, Moraliste?," Eighteenth-Century Music 11, no. 1 (2014): 79–110; David Tunley, François Couperin and "The Perfection of Music" (Aldershot, UK: Ashgate, 2004); and Clark and Connon, "The Mirror of Human Life." In addition, Ceballos, "Keyboard Portraits: Performing Character in the Eighteenth Century" (PhD diss., University of California Los Angeles, 2008), provides a broader contextualization for this practice across the long eigh-teenth century.

4. Although even the interpretation of this piece is not at all straightforward. As Clark and Connon write, "Couperin's stiff and somewhat exaggerated version [of the polonaise] perhaps be-trays the fact that, in contrast to the charming sincerity of the young princess, he found the East-ern European etiquette slightly ridiculous." Clark and Connon, "The Mirror of Human Life," 94.

5. On Couperin's connections to the comic opera of his day, see Jane Clark, "Aspects of the Social and Cultural Background," in Clark and Connon, "The Mirror of Human Life," 9–25.

not impossible, to ascertain, but Couperin's music provides for us something like the portraiture of an opera aria. Musical codes and conventions capture a snapshot of the exterior or interior life of a character — the harlequin's jesting or the lover's pumping blood. It is in this sense that Couperin's *Pièces de clavecin* have been drawn into comparison with the older textual character studies of La Bruyère or even the paintings of his contemporary Jean-Antoine Watteau (some of whose works even share titles in common with the *Pièces de clavecin*).[6] In the case of *L'Amphibie*, it is the amphibiousness of character itself that is the object portrayed, adding an additional layer of complexity to the entire endeavor.

But comparisons to opera arias, character studies, or painted portraits can only go so far. While the poetry of opera, the prose of a character study, and the imitation of the natural world in painting lent to those arts the power of mimesis, the musical materials Couperin employed generally were not accorded that same esteem in early eighteenth-century aesthetics. And apart from the titles, Couperin's harpsichord pieces only had musical materials to work with. The result is that no one in Couperin's own time — and much less in ours, though many have attempted — could give any definitive statement of what these character pieces depict. The *Pièces de clavecin* were published and performed in an era that was deeply suspicious of the mimetic capabilities of all music. And precisely because they were instrumental works, the *Pièces de clavecin* tested and played with that very suspicion.

The question of mimesis in eighteenth-century instrumental music is well worn. At one time, it was fashionable to think that instrumental compositions of this period obtained an effect entirely dissimilar to mimesis — that they were unencumbered by human meaning and were instead a link to something beyond it.[7] Then this view came under harsh and appropriate criticism for the way that it enshrined these compositions as timeless ineffable exercises in form.[8] The new fashion, accordingly, was to ensure that eighteenth-century

6. Ceballos, "François Couperin, *Moraliste?*"; Clark, "Aspects of the Social and Cultural Background," 19–20.

7. The classic point of reference for this view is Eduard Hanslick, *Vom Musikalisch-Schönen: Ein Beitrag zur Revision der Ästhetik der Tonkunst* (Leipzig: Rudolph Weigel, 1854).

8. For rich documentation of this entire intellectual movement and its exponents, see Mark Evan Bonds, *Absolute Music: The History of an Idea* (New York: Oxford University Press, 2014). In Bonds's own historiography, it was developments in philosophy — outside of music — that later effected a change in the conceptualization of instrumental music during the first few decades of the nineteenth century. See Bonds, *Music as Thought: Listening to the Symphony in the Age of Beethoven* (Princeton, NJ: Princeton University Press, 2006); this view is also represented in

instrumental music was replete with mimetic devices and therefore meant something in human terms. A growing body of scholarship now exists that tracks various mimetic conventions, topics, rhetorical tools, and references to other musical styles within the repertoire, wresting it from the ineffable and bringing it back down to earth.[9]

Neither of these scholarly impulses accurately captures the messy consternation of eighteenth-century critics writing about their period's instrumental music. When they did bother to write about it, they neither held it in high regard (much less a timeless, transcendent form) nor had the faintest idea of what it meant or imitated.[10] They treated it as a problem area within aesthetic theory, a deepening and sharpening of the general confusion surrounding the misfit of music with the doctrine of mimesis. They passed around phrases relating to this conundrum, such as the one that Bernard de Fontenelle is said to have cried out in impatience: "Sonata, what do you want from me?"[11]

Tomas McAuley, "Rhythmic Accent and the Absolute: Sulzer, Schelling, and the Akzenttheorie," *Eighteenth-Century Music* 10, no. 2 (2013): 277–286.Other scholars, most notably Emily I. Dolan, in *The Orchestral Revolution: Haydn and the Technologies of Timbre* (Cambridge: Cambridge University Press, 2013), have critiqued this view and have endeavored to demonstrate how musical practice and philosophy interacted during the long eighteenth century.

9. I refer here to the growth of what we now generally call, in twentieth-century terminology, topic theory. Among the many sources, see Leonard Ratner, *Classic Music: Expression, Form, and Style* (New York: Schirmer Books, 1980); Wye Jamison Allanbrook, *Rhythmic Gesture in Mozart: "Le Nozze di Figaro" and "Don Giovanni"* (Chicago: University of Chicago Press, 1983); Kofi Agawu, *Playing with Signs: A Semiotic Interpretation of Classic Music* (Princeton, NJ: Princeton University Press, 1991); Allanbrook, *The Secular Commedia: Comic Mimesis in Late Eighteenth-Century Music* (Berkeley: University of California Press, 2014); and Danuta Mirka, ed., *The Oxford Handbook of Topic Theory* (New York: Oxford University Press, 2014). Also important in understanding this historiographical transition is John Neubauer, *The Emancipation of Music from Language: Departure from Mimesis in Eighteenth-Century Aesthetics* (New Haven, CT: Yale University Press, 1986). Neubauer is interested in some of the same sources inspected in this study, though ultimately he finds that their claims can be understood within the broader rubric of mimesis.

10. The best documentation of the critical reactions to eighteenth-century instrumental music remains Bellamy Hosler, *Changing Aesthetic Views of Instrumental Music in 18th-Century Germany* (Ann Arbor, MI: UMI Research Press, 1981). Focusing on German sources, Hosler observes a move away from mimetic aesthetics and from an attempt at an *Affektenlehre* toward what he calls a *Seelenlehre*, or soul-oriented theory. I seek a further complication of Hosler's historiography by broadening the sources inspected and directing attention to language concerning the body in period criticism.

11. Jean-Jacques Rousseau, "Sonate," in *Encyclopédie ou dictionnaire raisonné des sciences, des arts et des métiers, par une société de gens de lettres*, ed. Denis Diderot and Jean le Rond d'Alembert, vol. 15 (Paris: Briasson et Le Breton, 1765), 348; see also Rousseau, "Sonate" in *Dictionnaire de musique* (Paris: Duchesne, 1768), 460.

The bulk of the period's criticism, as we have seen in chapters 1 and 2, concerned opera. Theorists asked how the music of the opera theater might work to raise the affects in opera audiences; they wondered how musical materials worked in conjunction with the poetry of the libretto, the stage drama, and other visual elements to aid in the mimesis of this multimedia art form. Even those who were most generous to the art of music within these debates construed it as an amplification of the other traditional forms of imitation present on the stage. For some theorists, it was the sonic materiality of music that rendered opera a dangerously sensuous art with a corporeal appeal. Musical sound distracted from the edifying work of the drama in serious opera, and in opera buffa it contributed to an embarrassment of sloppy embodiment depicting drunks and rogues with lusty songs in a haphazard Italian style.

So instrumental music — with no text or drama to amplify, no other mimetic art to underscore — incurred all of the reproaches of operatic music without reaping the benefits of opera's spectacularity. Indeed, instrumental music was for period critics a topic barely appropriate for discussion within aesthetic theory; that is why when they discussed it, they almost never referred to specific pieces of music. It was instead conceptualized as an extreme and therefore perhaps titillating practice because of its complete misfit with the doctrine of mimesis and with the early eighteenth-century understandings of how art was supposed to function in the world.

Even worse, eighteenth-century critics and musicians also realized that the style of instrumental music was changing before them. If all that instrumental music could offer was a sonorous and corporeal tickle, at least it should be unified in the way that it offered that sensation. Slowly, though, instrumental music began to take on the shape-shifting practices of comic opera, presenting one musical style after the next in rapid succession. Instrumental music — already nearly impossible to interpret — had become amphibious.[12]

Given this perplexing state of affairs, it is not surprising that some theorists grasped for what they could agree on about this expanding and changing practice sweeping Europe and growing more and more popular by the day.[13] There was some consensus at least that — as in opera — musical sound held

12. What I will be calling the amphibious style — my own take on what has long been called the classical style in late eighteenth-century instrumental music — is indebted not only to Couperin's fantastic title but also to Allanbrook's figurative use of the polyps and chameleons. See Allanbrook, *Secular Commedia*, esp. "Comic Flux and Comic Precision," 1–40.

13. I refer here to what was once called the "rise of instrumental music" but is better understood along the lines suggested by (and announced in the title of) Emily Dolan's *Orchestral Revolution*, see esp. 5–7.

a special relationship with the body. Instrumental music communicated in a corporeal way, even if it failed to edify or to morally improve its listeners, thus bypassing reason and heading straight to the flesh. It became possible, then, to understand instrumental music as obtaining a nondiscursive corporeal result on its listeners that might move them.[14]

For certain critics, such as Caspar Ruetz and Friedrich Melchior Grimm, this meant that the art of music was something other than mimetic. Music, for these theorists, had an exceptional capability to speak to the body, and it was precisely this ability that allowed it to communicate with the soul directly. Music was, in Ruetz's words, "not simply an imitation of nature, but nature itself."[15] In creating this solution for music, these authors also suggested a fascinating cryptodualism: although the soul was nonidentical with the body, music could move the former by means of its material encounter with the latter. In this model, the soul and body are musically connected but, as different entities, dual.[16] It was in this cryptodualist moment—inspired by the dilemmas of instrumental music—that the stage was set for the new attunement *Affektenlehre*.

Instrumental Music and Mimesis

It is easy enough for us to look back at Couperin's *Pièces de clavecin* and find imitations of his world everywhere: musical meters and rhythms help us to identify dance forms, which index social strata. We hear the gestures of a character type that we know from the theater or snatches of a convention that is associated with an operatic scene of pathos or joy. The same can be said of eighteenth-century instrumental sonatas and the growing repertoire of symphonic music, even if those works do not have Couperin's evocative titles (which both tempt us to analyze and give us some assistance with the task). From our vantage point, one can imagine an eighteenth century in which

14. Here I respond to Elisabeth Le Guin's inspiring work on corporeality in *Boccherini's Body: An Essay in Carnal Musicology* (Berkeley: University of California Press, 2006). While Le Guin creates images of performing and listening bodies in dialogue with eighteenth-century music, I hope to draw focus to the bodies imagined within the period's theory and criticism.

15. Caspar Ruetz, "Sendschreiben eines Freundes an den andern über einige Ausdrücke des Herrn Batteux von der Musik," in *Historisch-Kritische Beyträge zur Aufnahme der Musik*, by Friedrich Wilhelm Marpurg, vol. 1 (Berlin: J. J. Schützens Witwe, G. A. Lange, 1754), 292.

16. On cryptodualism, see especially Amy Cimini, "How to Do Things with Dualism: The Political Expedience of the Musical Mind-Body Problem," in "Baruch Spinoza and the Matter of Music: Toward a New Practice of Theorizing Musical Bodies" (PhD diss., New York University, 2011), 21–84.

critics were content to hear musical materials as approximations of mimesis, much as we do today.

But even if the period's cognoscenti were able to guess at what instrumental music was imitating, they were certainly not openly pleased about having to do so. Critics felt that mimesis should work in an unambiguous way, something closer to how it functions in painting or poetry; instrumental music just did not have the resources to succeed at this task. When faced with assessing this complex question in *Der vollkommene Capellmeister* (published in 1739, less than a decade after Couperin's fourth book of the *Pièces de clavecin*), Johann Mattheson expressed deep reservations. Instrumental music was for Mattheson the "young daughter" of vocal music; its distinction and powers were inferior to its governing predecessor.[17] Not only this, but its indefiniteness rendered it unlikely to achieve the main goal of musical composition, which was to arouse the affects in listeners. "It is much more difficult to write something for instruments in the correct way that would find good approbation, i.e., would move the listeners to this or that passion: because there are no words present in this case but only an empty language of tones. When people, upon hearing a sound or even a harmony, cannot conclude if it is fish or fowl, nothing can result."[18] Well, not quite nothing. Elsewhere Mattheson suggests that if musical sound could achieve anything on its own, it would be that "only the ears of the listeners . . . are tickled, but their hearts and thought are not aroused to a sufficient degree."[19] A sonic, material medium that spoke to the body without any content, instrumental music offered up an aesthetic curiosity: "an empty language of tones."

17. Johann Mattheson, *Der vollkommene Capellmeister* (Hamburg: Christian Herold, 1739), 204.

18. "Daß es viel schwerer auf Instrumenten etwas zu setzen, das rechte Art habe, und guten Beifall finde, d. i. die Gemüther der Zuhörer zu dieser oder jener Leidenschafft bewege: weil dabey keine Worte, sondern nur eine blosse Tonsprache vorhanden. Denn, daß ein Geräusche und auch eine Harmonie gehöret werde, daraus kein Mensch schliessen könne, ob es Fisch oder Fleisch sey, das macht die Sache nicht aus." Mattheson, *Der vollkommene Capellmeister*, 204. This translation is with reference to Allanbrook, *Secular Commedia*, 46–47. Mattheson later goes on to explain how the correct liturgical setting can work together with instrumental music in order to stir great passions; see Mattheson, *Der vollkommene Capellmeister*, 208–209.

19. "Den armen einfältigen und sich viel-dünckenden Zuhörern nur die blossen Ohren gekitzelt, nicht aber gehöriger Maassen das Hertz und Nachdencken rege gemacht werden." Mattheson, *Der vollkommene Capellmeister*, 20. Mattheson has just given the instruction—discussed in chapter 1—to "seek out a good, truly good poetic work in which nature is vividly painted, and strive to distinguish precisely the passions contained therein." Mattheson, *Der vollkommene Capellmeister*, 19. Since many composers do not know what they are painting, they only manage to tickle the ears of their listeners.

The mid-eighteenth century's chief exponent of the neoclassical doctrine of mimesis was Charles Batteux, and his landmark 1746 treatise *Les beaux arts réduits à un même principe* was, accordingly, rather suspicious of instrumental music. Batteux reached the subject of music in general within the third book of his treatise, where the principle of imitation is applied to the various arts. Poetry and painting come first; music and dance follow. Broadly put, Batteux endorsed a model in which musical sounds have an excellent ability to create affective responses in listeners; this they have derived from the naturally occurring tonal inflections of the impassioned speaking voice (a view similar to that proposed by Rousseau). When united with a text, musical sounds supplement the mimetic work of language by depicting an affective situation alongside it.[20] Nevertheless, the complete product must leave the listener confident in what has been collectively represented; a painter, after all, cannot simply throw bold colors haphazardly onto a canvas without depicting an object, and neither can the musician.[21] Erudite composers could satisfy themselves by working out complex harmonic designs according to mathematical principles, but, Batteux said, "if they don't signify anything, I would compare them to the bodily movements of orators, which are only signs of life."[22] Even texted music risked, in its vagueness, comparison with bare bodies.

When Batteux finally arrived at the back-alley topic of instrumental music, his initial assessment was equivocal: "Music can be meaningful in the symphony, where it has but half a life."[23] Instrumental music might actually have some vague ability to communicate on its own, in this view, but ultimately without a text, the art of music was severely curtailed. "Add the other half of its being," Batteux continued, "and it is song, where it becomes a painting of the human heart."[24] Batteux concluded the chapter with two definitive statements: music, united with a text, had the ability to produce "a type of ordered discourse" [*discours suivi*].[25] But whatever was puzzling or unclear was ineffective. No matter how well the composition fell into accord with theories of

20. See Charles Batteux, *Les beaux arts réduits à un même principe* (Paris: Durand, 1746), 250–259.

21. Batteux, *Les beaux arts*, 263.

22. "S'ils ne signifient rien, je les comparerai à ces gestes d'Orateurs, qui ne sont que des signes de vie." Batteux, *Les beaux arts*, 265.

23. "La Musique étant significative dans la symphonie, où elle n'*a qu'une demi-vie.*" Batteux, *Les beaux arts*, 267.

24. "*Que la moitié de son être*, que sera-t'elle dans le chant, où elle devient le tableau du cœur humain?" Batteux, *Les beaux arts*, 267.

25. Batteux, *Les beaux arts*, 268.

harmony, no matter how well composed, it was very possible to create music that imitated nothing and that meant nothing at all.[26]

Reservations like this were common, even among thinkers who extolled the ability of opera to arouse the affects. Among them was none other than Rousseau, whose article "Sonate" for the *Encyclopédie* betrayed a huge anxiety on the topic of mimesis in instrumental music. The short article is only four paragraphs long, and the first three consist in a terse definition for the term and a hurried summary of its typical form. In the final paragraph, nearly the length of the first three combined, Rousseau unleashed his worries. Instruments, he suggested, were overtaking voices in popularity, making sonatas all the more fashionable; still, this fashion could not last. After all, he reminded his readers, music is an art of imitation, and without a text, there is no way to indicate the object imitated. "To know what all this overwhelming balderdash [*tous ces fatras*] of Sonatas is trying to say, it would be necessary to do as the crude artist does, who is obliged to write underneath his images 'This is a man,' 'This is a tree,' 'This is an ox.' I will never forget the words of the celebrated Fontenelle, who found himself worn out by these ceaseless symphonies at a concert and in a transport of impatience cried out aloud, 'Sonata, what do you want from me?'"[27] Rousseau's *Encyclopédie* entry marks the point at which Fontenelle's celebrated remark entered print circulation. Its immediate context is striking, not only for the exasperation that Rousseau used Fontenelle's words to channel but also because of the aesthetic analogy the former drew in order to prepare the latter's quip. In order for instrumental sonatas to be intelligible, Rousseau suggested, they would require textual labels as though they were indecipherable paintings. They communicated something, certainly, but without the aid of a text — without the assistance of a more traditionally mimetic art — pieces of instrumental music were little more than incomplete, indecipherable attempts at imitation.

Over the course of the eighteenth century, two central points of agreement emerged in the varied remarks of critics concerning instrumental music. The first was the basic doubt that untexted music had the ability to imitate nature

---

26. Batteux, *Les beaux arts*, 268–269.

27. "Pour savoir ce que veulent dire tous ces fatras de *sonates* dont nous sommes accablés, il faudroit faire comme ce peintre grossier qui étoit obligé d'écrire au — dessous de ses figures, *c'est un homme, c'est un arbre, c'est un boeuf.* Je n'oublierai jamais le mot du célebre M. de Fontenelle, qui se trouvant à un concert, excédé de cette symphonie éternelle, s'écria tout haut dans un transport d'impatience, *sonate, que me veux-tu?*" Rousseau, "Sonate" (*Encyclopédie*), 348; see also Rousseau, "Sonate" (*Dictionnaire*), 460.

as the other arts did. This meant that its main appeal was strictly material and corporeal, rendering it useless in a traditionally didactic sense. Even Christian Gottfried Krause would admit, "No one says: that was informative music. . . . Try as you will to persuade someone to love his neighbor through tones; you will not succeed."[28] Instrumental music, then, was only useful for setting the background for some other main attraction — perhaps as a curtain-raising overture or, as Johann Philipp Kirnberger put it, "for dances, marches, and other festive acts."[29] Here, at least, instrumental music needed only to create some vague sonic scenery as stage dressing.

The trouble was that even while theorists worried over instrumental music's mimetic capabilities, they noticed a fundamental change in its style. Composers of instrumental music wanted to learn how to make their sonatas sing like the popular characters of comic opera; instrumental music began to take on the patchwork, picaresque style of a Rameau's nephew. Instrumental music was problematic not only for its indefiniteness but also for its amphibiousness.

The Amphibious Style

If we take another look at Couperin's *L'Amphibie* and compare it with the other works in the *Pièces de clavecin*, we will notice several formal aberrations. *L'Amphibie* contains eight distinct sections, partitioned from each other not only by markings (Couperin moves through *noblement, coulé, gayment, modérément, vivement, afectueusement,* and *marqué*) but also through changes in the rhythmic profile, texture, and pace of events. In addition to these, Couperin shifts between keys and effectively changes the meter in some cases. All of this is done in order to make each section sound distinct from the others. In other works of the *Pièces de clavecin*, two contrasting or complementary styles were enough — many had only one. *L'Amphibie* is a marked exception — a grand passacaglia that takes as its topic the idea of change and mutation and therefore requires a different kind of formal process than the other works published alongside it.

But as the eighteenth century progressed, more and more music became

---

28. "Niemand sagt: das war eine lehrreiche Musik. . . . Bemühet euch, wie ihr wollt, jemand in Tönen zu überreden, er solle seinen Nächsten lieben; es wird euch nicht gelingen." Christian Gottfried Krause, *Von der musikalischen Poesie* (Berlin: Johann Friedrich Voß, 1752), 41–42.

29. "Dadurch wird der Gebrauch der Instrumentalmusik ihrer Natur nach vornehmlich auf die Tänze, Märsche und andre festliche Aufzüge eingeschränkt." Johann Philipp Kirnberger, "Instrumentalmusik," in *Allgemeine Theorie der schönen Künste*, by Johann Georg Sulzer, 2 vols. (Leipzig: M. G. Weidmanns Erben und Reich, 1771–1774), 1:559.

amphibious. *L'Amphibie* shared much with the comic opera characters that were newly gaining popularity across Europe in the early part of the eighteenth century. Alongside the rancorous debates about opera, composers of instrumental music were quietly learning tricks from the comic style about rapid modulations and shifts in affect; and as they began to favor this style above others, commentators took note and castigated them for creating such unruly music. The conservative French critic Noël-Antoine Pluche, for instance, thought as poorly of pieces written in this jumbled manner as he did of the comic opera characters they echoed.

> One would never have a good opinion of a soul who passed from sadness to great clamors of laughter, and from banter to a grave manner, then to a tender one, to anger, and to rage without having a single subject to laugh or be upset about. But are sonatas and many other kinds of music anything other than what we have just said? They are a kind of music just as marbled paper is a painting. . . . They are most like the studies made by young painters of different attitudes and the different passions of humanity. They are more properly a way of forming technique, and less pleasing for the public.[30]

Pluche's angry condemnation of the amphibious instrumental style is a fantastic parallel to Diderot's depiction of Rameau's nephew himself—always one yet never the same, vacillating between affective extremes. But beyond this convenient homology, there is also a crucial slippage within Pluche's text that betrays yet a further complexity surrounding instrumental music and affect during the eighteenth century. In order for a critic like Pluche to complain of stylistic hybridity in instrumental music, that critic first had to admit that different styles themselves were identifiable within the mixture. These were either named or, as in Pluche's case, analogized such that readers would have some idea of the different affective states offered up by the music in question. Pluche finally arrives at this point toward the end of the quotation: instrumental music was something like the "studies made by young painters of . . . the

---

30. "Mais on n'eut jamais bonne opinion d'un esprit qui passe de la tristesse aux grands éclats de rire, & du badinage à l'air grave, à l'air tendre, à la colère, & à la rage sans avoir aucun sujèt de rire ni de se fâcher. Or les sonates & bien d'autres musiques sont-elles autre chose que ce que nous venons de dire? Elles sont une musique comme le papier marbré est une peinture . . . Elles sont plûtôt comme les études que font les jeunes peintres des différentes attitudes & des différentes passions de l'homme. Elles sont propres pour former l'artifice, mais peu réjouissantes pour le public." Noël-Antoine Pluche, *Le spectacle de la nature, ou entretiens sur les particularités de l'histoire naturelle, qui ont paru les plus propres à rendre les Jeunes-Gens curieux, & à leur former l'esprit*, vol. 7 (Paris: Veuve Estienne et Fils 1747), 116.

different passions." Perhaps, then, the affective portraiture possible in instrumental music was the result of its many and frequent juxtapositions.

Critiques of the amphibious style's hybridity therefore betrayed the underlying belief that instrumental music had some capacity to raise the affects in listeners, though theorists were confused about how. The nature of
that capacity was not mimesis as in the other arts — that much was clear. But
something about this new amphibious music was reaching its auditors, and
its hodgepodge nature made the dilemma that much more vexing for them.

As the century wore on, the amphibious style was no longer the exception —
it was the rule. Already in 1739 Mattheson complained, "There is in the writing of many self-instructed composers such a mishmash [*Mischmasch*] to be
found, as if everything were deteriorating into an amorphous clump. And I
think that one would find many who, upon being asked in which style this or
that piece was set, would be very embarrassed to answer."[31] Or, in the words of
Johann Adolf Scheibe, "In general, one throws together many different kinds
of assorted individual pieces in a heap, and writes at will above it the first name
that strikes the composer."[32] Instrumental music was not quite like marbled
paper then, as Pluche first suggests in the previous quotation, but much more
like a collage of passion portraits. Stylistic differences could emerge precisely
because they had been pasted closely together.

In order to understand in greater detail how this worked in the compositions of the day, consider the opening of Haydn's Symphony no. 57 (1774).
Haydn wrote the first measure for strings alone, whispering a detached,
repeated-note figure in which the first pitch glides quickly up to the next — a
kind of slide figure. The meter is a slow, deliberate 3/4, which gives each
repetition of the slide figure some space to breathe. In an attention-grabbing
contrast, this subdued opening is answered by the entire orchestra in full volume and in a much higher register. This alternation occurs once more before
we hear the first real melody; again the dynamic level is hushed, and now
the violins play a long, drawn-out, and lyric line. This sounds like a melody

31. "Denn es ist bereits bey vielen selbstgewachsenen Componisten ein solcher Mischmasch
in der Schreib-Art anzutreffen, als ob alles in einen ungestalten Klumpen verfallen wollte. Und
ich glaube, daß man ihrer eine Menge fünde, die, auf Befragen, in welchem Styl sie dieses
oder jenes setzten, mit der Antwort sehr verlegen seyn würden." Mattheson, *Der vollkommene
Capellmeister*, 93.

32. "Ueberhaupt aber wirft man vielerley besondere Arten einzelner Stücke in einen Hauf-
fen, und schreibet nach belieben einen Namen darüber, welcher dem erfahrnen Componisten
zuerst einfällt." Johann Adolph Scheibe, *Der critische Musicus*, vol. 1 (Hamburg: Thomas von
Wierings Erben, 1737–1738), 109. See also Danuta Mirka's discussion of this quotation in her
introduction to *The Oxford Handbook of Topic Theory*, 5–8.

someone might sing, and it is accompanied by a gentle pulsation in the lower string instruments. But this quickly comes to a halt after just two phrases, and we return to the contrasting call and answer that opened the piece. Before the slow introduction concludes, Haydn finds a way of combining the lyrical melody and the slide figure, writing them on top of each other. But this is not enough, since it is only a mere introduction to yet another set of contrasts. The Allegro proper of the symphony pits celebratory, bubbling enthusiasm against unanticipated bolts from the blue:[33] detached, jagged lines running from high to low, suggesting stormy seas. Tempest figures yield to a slow hush and finally build to a concluding fanfare with the entire orchestra in celebratory rhythms. Already we have seen contrast after contrast in this amphibious style, and this is only the first part of the first movement of the symphony. It will be followed by three more, contrasting movements — each with its own interior sets of juxtapositions.

Haydn's amphibiousness in Symphony no. 57 is impressive, but it is by no means the most frequently discussed of the period. When scholars of our own day seek to illustrate the stylistic juxtapositions of classic eighteenth-century instrumental music, they typically turn to the first movement of the celebrated Mozart Piano Sonata in F Major, K. 332 (1784). This work has become, as Wye J. Allanbrook put it, "the paradigm piece for topical analysts," and with a close look it is easy to see why.[34] Analyses of the movement point out that the opening melody — a lyrical, soaring line that sounds as though it belongs in an opera aria — almost immediately gives way to a break in texture and the onset of imitative counterpoint (which may itself be a parody of the learnedness that counterpoint requires). After a short tag ending that brings the counterpoint to a close, Mozart interjects music that allows the keyboard to temporarily become pairs of hunting horns; here he evokes notions of distance and rustication. But the countryside is soon covered in dark clouds, and the next passage is all storm and tragedy, with the keyboard quickly ascending and descending in the minor mode. All of this, and we have only heard the first thirty measures of the opening in the first movement.[35]

Recent scholars have been drawn to K. 332 and pieces like it precisely because of the dramatic, amphibious contrasts they make evident. In order

---

33. I borrow this phrase from Joseph Dubiel, "Senses of Sensemaking," *Perspectives of New Music* 30, no. 1 (1992): 210–221, where it is also used in the context of a Haydn analysis.

34. Allanbrook, *Secular Commedia*, 111.

35. On this movement, see also Agawu, *Playing with Signs*, 44–48; Kofi Agawu, *Music as Discourse: Semiotic Adventures in Romantic Music* (New York: Oxford University Press, 2009), 44; and Ratner, *Classic Music*, 222.

to identify, describe, and discern the different topical references of this instrumental music, they focus on works that parade one style after another, allowing the contrasts to shine more vividly precisely for their propinquity. For the most part, the goal of these scholars is clarity in identification and labeling. And there is something in the way that they are drawn to this classic, amphibious style that is similar to the manner in which eighteenth-century critics were struck by it; both sets of thinkers recognize that the rule of constant change is worthy of discussion.

But while recent scholarship uses the form of topical juxtaposition as a way to confidently catalogue each referent, eighteenth-century critics wrote of it primarily to communicate their exasperation and confusion. The amphibious style gave eighteenth-century thinkers license to complain of disorder in this music. And because they were befuddled by the "assorted individual pieces" that were thrown "in a heap," they began to experiment with new ways of theorizing the connection between musical materials and their affective import.[36]

Pluche, for instance, did more than simply reprimand the amphibious style for its inconstancy. Instead, he was given to animating this musical practice in long, colorful strains of analogy. This new disorderly music was like an individual "who passed from sadness to great clamors of laughter." But Pluche deepens this analogy as his critique picks up steam. Finally the amphibious style becomes a cartoonish avatar for all of its perceived shortcomings and is made to perform them in the lines of Pluche's printed text:

> At first peaceful, then violent, all of a sudden he stops. His bow moves by jumps, by leaps. Then come the sighs, and then the thunder, then the echoes. He seems to flee, and one can't hear him anymore. Little by little he gets closer, rolls, soars, climbs, falls, and bounces back. Next he walks humming, twittering, hopping, fluttering, pirouetting, flitting. When he stops the brusque airs and the snippets of birdsong, it is only in order to deliver you the cries of a whole farmyard, the noise of canons and bombs, the scraping of a roasting spit, or the clattering of wagons. Therefore he either imitates nothing or imitates everything for no reason. Of all that produces sound in nature, the human voice and the expression of the heart are what he imitates the least.[37]

36. Scheibe, *Der critische Musicus*, 109.

37. "D'abord paisible, puis emporté, tout-à-coup il s'arrête. Son archèt va par bonds, par sauts: viennent les soupirs: viennent les tonnerres: viennent les échos. Il semble fuir: on ne l'entend plus. Peu-à-peu il se rapproche, roule, plane, grimpe, tombe & se reléve. Il marche ensuite frédonnant, gasouillant, sautillant, voletant, pirouettant, papillonnant. S'il quitte les airs

Grasping for a way to understand this disordered musical practice, Pluche scripted a reversal in which he employed mimetic, imagistic writing in order to accuse instrumental music of lacking mimesis in sound. As a result, he conjured up a bizarre comic opera character, or a Rameau's nephew cycling through incredible scene contrasts, who "imitates nothing or imitates every-thing for no reason."[38]

Listening to instrumental music was like witnessing the actions of a human without interior content or a performing body without a soul. Pluche, along with many other critics of the period, developed a troped and elaborated ver-sion of the older concern that music was all too sensual and made too great an appeal to the body; these critics used the figure of the body to help them understand the confusions of the amphibious style. In so doing, they imagined instrumental music as its own inanimate yet performing body. To them it was all mechanical gymnastics, like a puppet or a picaro without any interior depth. The supposed body — its material reality — was the only thing that held it together. And for that reason, it could only ever make a skin-deep appeal to the listener.

Pluche was certainly not the first to make this criticism or even the most pointed in its execution. Mattheson had already limned it when he wrote, at the end of his mimetic *Affektenlehre* taxonomy, about the possibility of unin-spired musical composition. "Even if its outward appearance is more beautiful than Venus, it would still only be a beautiful body without an intelligent soul. Here we have charming notes and lovely sounds but no heart-moving song."[39] In this passage, Mattheson discusses the possibility for banality in all musical composition, but nevertheless the dualism in his remark leads him to suggest

---

brusques & les déchiquetures de la voix des oiseaux; ce sera pour vous livrer les cris de toute une basse cour, le bruit de canon & des bombes, ou le raclement des tournebroches, ou le fracas des charrettes. Ainsi ou il n'imite rien, ou le contrefait tout à propos de rien. De tout ce qui fait bruit dans la nature la voix humaine & l'expression du cœur est ce qu'il imite le moins." Pluche, *Le spectacle*, 118.

38. Published well before Diderot began work on his famous dialogue, this passage in Pluche might well have served as one point of inspiration for *Rameau's Nephew* (although I am not aware of any secondary literature in the wealth of writing on Diderot's text that brings the two into conversation). At the very least, Pluche's figure is an excellent example of what Sianne Ngai calls "the zany." See Ngai, "The Zany Science," in *Our Aesthetic Categories: Zany, Cute, Inter-esting* (Cambridge, MA: Harvard University Press, 2012), 174–232; and also chapter 2 of this book.

39. "Das heisset nun nichts anders, ob es gleich, dem äusserlichen Ansehen nach, schöner als die Venus wäre, denn ein feiner, niedlicher Leib, ohne eine verständige Seele; es sind an-genehme Noten, liebliche Klänge, ohne hertzrührenden Gesang." Mattheson, *Der vollkommene Capellmeister*, 20.

that such lacking music might only graze the body of its listeners. "Is it therefore any wonder that in these pieces . . . the poor listeners only have their ears
tickled?" he opined.[40]

Still other critics of instrumental music imported an explicit mind-body
dualism in order to associate this amphibious practice with low corporeal
tricks. When Johann Christoph Gottsched translated Batteux's *Les beaux arts
réduits à un même principe* for the German-speaking world, he drew attention
to the dualism already lurking in the background of the French theorist's text,
expanding and embellishing it in his commentary. While Batteux had allowed
that the music of the symphony might have "but half a life," Gottsched's remarks on the same passage construed this "half a life" in various scenes of
corporeal performance.

> In this passage, we hear that music, without a text or dance, is only a
> dead thing — only a body without a soul. Why? One understands or
> rather guesses at only half of what was played if no gestures or words
> accompany it that can truly clarify what the tones ought to say. It is just
> like the bare gestures of the old pantomimes when they attempted to
> depict tragic apparitions. One must first hear the text before, recited
> by another actor, if one is to understand the pantomime. Bare music
> [*eine bloße Musik*] expresses itself just as imperfectly when its verses
> or dances are missing that it should be considered nothing other than
> bare *Charivari*, which only resembles the chirping of birds.[41]

Gottsched proposes several important analogies in this passage, each time
slightly adjusting his understanding of instrumental music. He opens the
commentary with the application of an explicit dualism by means of interpreting Batteux's "half a life" comment: instrumental music has only the cor-

40. "Ist es demnach ein Wunder, daß bey so gestalten Sachen, da die wahre Natur-Lehre des
Klanges, samt der dahin gehörigen Wissenschafft von den menschlichen Gemüths-Bewegungen,
gänzlich unter der Banck lieget, den armen einfältigen und sich viel-dünckenden Zuhörern nur
die blossen Ohren gekitzelt." Mattheson, *Der vollkommene Capellmeister*, 20.

41. "Da hören wir, daß eine Musik, ohne Text, oder Tanz, nur ein todtes Ding, nur ein Körper, ohne Geist ist. Warum? Man versteht oder erräth es vielmehr nur halb, was gespielet wird;
wenn nicht entweder Gebärden, oder Worte dazu kommen, die das deutlicher erklären, was
die Töne sagen sollen. Sie ist wie die bloßen Gebärden der alten Pantomimen waren, wann sie
tragigische Auftritte vorstellen wollten, man mußte vorher die Worte davon, von einem andern
Schauspieler haben hersagen hören, wenn man den Pantomimen verstehen sollte. Eben so
unvollkommen dräcket eine bloße Musik sich aus, wenn ihr Verse, oder Tänze fehlen: Dafern
sie anders nicht ein bloßes Charivari seyn soll, das nur dem Zwitschern der Vögel gleicht."
Johann Christoph Gottsched, *Auszug aus des Herrn Batteux schönen Künsten aus dem einzigen
Grundsatze der Nachahmung hergeleitet . . .* (Leipzig: Bernhard Christoph Breitkopf, 1754), 202.

poreal half of life; it is essentially a dead yet performing body. But he soon leaves this grim image behind for something slightly more human: a deficient, confused pantomime performance without any prefaced text. The final pronouncement, however, shifts instrumental music over to the domain of the uncontrolled and uninterpretable. It finally becomes, in Gottsched's commentary, the equivalent of nonhuman corporeal performance in the chirping of birds.

Far from an unambiguously mimetic medium that was simply in need of interpretive work, instrumental music was for many period critics a messy dilemma. Not only was it clearly lower in merit than texted music, but it had also begun to complicate the issue of mimesis with its penchant for stylistic hybridity. Still, in their best efforts to find in this practice something that resembled meaning, theorists drew comparisons to other corporeal performances in which any straightforward imitation was obscured: the antics of a zany Rameau's nephew, the movements in an old pantomime stripped of its text, or the chirping of birds — anything that might have suggested to them a performance of a body without interior content.

"Not Simply an Imitation of Nature, but Nature Itself"

Nevertheless, amid the confusions created by instrumental music and the amphibious style, there was a group of theorists at work on reconceptualizing the affective power of music. While these theorists might not have had the focus of their concerns directed at instrumental music per se, they took their cues from the debate surrounding it. Perhaps it was not a liability at all that music without a text was said to speak to listeners' bodies. Perhaps this distinctively corporeal relationship gave to it a special purchase on affective transmission. In different ways, Johann Adam Hiller, Caspar Ruetz, and Friedrich Melchior Grimm created something new out of the explicitly dualist pronouncements against music's corporeal appeal. For these thinkers, music's ability to touch the body was precisely what allowed it to move the soul.

Hiller contributed his 1754 "Abhandlung von der Nachahmung der Natur in der Musik" to Marpurg's *Historisch-Kritische Beyträge*, where a critical conversation concerning the reception of Batteux's views within musical circles was taking place.[42] Hiller's article, which extolled Batteux and denigrated instrumental music, would seem an unlikely place to turn for a new view on

---

42. Johann Adam Hiller, "Abhandlung von der Nachahmung der Natur in der Musik," in *Historisch-Kritische Beyträge zur Aufnahme der Musik*, ed. Friedrich Wilhelm Marpurg, vol. 1 (Berlin: J. J. Schützens Witwe, G. A. Lange, 1754) 515–543.

the relationship between music and affect. But in the essay, Hiller elaborated and qualified Batteux in such a way that the raw material of musical sound, for this German critic, was understood to "reach the heart immediately and without circumlocution."[43] Hiller associated pictures and ideas — the traditional objects of mimesis — with the mind. The heart, the seat of the affects, held a special relationship with musical sounds. Thus music, the art of sounds, made a direct appeal to the corporeal interior of the listener. "Music," Hiller suggested, "has secret passages to the heart that we have not yet discovered, and that we cannot block in order to guard it."[44] It would seem that Hiller had to create an alternative architecture of affective arousal in order to account for the work of music in moving the soul to the affects.

The same basic conceit — wherein music is said to access a unique conduit through the body to the interior of the listener — was also an important feature of Ruetz's contribution to Marpurg's journal.[45] But Ruetz, by contrast to Hiller, arrived at this conclusion in the midst of an outright attack on Batteux's theory of imitation. Ruetz distrusted Batteux's system for the arts and perceived an acute weakness in its ability to account for music. Not only did he find Batteux laughably incompetent at interpreting and employing music theory, but he also thought the French theorist's understanding of imitation a poor fit for music's powers. It seemed absurd to Ruetz that musical sound should be required to live up to the imitative capabilities of the other traditionally mimetic arts. Would not critics, comparing music to poetry and painting, "demand from music things that are totally contrary to its nature?" he asked. "Could they not arrive at the idea of requiring that music should represent first a house, now a bridge, now a flower, now a shrub, and soon even a squirrel?"[46] That music should be assessed along the lines of these capabilities seemed to Ruetz a failure on the part of Batteux's systematic effort to develop universally applicable rules for all of art.

To Ruetz, music pointed beyond the received understandings of signification within the day's aesthetic theory. Specifically, Ruetz took careful aim at

43. "Es wird so gleich dafür erkannt, und gelanget unmittelbar und ohne Umschweif zu dem Herzen." Hiller, "Abhandlung," 521.

44. "Die Musik hat geheime Zugänge zu dem Herzen, die wir noch nicht entdecket haben, und die wir vor ihr zu beschützen nicht im Stande sind." Hiller, "Abhandlung," 523.

45. Caspar Ruetz, "Sendschreiben eines Freundes an den andern über einige Ausdrücke des Herrn Batteux von der Musik," in Marpurg, *Historisch-Kritische Beyträge*, vol. 1, 273–311. For a more extended treatment of Ruetz's essay, see Hosler, *Changing Aesthetic Views*, 124–130.

46. "Werden sie nicht Dinge von der Musik verlangen, die ihrer Natur ganz zuwider sind? Könten sie nicht den Einfall bekommen, von der Musik zu fordern, daß sie bald ein Haus, bald eine Brücke, bald eine Blume, bald eine Staude, ja bald ein Eichhörnchen vorstellen soll?" Ruetz, "Sendschreiben," 275–276.

a passage of Batteux's treatise in which the French theorist struggled to cate-
gorize music as either a natural or an arbitrary sign. "Of course the words in
a language are arbitrary," Ruetz writes, "and there may occasionally be other
expressions and signs of our thoughts and feelings that are neither natural nor
artificial," highlighting the same confusion Batteux had encountered.[47] But
Ruetz took the dilemma one step further in order to propose a new solution.
Perhaps, he ventured, the problem was not with music at all but with how
the natural sign—and all of signification—was thought to be rooted in the
natural world. "[Music] is not simply an imitation of nature, but nature itself,
since it is just as grounded in nature to speak through singing and harmonic
tones as it is through words, rhetorical speeches, and gestures. It simply generates feeling in us, and thousands of other feelings of which a musical heart
is capable are music's own property, which no speaker nor poet can arouse
by his words or moving declamation."[48] Here Ruetz begins to suggest that
the art of music holds a special relationship with the corporeal interiors of
musical listeners. It is through this relationship that musical sound is able to
arouse distinctive affective experiences that are not achievable through any
other aesthetic medium. He continues: "In this last case music is no copy
of nature, but the original itself. It is a universal language of nature that is
accessible only to harmonious souls. And its distinctive expressions, which
it does not borrow from other things, have a secret understanding with these
souls."[49] In this statement, Ruetz completely remaps the theory of the natural
sign. Music does not function through imitations of nature, and it does not
borrow its powers from reproductions of natural objects. Instead, music itself
is a natural conduit for affect. It is possible to read Ruetz along the lines of the
more explicitly materialist theory of his French contemporary Élie-Catherine
Fréron;[50] he hints, in this passage, toward the idea that it could be music's

47. "Freylich sind die Worte in einer Sprache willkuhrlich; und es mögen hin und wieder
noch andere Ausdrücke und Zeichen unserer Gedanken und Empfindungen seyn, die weder
natürlich noch kunstlich sind." Ruetz, "Sendschreiben," 290.

48. "Sie ist nicht allein eine Nachahmerin der Natur, sondern die Natur selbst; indem es so
wohl in der Natur gegründet ist, durch singende und harmonische Töne zu reden, als durch
Worte, rednerischen Vortrag und Gebärden. Sie macht uns eben das Empfinden; und tausend
andere Empfindungen, deren ein musikalisches Herze fähig ist, und die kein Redner, noch Poet
durch seine Worte und bewegliche Declamation erwecken kann, sind ihr Eigenthum." Ruetz,
"Sendschreiben," 292–293.

49. "In diesen lezten ist die Musik keine Copie der Natur, sondern das Original selbsten.
Sie ist eine allgemeine Sprache der Natur, die nur den harmonischen Seelen verständlich ist.
Und ihre eigenthümliche Ausdrücke, welche sie nicht von andern Dingen entlehnet, haben
ein geheimes Verständniß mit diesen Seelen." Ruetz, "Sendschreiben," 293. See also Hosler's
translation of this passage in *Changing Aesthetic Views*, 126.

50. On Fréron's materialist theory of musical affect, see chapter 2.

sonic status—that is, the fact that music "is nature itself"—that allows it access to the soul through the human interior.

For both thinkers, then, music had direct access to the listener through its
"secret passages [geheime Zugänge]" to the heart—the seat of the affects for
Hiller—or its "secret understanding [geheimes Verständniß]" with the soul in
Ruetz. Unlike the explicit dualisms that associated music (especially instrumental music) with the body, this figure by contrast had a cryptodualist aspect.
Ruetz and Hiller posited that music was the connecting medium between the
human body and the soul's affective arousal; but if in these theories music
was what stitched the two different entities together, then they must therefore
have been fundamentally distinct. Music, with its ability to penetrate into the
body, could by this means move the soul. The soul and body were therefore
musically coupled but nevertheless nonunified, unidentical, dual.

This cryptodualism is precisely what Ruetz and Hiller shared with Friedrich Melchior Grimm, whose entry "Poeme lyrique" for the *Encyclopédie*
spent a great deal of effort distinguishing the aesthetic power of music from
that of language. The two, on Grimm's account, were parallel systems: "Music is a language," he writes plainly.[51] But in Grimm's thinking, music was
more than language's double. Instead it put into operation a metalinguistic
function as a "universal language" since it spoke "the language of all nations
and all ages."[52] Rather than simply duplicating the power of language's sym-
bolic signification, music operated on our faculties directly. "[Music] strikes
our organs and our imagination immediately. It is also by its very nature the
language of feeling and the passions. Its expressions, going straight to the heart
without passing, so to speak, through the mind, must produce effects known in
no other idiom. . . . This is the power that music has in common with gesture,
that other universal language. Experience teaches us that nothing commands
the soul more imperiously or moves it more strongly than these two ways of
speaking to it."[53] The corporeal art of gesture and the sonic art of music, then,
spoke like language but made their appeal "straight to the heart without pass-

51. "La Musique est une langue." Friedrich Melchior Grimm, "Poeme lyrique," in Diderot
and d'Alembert, *Encyclopédie*, vol. 12, 824.

52. "La langue du musicien . . . parle la langue de toutes les nations & de tous les siecles."
Grimm, "Poeme lyrique," 824.

53. "Une langue universelle frappant immédiatement nos organes & notre imagination,
est aussi par sa nature la langue du sentiment & des passions. Ses expressions allant droit au
cœur, sans passer pour ainsi dire par l'esprit, doivent produire des effets inconnus à tout autre
idiome. . . . C'est un pouvoir que la musique a de commun avec le geste, cette autre langue
universelle. L'expérience nous apprend que rien ne commande plus impérieusement à l'ame, ni
ne l'émeut plus fortement que ces deux manieres de lui parler." Grimm, "Poeme lyrique," 824.

ing, so to speak, through the mind." Thus music, for Grimm as for Hiller and Ruetz, performed a paradigmatic cryptodualism. It was this immediate ability of music to strike our bodily organs that allowed it forcefully to encounter the separate entity of the soul.

By the middle decades of the eighteenth century, the stage was set for a new theory of affect pitched to musical sound. The consternation surrounding instrumental music further amplified the debates over the music of the opera theater. Instrumental music was not only incredibly vague but also stylistically amphibious, shape-shifting, and dissimulating; this practice seemed flagrantly to contradict the day's prevailing aesthetic theory of imitation. Critics therefore doubled down on their older concerns about the sensual appeal of musical art. Instrumental music was equated with the body and was said to make its impact there. Some theorists, such as Mattheson and Gottsched, described instrumental music as a performing body devoid of a soul. It was this explicit dualism, associated especially with critiques of instrumental music, that helped to make possible the formation of a different, cryptodualist explanation of music's power to arouse the affects. Perhaps, theorists postured, the link between musical sound and the human interior was exactly what allowed it to reach the soul of the listener. Perhaps music did not imitate nature at all but was a natural vehicle itself, transmitting affect to its auditors in a direct, immediate, corporeal way. A novel theory of affective attunement was ascendant.

4

The Attunement *Affektenlehre*

As the penultimate movement of Beethoven's Fifth Symphony draws to its end, the texture of the performing orchestral instruments thins out. A skeleton crew of strings, bassoon, and oboe quietly trade the movement's signal four-note motive, which is itself a transformation of the four-note gesture that opens this symphony. In a Gothic, somewhat creepy style, the four-note motive is treated to fragmentation as the violins pluck soft pizzicato against the lean sound of the double-reed instruments.[1] The overall effect is dry and hollow. Then the strings begin to play a solid, sustained chord at a low dynamic level, the timpani pulsing in the background. The harmonic motion has reached stasis here.

From the lower register of the first violins, the melody that opened the movement rises, then gently arches and falls again. The violins repeat this pattern, slowly climbing out of the low pitches, reaching upward, and gaining in volume as they expand the range of the music. While they continue their ascent and begin to play in the singing register of the instrument, they are joined by wind instruments on sustained pitches—bassoons first, then oboes, then horns, trumpets, and flutes. This powerful crescendo on dominant harmony creates the effect of something rushing quickly toward the listener;[2] then sud-

---

1. On the topical references of this movement, see Susan McClary, "In Praise of Contingency: The Powers and Limits of Theory," *Music Theory Online* 16, no. 1 (2010), www.mtosmt .org/issues/mto.10.16.1/mto.10.16.1.mcclary.html.

2. Deirdre Loughridge, *Haydn's Sunrise, Beethoven's Shadow: Audiovisual Culture and the Emergence of Musical Romanticism* (Chicago: University of Chicago Press, 2016), 223–225.

denly and without a break the opening theme of the symphony's finale begins: the full orchestra outlines a powerful C major triad. The style is heroic with an allegro tempo and martial rhythms. The bright, triumphant radiance of the music in this new movement is an inversion of the dark creepiness heard less than sixty seconds before. But these different topical worlds are related to each other through the motivic material, which—with its familiar rhythms and patterns—now works its way through the finale's buoyant themes.

The tight interconnection of the motives in Beethoven's Fifth Symphony was a striking and vital feature of the work for one of its first and most noted reviewers, E. T. A. Hoffmann. Writing in 1810 for Leipzig's *Allgemeine musikalische Zeitung*, Hoffmann emphasized how Beethoven's music had created a single response in its auditors. Even while the topical reference could change dramatically from one moment to the next, for Hoffmann it was "chiefly the intimate relationship of the individual themes to each other that generates the unity that is able to keep the heart of the listener held in *one* attunement [*Stimmung*]."[3] For Hoffmann, this singular, attuned condition was longing— *Sehnsucht*. Beethoven's music "wipes out everything in us but the pain of infinite *Sehnsucht*, in which every desire that quickly ascended in jubilant tones sinks down and perishes."[4] The carefully linked structures in Beethoven's music created for the listener an immersive, subjective state capable of drowning out all else, superseding any of the symphony's momentary affects or expressions.

Both Beethoven's symphony and Hoffmann's review have attracted considerable commentary since the early nineteenth century and have been made to say countless things about each other. In a recent, compelling study, Deirdre Loughridge explains how Hoffmann's review of the symphony draws on imagery associated with the optical entertainment of the phantasmagoria show, characterizing the Fifth Symphony as "an experience of the spirit world as real, alien, and ever ready to return."[5] For Heinrich Schenker, Hoffmann's review was musically unsophisticated and nothing other than a spiritual exercise; for later critics such as Carl Dahlhaus, the same review was responsible

---

3. "Ist es vorzüglich die innige Verwandtschaft der einzelnen Themas untereinander, welche jene Einheit erzeugt, die des Zuhörers Gemüth in *einer* Stimmung festhält." E. T. A. Hoffmann, "Recension," *Allgemeine musikalische Zeitung* (Leipzig), July 4–11, 1810, col. 658 (emphasis in original).

4. "Und alles in uns vernichten, nur nicht den Schmerz der unendlichen Sehnsucht, in welcher jede Lust, die, schnell in jauchzenden Tönen emporgestiegen, hinsinkt und untergeht." Hoffmann, "Recension," col. 633.

5. Loughridge, *Haydn's Sunrise*, 230.

for inaugurating a tradition in which the only meaningful appreciation of the Fifth Symphony is achieved through structural analysis of its music.[6]

Hoffmann's insistence on a singular state of attunement, however, is also the outcome of a particular tradition within affect theory. For Hoffmann, Beethoven's music generated more than a simple series of mimetic representations; instead, its varied forms of the unified thematic material "revealed to people a world . . . in which they leave behind all feelings circumscribed by definable ideas in order to give themselves over to the unutterable."[7] Beethoven's music attuned its audiences to a nondiscursive state — a state opposed to the definite, linguistically mediated domain of thoughts and feelings. Here, in Hoffmann's review, was a mature manifestation of the *Affektenlehre* tradition. This new stage of the *Affektenlehre* was no longer mimetic, and its authors no longer made specific claims about direct relationships between musical materials and specific emotional states or feelings. Instead, Hoffmann and other early nineteenth-century critics held an understanding of attunement that more closely resembles twenty-first-century affect theory. Nondiscursive and immediate, this kind of affective experience is best captured in Hoffmann's term for it: *Stimmung*, which translates to "mood" or "attunement." Hoffmann's review represents the final stage of the attunement *Affektenlehre* tradition, in which affect retreated to the interiors of listening subjects and took on characteristics associated with the ineffable.[8] The result of decades of transformation within late eighteenth-century aesthetic theory and music theory, it is a pendant to our contemporary understanding of affect.

In the middle decades of the eighteenth century, several philosophers had simultaneously — and seemingly unrelatedly — turned to the figure of sympathetic resonance as a resource for describing the operation of affect on the body. Grounded in the empirical physics of sound vibration, sympathetic res-

6. Heinrich Schenker, *Der Tonwille: Pamphlets / Quarterly Publications in Witness of the Immutable Laws of Music* (1921–1924), ed. William Drabkin, vol. 2 (New York: Oxford University Press, 2004), 26; Carl Dahlhaus, *The Idea of Absolute Music*, trans. Roger Lustig (Chicago: University of Chicago Press, 1989), 69; on the reception history of Hoffmann's essay more generally, see Loughridge, *Haydn's Sunrise*, 228–231.

7. "Die Musik schliesst dem Menschen ein unbekanntes Reich auf; eine Welt . . . die ihn umgiebt, und in der er alle durch Begriffe bestimmbaren Gefühle zurücklässt, um sich dem Unaussprechlichen hinzugeben." Hoffmann, "Recension," col. 631.

8. It may be fair to say that both affect and music share certain paradoxes with the ineffable, particularly their mutual relationship, often posed in antithesis, to language. My understanding of the paradoxes of the ineffable and Hoffmann's place within that tradition has been shaped by Michael Gallope, *Deep Refrains: Music, Philosophy, and the Ineffable* (Chicago: University of Chicago Press, 2017).

onance made for a convenient analogy or description of affective mediation and even, for some authors, a cryptodualist model of mind-body interaction. At the same time, debates on opera, as we have seen, had catalyzed a new set of questions within aesthetic theory about the ability of music to evoke the affects. One result of these quarrels was a theory of affective attunement: music, through its physical reality as sound vibration, could generate sympathetic resonances or attunements in the bodies or interiors of its auditors, thereby placing them in affective states.

Many early adopters of this new attunement view of musical affect attempted to reconcile it with the inherited mimetic *Affektenlehre* tradition, and some sought a hybridization with older theories predicated on the operation of bodily nerve fluid or animal spirits. But the mature articulation of this theory — in the writings of Antonio Planelli, Michel-Paul-Guy de Chabanon, Wilhelm Heinrich Wackenroder, and later critics — offered a nonrepresentational, nondiscursive understanding of affect that relied on autonomic corporeal responses to music. This amounted to a transformation within aesthetic theory that granted to music a special mode of evoking affect in subjects and thoroughly associated the experience of affect with music.

Human Instruments: The Prelude to Affective Attunement

What prepared the full articulation of the attunement *Affektenlehre* was a series of developments within the philosophy of sensation that took place in mutual influence with the history of music theory. Indeed, as early a thinker of sense perception as David Hume would borrow from the domain of music in adopting the figure of string vibration. Hume employed this figure as an explanatory mechanism in his "Dissertation on the Passions," first published with *Four Dissertations* (1757), which continues his general philosophical project of a complete, Newtonian understanding of human nature.[9] For this reason, the passions are said not to be of the soul but rather of the mind, which for Hume is an entity with describable anatomical and operational properties.[10] Already in the third paragraph of the first section in the treatise,

9. David Hume, *Four Dissertations* (London: A. Millar, 1757). I have consulted the critical edition in Hume, *"A Dissertation on the Passions" and "The Natural History of Religion": A Critical Edition*, ed. Tom L. Beauchamp (Oxford, UK: Clarendon, 2007).

10. For an account of the slow shift away from the Aristotelian natural science of the soul to the Enlightenment sciences of human nature — in which mind begins to supplant the role of soul — see R. W. Serjeantson, "The Soul," in *The Oxford Handbook of Philosophy in Early Modern Europe*, ed. Desmond M. Clarke and Catherine Wilson (Oxford: Oxford University Press, 2011), 119–141; William Edward Morris and Charlotte R. Brown, "David Hume," in *The Stanford*

Hume is in the position of having to describe how the various passions follow on from each other in succession.

> Now, if we consider the human mind, we shall observe, that, with regard to the passions, it is not like a wind instrument of music, which, in running over all the notes, immediately loses the sound when the breath ceases; but rather resembles a string-instrument, where, after each stroke, the vibrations still retain some sound, which gradually and insensibly decays. . . . The passions, in comparison, are slow and restive: For which reason, when any object is presented, which affords a variety of views to the one and emotions to the other; though the fancy may change its views with great celerity; each stroke will not produce a clear and distinct note of passion, but the one passion will always be mixed and confounded with the other.[11]

Hume inherits the notion of the human interior configured as a string instrument from the *musica humana* tradition and elaborates a metaphorical connection between the tunings and soundings of this instrument and the operations of the affects.[12] He further develops this notion with reference to the physical properties of sound vibration, allowing these properties to explain the connection or enchaining of the affects to each other.

Two features of this description in Hume's theory increased in relevance over the course of the century. The first is the idea of the human interior as a vibrating instrument that is played on by the outside world; the second is the notion that each affect calls forth others, one leading to the next. Both of these were central to the staunchly materialist account of the affects found in Diderot's *Le rêve de d'Alembert*, in which Diderot stages a fictional conversation between himself and his fellow encyclopedist. When d'Alembert quizzes Diderot on how the mind has the ability to be occupied with more than one thing at a time, Diderot responds in musical terms.

> I have sometimes compared the fibers of our organs to vibrating, sensitive strings. The vibrating, sensitive string oscillates and resonates for a long time after one has plucked it. . . . But these vibrating strings have yet another property; they can make others tremble; and it is thus that one idea calls up a second, these two a third, all three a fourth, and so on. . . . This instrument makes surprising leaps, and an idea awakened

---

Encyclopedia of Philosophy (Spring 2017 Edition), ed. Edward N. Zalta, accessed April 4, 2017, https://plato.stanford.edu/archives/spr2017/entries/hume/.

11. Hume, *Dissertation on the Passions*, 4.

12. For other predecessors within this tradition, see chapter 2 of this book.

can sometimes resonate with a harmonic that is at an incomprehensible interval. If this phenomenon is observable in between two sonorous strings that are separate and inert, why would it not be found between items that are living and related — between continuous and sensible fibers?[13]

To this, d'Alembert eventually parries, "You are trying to eliminate the distinction between mind and matter."[14] Such was Diderot's materialism. The notion of "idea" (*idée*) in this passage seems to follow on from Locke's view of the same term, which corresponded to both perceptions and acts of perceptions.[15] For Diderot, these phenomena were, in any case, analogous with automatic corporeal processes of resonation with the exterior world, a characteristic they share with the affects. Diderot and d'Alembert go on in the dialogue to develop the image of the human instrument, which results in a lengthy comparison between philosophers and clavichords. Diderot explains, "We are all instruments gifted with sensibility and memory. Our senses are so many keys that are struck by nature that surrounds us, and that often strike themselves, and this, in my judgment, is all that would take place in a clavichord organized as you and I are."[16] In Diderot's radical vision, all that prevents humans from being roughly equivalent with objects is their capacity for sensation and memory. Vibration serves here as the interstice: it mediates between external and internal but also demonstrates the fundamental continuity between human and nonhuman.

13. "Je le pense ; ce qui m'a fait quelquefois comparer les fibres de nos organes à des cordes vibrantes sensibles. La corde vibrante sensible oscille, résonne longtemps encore après qu'on l'a pincée. . . . Mais les cordes vibrantes ont encore une autre propriété ; c'est d'en faire frémir d'autres ; et c'est ainsi qu'une première idée en rappelle une seconde ; ces deux-là une troisième ; toutes les trois une quatrième, et ainsi de suite. . . . Cet instrument a des sauts étonnants, et une idée réveillée va faire quelquefois frémir une harmonique qui en est à un intervalle incompréhensible. Si le phénomène s'observe entre des cordes sonores, inertes et séparées, comment n'aurait-il pas lieu entre des points vivants et liés, entre des fibres continues et sensibles?" Denis Diderot, *Le rêve de d'Alembert*, in *Œuvres philosophiques*, ed. Michel Delon with Barbara de Negroni (Paris: Gallimard, 2010), 351.

14. This is how Jacques Barzun and Ralph H. Bowen render the passage in Denis Diderot, *Rameau's Nephew and Other Works*, trans. Barzun and Bowen (Indianapolis: Hackett, 1956), 100. "Vous en voulez à la distinction des deux substances." Diderot, *Le rêve de d'Alembert*, 351.

15. See Pauline Phemister, "Ideas," in *The Oxford Handbook of Philosophy in Early Modern Europe*, ed. Desmond M. Clarke and Catherine Wilson (Oxford: Oxford University Press, 2011), 142–159.

16. "Nous sommes des instruments doués de sensibilité et de mémoire. Nos sens sont autant de touches qui sont pincées par la nature qui nous environne, et qui se pincent souvent elles-mêmes. Et voici, à mon jugement, tout ce qui se passe dans un clavecin organisé comme vous et moi." Diderot, *Le rêve de d'Alembert*, 352.

During the latter half of the eighteenth century, the figure of the resonant human interior as instrument developed along several related but separate axes. In the first, the instrument and its tuning came to represent the relationship between the mental faculties. This idea reached full expression in Immanuel Kant's *Critique of Judgment* (1790), in which the faculties of the understanding and the imagination are said to be in reciprocal attunement (*Stimmung*) and accordance (*Zusammenstimmung*) with each other.[17] In judgments of beauty, the activity of the imagination is not constrained by the rules of the understanding (as it otherwise is in cognition) but rather enters into free play with the understanding and subsequently finds itself in attunement with this faculty.[18] Johann Gottfried Herder's metacritique of Kant, written in dialogue form in *Kalligone* (1800), returns us to a more familiar scene. Here, the instrument and its resonances are not restricted to the human interior but are, instead, the interface through which humans come to know the external world and are moved to affective responses.

A: And tones that grow or diminish in power, that rise or fall, that are slower or faster, more serious or jocular, that are pressing or retreating, harsh or soft, evenly or unevenly progressing, that is, pulses, beats, breaths, waves, emotion, and pleasure, how do these affect our mind?

B: Homologous movements, as all music evinces concomitant involuntary impressions in our affects. The passion in us . . . rises and sinks, it leaps or creeps and treads slowly. Now it is pressing forward, now

17. Immanuel Kant, *Critik der Urtheilskraft* (Berlin: Lagarde und Friederich, 1790); facsimile edition in *Critik der Urtheilskraft*, with introduction by Lewis White Beck (London: Routledge/ Thoemmes, 1994), § 9, p. 31; Kant, *Critique of Judgment*, trans. Werner S. Pluhar (Indianapolis: Hackett, 1987), 62–63. On this aspect of Kant's thinking in the *Critique of Judgment*, see Henry Allison, *Kant's Theory of Taste* (Cambridge: Cambridge University Press, 2001), 110–118.

18. In the dominant historiography of *Stimmung*, Kant's is the first true aesthetic use of the term, after which it develops the distinct meaning it takes on through the nineteenth-, twentieth-, and twenty-first centuries as "mood" or "atmosphere." The thinking in this historiographical strand is that *Stimmung*, as attunement, is not technically related to its antecedents in historical music theory. I would encourage a broader view of attunement that is not restricted to the German term *Stimmung* and see Kant's use of the term as very much a part of a broader tradition that understands the human interior to be tuned, harmonized, and ordered, a tradition that grows out of *musica humana*. The historiography I refer to earlier begins with David Wellbery, "Stimmung," in *Historisches Wörterbuch Ästhetischer Grundbegriffe*, ed. Karlheinz Barck et al., vol. 5 (Stuttgart: Metzler, 2003), 703–733; and is further developed in Hans Ulrich Gumbrecht, *Atmosphere, Mood, Stimmung: On a Hidden Potential of Literature*, trans. H. Erik Butler (Stanford, CA: Stanford University Press, 2012); and Erik Wallrup, *Being Musically Attuned: The Act of Listening to Music* (Farnham, UK: Ashgate, 2015).

retreating, now weaker and now stronger moved. Its movement, its step changes with each modulation, with every apt accent let alone change of key. Music plays a clavichord within us, which is our own innermost nature.[19]

In critiquing Kant, Herder drew on the alternative strand of human instrumentality running through eighteenth-century thought: the notion of the human as an instrument composed of sensitive strings that vibrate in sympathetic resonance with musical sounds.[20]

Doctrines of Affective Attunement

Interwoven with these strands of thinking on the sonorous human instrument was a new thread of the music theoretical *Affektenlehre*. As the midcentury opera quarrels put increasing pressure on theorists to account for the aesthetic capacities of musical sound, theorists began to make innovative recourses to vibration, anatomy, and attunement. In the middle decades of the century, theorists used the image of the affectively attuned listener as one of a great number of explanatory mechanisms, and there was no consistency in the physiological claims they used to support it. Gradually, theorists shifted away from figural and metaphorical language; the body's nerves eventually became their explicit focus and the most important part of this theory's recourse to physiology, as theorists attempted to update the older mimetic *Affektenlehre* tradition with their new mechanism of attunement.[21] By the century's end, the

19. "A. Und wachsende oder abnehmende, steigende oder sinkende Töne, ein langsamer oder schneller, ernsthafter oder hüpfender, andringender, zurückweichender, hart-oder weicher, gleich-oder ungleichmässiger Fortgang der Töne, d. i. der Stöße, Schläge, Hauche, Wellen, der Rührungen und Vergnügen, was wirken sie auf unser Gemüth? B. Gleichartige Regungen, wie jeder die Musik begleitende unwillkührliche Ausdruck unsrer Affekten zeigt. Das Leidenschaftliche in uns . . . hebet sich und sinkt, es hüpft oder schleicht und schreitet langsam. Jetzt wird es andringend-, jetzt zurückweichend-, jetzt schwächer-, jetzt stärker gerührt; seine eigne Bewegung, sein Tritt verändert sich mit jeder Modulation, mit jedem treffenden Accent, geschweige mit einer veränderten Tonart. Die Musik spielt in uns ein Clavichord, das unsre eigne innigste Natur ist." Johann Gottfried Herder, *Kalligone*, vol. 1 (Leipzig: Johann Friedrich Hartknoch, 1800), 116–117.

20. On Herder's clavichord listener and its significance for the theory of timbre, see Emily I. Dolan, *The Orchestral Revolution: Haydn and the Technologies of Timbre* (Cambridge: Cambridge University Press, 2013), 83–89.

21. The growing interest in the relationship between musical vibration and the human nervous system during the eighteenth century has been well documented. See especially the papers collected in James Kennaway, ed., *Music and the Nerves, 1700–1900* (New York: Palgrave Macmillan, 2014).

attunement *Affektenlehre* had lost all of its mimetic components, and — in the thinking of some theorists — musical affect was said to work through vibration and body alone.[22]

When Christian Gottfried Krause published *Von der musikalischen Poesie* in 1752, the *querelle des bouffons* had already begun in Paris. At first blush, Krause would seem to hold a view very similar to that put forth by Élie-Catherine Fréron, who believed that musical sounds had the power to arouse the affects by vibrating those human nerves that happened to be tuned in unison with them. As Krause put it, "the soul is like a stringed instrument, which resonates when one provides the tone of one of its strings, although the string itself was not touched."[23] But Krause goes on to explain that the "motions of the soul" have exact relations with "the condition of our blood and blood vessels."[24] The different kinds and stages of love, for instance, accordingly generate "different surges of the blood."[25] Music arouses the affects by vibrating in sympathy with "the natural tension of the veins in [the] ears."[26] This more general picture of the human interior as a zone for sympathetic vibration was also a major theme of the criticism on all sides of the *querelle des bouffons* and made its way into Joseph-Louis Roger's *Tentamen de vi soni et musices in corpore humano* (1758). For Roger, "the influence that music exerts over us depends in part on

---

22. The emergence of what I call the attunement *Affektenlehre* bears some resemblance to transformations related in other historical accounts of this period. Kevin Barry, for instance, relates the emergence of the "empty sign" in eighteenth-century aesthetic thought. Examining the cross-pollination between poetic theory and musical aesthetics, Barry identifies "a recurrent figure of language as a kind of music that is heard as if it were the more intense insofar as it is the more empty." Barry, *Language, Music, and the Sign: A Study in Aesthetics, Poetics, and Poetic Practice from Collins to Coleridge* (Cambridge: Cambridge University Press, 1987), 17. While it is clear that the new attunement *Affektenlehre* theories are related to the tradition Barry describes, I would emphasize that some of these theorists eschew any discussion of signification altogether, preferring instead to describe how music has the material ability to bypass its typical workings. For Erik Wallrup, an older sense of *Affekt*, grounded in the doctrine of imitation or mimesis (what I have called the mimetic *Affektenlehre*), gives way to a discourse of *Stimmung*, or attunement; though for Wallrup, affect is nonequivalent to *Stimmung*, since the former entails an object and the latter has no object proper to it. Wallrup, *Being Musically Attuned*, esp. 156–161.

23. "Die Seele ist, wie ein besaitetes Instrument, welches mitklingt, wenn man einen Ton angiebt, den eine von dessen Saiten hat, obgleich die Saite selbst nicht berühret worden." Christian Gottfried Krause, *Von der musikalischen Poesie* (Berlin: Johann Friedrich Voß, 1752), 79.

24. Krause, *Von der musikalischen Poesie*, 80.

25. "Bey den Stufen der verschiedenen Arten der Liebe eräugnen sich verschiedene Wallungen im Geblüte." Krause, *Von der musikalischen Poesie*, 90.

26. "Der natürlichen Spannung ihrer Adern im Ohr." Krause, *Von der musikalischen Poesie*, 79.

the greater or lesser facility with which the viscera, the bones, the nerves, and the humors of the human body resonate and tremble."[27] Krause and Roger share with Fréron the belief that certain parts of the human body are tuned and ready to sound in sympathy with the vibrations of music. But just what these parts were and how they interfaced with the rest of the human animal's internal workings was as yet inconsistent.[28]

These widely varying physiological explanations of the human instrument coexisted with the mature stages of the mimetic *Affektenlehre* tradition, in which theorists continued to postulate direct, mimetic links between the formal materials of musical sound and the affective responses of listeners. By the latter decades of the eighteenth century, some theorists had ventured a synthesis: a mimetic *Affektenlehre* that borrowed from the imagery of the human instrument in order to explain the transmission of affect from music to auditor. For Daniel Webb, whose *Observations on the Correspondence between Poetry and Music* (1769) drew on theories of the nerves as well as the animal spirits, the relationship was entirely a question of corresponding movements. "When, therefore, musical sounds produce in us the same sensations which accompany the impressions of any one particular passion, then the music is said to be in unison with that passion," he ventured.[29] Johann Georg Sulzer and his collaborators J. A. P. Schultz and Johann Philipp Kirnberger adopted a similar view, again intermixing the action of the nerves with that of the circulatory

27. "Car l'influence que la musique exerce sur nous dépend en partie de la facilité plus ou moins grande qu'ont les viscères, les os, les nerfs et les humeurs du corps humain à résonner et à frémir." Joseph-Louis Roger, *Traité des effets de la musique sur le corps humain* (1758), trans. Étienne Sainte-Marie (Paris: Brunot; Lyon: Reymann et Compe and J. Roger, 1803), 29.

28. For a detailed study of the French sources relating to this messy period in the history of the *Affektenlehre*, see Downing A. Thomas, "Heart Strings," in *Aesthetics of Opera in the Ancien Régime, 1647–1785* (Cambridge: Cambridge University Press, 2002), 179–200. In yet another, divergent adaptation of the vibrating-string metaphor, Gotthold Ephraim Lessing proposed that actors evoked parallel but differing affects in their audiences by means of sympathetic resonance. In this fashion, if the string of the actor reverberates with sorrow, the string of the audience member might ring with pity. See Lessing to Moses Mendelssohn, Leipzig, February 2, 1757, in Lessing, *Werke und Breife*, vol. 3, *Werke, 1754–1757*, ed. Conrad Wiedemann (Frankfurt am Main: Deutscher Klassiker Verlag, 2003), 713–714. On actors and the figure of sympathetic resonance, see also Joseph Roach, *The Player's Passion: Studies in the Science of Acting* (Ann Arbor: University of Michigan Press, 1993).

29. Daniel Webb, *Observations on the Correspondence between Poetry and Music* (London: J. Dodsley, 1769), 7–8. A later account in this same hybrid format, drawing on Webb, can be found in Carl Ludwig Junker, "Tonkunst," in *Betrachtungen über Mahlerey, Ton- und Bildhauerkunst* (Basel: Karl August Serini, 1778), 63–69, esp. 64–65. On Junker's theories, see Bellamy Hosler, *Changing Aesthetic Views of Instrumental Music in 18th-Century Germany* (Ann Arbor, MI: UMI Research Press, 1981), 168–177.

system. For these theorists, "the vivacity of the passions is derived from the play of the nerves and the quick coursing of the blood . . . since [music] is bound up with the movement of air, which impacts the highly excitable nerves of hearing, so it also affects the body."[30] In order to invoke the affect of joy, then, the composer simply writes in "full tones with a speed that is not rushed, and moderate shades of louder and softer, lower and higher pitch," whereas "sadness expresses itself in slower terms."[31] The only major separation between these theorists and their predecessors in the mimetic *Affektenlehre* tradition is their postulation of music's direct transference to the human body by means of sympathetic vibration.

In drawing a grand set of homologies between the motions of musical sound vibrations, the motions of the human instrument, and the motions of the affects, theorists in the late eighteenth century had effectively eliminated a step in the traditional mimetic theory of representation. As an art form, music in this new hybrid *Affektenlehre* was not said to create representations; it was instead working in a direct and immediate way on our capacity to experience affect. Some theorists attempted to rescue the older mimetic theory of art, describing this direct transference as a sort of imitation in its own right. This compromise view is most clearly set out in Johann Jakob Engel's *Ueber die musikalische Malerey* (1780), a lengthy tract on musical representation. Engel's understanding of music's affective force closely follows the theories of attunement set out by his contemporaries: "All passionate representations of the soul are inseparably linked with a corresponding movement of the nervous system. . . . The influence is reciprocal; the same path that leads from the soul to the body leads back from the body to the soul. Through nothing else but sound can the shock [of the nervous system] be so steady, so powerful, and so diversely manifested."[32] In this passage, Engel has also availed him-

---

30. "Mas weiß, daß die Lebhaftigkeit der Empfindungen von dem Spiehl der Nerven, und dem schnellen Laufe des Geblüthes herkommet: daß die Musik würklich auf beyde würke, kann gar nicht geläugnet werden. Da sie mit einer Bewegung der Luft verbunden ist, welche die höchst reizbaren Nerven des Gehörs angreift, so würket sie auch auf der Körper." Johann Georg Sulzer and Johann Peter Schulz, "Musik," in *Allgemeine Theorie der schönen Künste*, by Sulzer, 2 vols. (Leipzig: M. G. Weidmanns Erben und Reich, 1771–1774), 2:789.

31. "Die Freude spricht in vollen Tönen mit einer nicht übertriebenen Geschwindigkeit, und mäßigen Schattirungen des starken und schwächern, des höhern und tiefen in den Tönen. Die Traurigkeit äußert sich in langsamen Reden." Johann Georg Sulzer and Johann Philipp Kirnberger, "Ausdruk in der Musik," in Sulzer, *Allgemeine Theorie*, 1:110.

32. "Alle leidenschaftlichen Vorstellungen der Seele sind mit gewissen entsprechenden Bewegungen im Nervensystem unzertrennlich verbunden. . . . Die Einwürkung ist gegenseitig;

self of vibration's mediating capacity in order to link the body and the soul, forging a provisionary cryptodualism in the midst of his theory of musical affect. But beyond this, Engel makes a plea for the continued relevance of musical mimesis. In addition to acknowledging the existence of the direct painting of audible objects in music, Engel goes on to insist, "The composer still paints . . . when he imitates neither a part nor a feature of the object itself, but rather the impression that this object tends to make on the soul. Through this means, musical imitation obtains its greatest extent."[33] For Engel, as for some late eighteenth-century theorists, attunement was simply another form of mimesis: it was an imitation of an affective response, designed to duplicate itself in the listener.

Nevertheless, as theorists began to train their focus on the body, its interior parts, and its autonomic processes, the theory of musical affect was shifting away from descriptions of musical objects and their role in evoking affective responses. For Antonio Planelli, who was both a scientist and a writer on opera, the experience of musical affect was tightly related with the actions of the "diathetic nerves [*Nervi Diatetici*]."[34] These, he proposed, are the category of nerves that control emotion. They are located in the chest, the stomach, and—most importantly—the various parts of the face. For Planelli, the involuntary motions of these body parts are bound up with the corporeal experience of affect. "Each emotion has its own particular physiology," he explained.[35] The action of weeping, linked to the affect of sadness, corresponds to a particular action of the diathetic nerves; the same can be said of laughter or of a quavering and halting voice. Music holds a special relationship to these nerves mediated through sympathetic resonance.

> It seems beyond obvious that our nerves, like so many strings of an instrument, have a determined pitch. And in acoustics it is an unquestioned principle that a sound will necessarily set in motion whatever

---

eben der Weg, der aus der Seele in den Körper führt, führt zurük aus dem Körper in die Seele. Durch nichts aber werden diese Erschütterungen so sicher, so mächtig, so mannigfaltig bewirkt, als durch Töne." Johann Jakob Engel, *Ueber die musikalische Malerey* (Berlin: Christian Friedrich Voß und Sohn, 1780), 18–19.

33. "Der Tonsetzer malt noch . . . indem er weder einen Theil, noch eine Eigenschaft des Gegenstandes selbst, sondern den Eindruk nachahmt, den dieser Gegenstand auf die Seele zu machen pflegt. Durch dieses Mittel erhält die musikalische Nachahmung ihren weitesten Umfang." Engel, *Ueber die musikalische Malerey*, 12.

34. Antonio Planelli, *Dell' opera in musica* (Naples: Donato Campo, 1772), 106.

35. "Ogni passione à la sua fisonomia particolare." Planelli, *Dell' opera in musica*, 108.

bodies are found in the vibrational zone that it produces in the air, if these bodies possess a determined pitch and it is precisely the unison or another consonant sound. . . .

Because of the correspondence between the movement of [the nerves] and the passions of the soul, their oscillations will arouse that passion that corresponds to the given motion produced in them.[36]

Working through the sonorous attunement of autonomic, corporeal processes, musical affect was for Planelli more a science of the human body than it was a science of musical composition or an aesthetic practice. Vocality and human expression — while once evocative of musical affect under the aegis of mimesis, as in Rousseau's writings — are for Planelli understood as components of affective response. They have migrated entirely from the side of the affecting object to the affected subject. Planelli is, therefore, a theorist firmly in the attunement *Affektenlehre* tradition, a theorist for whom musical affect is delivered through an immediate experience of sound vibration that stirs the workings of the human instrument.

Straightforward rejections of the mimetic aesthetic framework for music had been a part of critical discourse since the *querelle des bouffons*, but they increased in frequency and fervor as the century drew on. While the English critic James Beattie acknowledged some "relation at least, or analogy, if not similitude, between certain musical sounds, and mental affections," he nevertheless hesitated to include music alongside the other mimetic art forms.[37] "In fact, I apprehend, that critics have erred a little in their determinations upon this subject," he wrote, "from an opinion, that Music, Painting, and Poetry are all imitative arts. I hope at least I may say, without offence, that while this was my opinion, I was always conscious of some unaccountable confusion of thought, whenever I attempted to explain it in the way of detail to others."[38] For Beattie, as for many other eighteenth-century thinkers, the

36. "Sembra in oltre manifesto, che il nostri nervi, come altrettante corde d'uno stromento, abbiano un tuono determinato. É nell'Acustica un indubitato principio, che un suono qualunque metta necessariamente in moto tutti que'corpi, che si trovano dentro la sfera dell'ondeggiamento, ch'egli forma nell'aere, se questi corpi abbiano un determinato tuono, e propriamente l'unisono, o altro consonante a quel suono. . . . E per quella corrispondenza, che passa tra il movimento di questi e le passioni dell'animo, il loro *oscillamento* ne desterà quella passione, che corrisponde a quel dato moto prodotto in essi." Planelli, *Dell' opera in musica*, 109–110.

37. James Beattie, "An Essay on Poetry and Music, as They Affect the Mind: Written in the Year 1762," in *Essays* (Edinburgh: William Creech; London: E. & C. Dilly, 1776), 143.

38. Beattie, "Essay on Poetry and Music," 128.

theory of mimesis was found lacking in the context of an art as complex and abstract as music.

The extreme French critic Pascal Boyer took these complaints a step further, denying that music had even the capability to imitate or mimetically reproduce the passions. "A composer who pretends to copy the passionate accents of nature is as ridiculous as someone who wants to form all words imaginable with three letters of the alphabet."[39] For Boyer, it seemed absolutely absurd that music could ever have the power to raise the passions in audiences unless it could be said to capture the sounds of those passions mimetically. This, in Boyer's view, it simply did not do. "Does anyone who is affected search for accompanists?" Boyer asked. "Or indeed does he have an orchestra in his chest? Is his voice double, triple, or quadruple? Does one create chords when one speaks?"[40] Boyer disqualified music on the basis of its inability to imitate either impassioned cries or the passions connected to them. Music, in his thinking, did not have the resources to perform either task.

Nevertheless, theorists understood that they had to account for the aesthetic force of music in some fashion. Music — now taken seriously by many writers of aesthetic theory — had created something of an explanatory crisis. By the century's end, some were building on Fréron's early proposal that the mechanism of attunement could both account for music's power and also relieve from criticism the burden of explaining music within the ill-fitting rubric of mimesis. For Michel Paul Guy de Chabanon, the two tasks were intimately related. His criticisms of the mimetic framework were familiar. "What more extraordinary things need one advance about music, now that it has been forgotten that its principal component is melody? All the power of the art, it was said, consisted in imitating the inarticulate cry of the passions. But how can a song be made from a cry?"[41] Chabanon, like Boyer, invoked

39. "Un compositeur qui pretend copier les accens passionnés de la nature, est donc aussi ridicule que quelqu'un qui voudroit former tous les mots imaginables avec trois lettres de l'Alphabet." Pascal Boyer, *L'Expression musicale, mise au rang des chimères* (1779; repr., Geneva: Minkoff, 1973), 8.

40. "D'ailleurs, quiconque est affecté cherche-t-il des Accompagnateurs? Ou bien a-t-il une Orchestre dans sa poitrine? La voix est-elle double, triple, quadruple? Fait-on des accords lorsqu'on parle?" Boyer, *L'Expression musicale*, 16–17.

41. "Que n'a-t-on point avancé d'extraordinaire sur la Musique, du moment qu'on a perdu de vue que son principe constitutif est la mélodie? Toute la puissance de cet Art, a-t-on dit, consiste à imiter le cri inarticulé des passions. Mais d'un cri, comment fait-on un chant?" Michel Paul Guy de Chabanon, *Observations sur la musique et principalement sur la metaphysique de l'art* (Paris: Pissot, 1779), 64.

Rousseau's basic framework—in which melody mimetically reproduced the natural cries of the passions—for harsh criticism. Most significantly, Chabanon did not hear anything like what Rousseau proposed was at work in the music of his contemporaries. "This brings us to a natural observation. If music were essentially an art of imitation, the melody, the accompaniment, everything should unanimously play a part in imitating. However, we see that in the most moving arias, in the most touching adagios, the accompaniment removes itself from imitation and plays melodiously around the subject. In pieces where the accompaniment endeavors to paint effects, the top part is liberated of this imitative function and is brought back to simply singing."[42] The music of Chabanon's day was not univocal—it was textured, packed with different affective shadings and topical references, and built out of multiple conventions all stacked together. The object of his inspection simply did not support the received theory meant to explain it. Music, it seemed to Chabanon, must function in some nonmimetic fashion, attuning its listeners to an affective state through its immediate, nonrepresentational access to the body's autonomic systems. "Man, believe me," he wrote, "is nothing other than an instrument; his fibers respond to the lyrical instruments that strike and interrogate them."[43]

In Chabanon's thinking, the attunement *Affektenlehre* had displaced its older mimetic predecessor and the general theory of mimesis along with it.[44] Responding to a crisis of representation generated by music, theorists offered a distinctively sonic paradigm for affect that was premised not on the music's

42. "Ceci nous conduit à une observation naturelle. Si la Musique étoit essentiellemet un Art d'imitation, le chant, les accompagnemens, tout devroit unanimement concourir à imiter. Cependant nous voyons dans les Airs les plus pathétiques, dans les *adagio* les plus touchans, l'accompagnement s'écarter de l'imitation & se jouer mélodieusement autour du sujet: dans les morceaux où l'accompagnement s'efforce de peindre des effets, la partie supérieure s'affranchit de cette fonction imitatrice, & se réduit simplement à chanter." Chabanon, *Observations sur la musique*, 213.

43. "L'homme, croyez-moi, n'est qu'un instrument; ses fibres répondent aux fils des instrumens lyriques qui les attaquent & les interrogent." Chabanon, *Observations sur la musique*, 73.

44. Again, my view differs from those of other recent commentators on this issue, who see a perpetuation of the mimetic framework even in the views of those who explicitly reject it. Downing A. Thomas, for instance, writes, "Indeed, if mimesis is understood as a form of compulsive modeling or as a 'sympathetic resonance' that occurred when our minds and bodies come into contact with musical sound, then the distinction between music as physical 'science' and music as a language with moral effects becomes less pronounced." Thomas, *Aesthetics of Opera*, 187. Although I understand Thomas's historiographical impulse, I am drawn to underline the conceptual differences that the period thinkers themselves articulated. On this topic, see also the discussion of mimesis in chapter 2 of this book.

content but rather on its physical medium of sound vibration. In this new attunement *Affektenlehre* — the operation of which could be specified through references to the human body and its interior — the challenge of explaining musical affect with detailed references to musical objects had receded. With a belief in a human instrument made out of the autonomic nervous system, all that musical affect required was the physical certainty of sympathetic resonance.

The final stages of the attunement *Affektenlehre* tradition, at the turn of the nineteenth century, were its most mannered phase. The image of the human instrument tuned to musical sound came to represent a numinous kind of aesthetic attention. In a 1792 letter he wrote to his friend Ludwig Tieck, the young Wilhelm Heinrich Wackenroder explained two different types of listening. In the first type, Wackenroder attentively observes each musical gesture, endeavoring to completely eliminate exterior thoughts, "guzzling in the tones."[45] This first type of listening he can only sustain for a single hour at a time. In the second type, Wackenroder derives pleasure not directly from the music or its references but rather from the altered state it affords. Listening this way, he writes, "I no longer hear the emotion that prevails in the piece, but rather my thoughts and fantasies are carried off, so to speak, on the waves of melody and lose themselves in a distant recess. It is peculiar: when I am set into this attunement [*Stimmung*], I can best reflect aesthetically on music as I hear it."[46] For Wackenroder, this state of musical attunement exceeds even the specific emotional content of the music. Although the condition is afforded by music's sonorous unfolding, it is nevertheless completely untethered from the particularity of the musical object and located instead within the singular, subjective experience of the listener.

Wackenroder's numinous, detached attunement bears resemblance to the elevated state that Hoffmann later described in his 1810 review of Beethoven's Fifth Symphony. These critics share a view of musical attunement brought about through specific music but nevertheless exceeding both discursive codification and any relation to that music's moment-to-moment specificity. For Hoffmann, this could result — as in his review of the Fifth Symphony — in

---

45. "Dieses geizige Einschlürfen der Töne." Wilhelm Heinrich Wackenroder to Ludwig Tieck, May 5, 1972, in Wackenroder, *Werke und Briefe*, ed. Gerda Heinrich (Munich: Carl Hanser, 1984), 368.

46. "Dann höre ich nicht mehr die Empfindung, die in dem Stücke herrscht, sondern meine Gedanken und Phantasien werden gleichsam auf dem Wellen des Gesanges entführt, und verlieren sich oft in entfernte Schlupfwinkel. Es ist sonderbar, daß ich, in diese Stimmung versetzt, auch am besten über Musik als Ästhetiker nachdenken kann, wenn ich Musik höre." Wackenroder to Tieck, 368.

a single state of infinite *Sehnsucht*. In his other forms of criticism, however, Hoffmann describes a higher-order sort of attunement that gives way, by contrast, to bliss. The protagonist of "The Enemy of Music" (a story first published in the *Allgemeine musikalische Zeitung* and later included in *Kreisleriana*) is a misunderstood novice whose appreciation for music is so deep that his friends and family mistake it for disdain. He describes a typical confusion:

> I only know that such a voice and such singing as that of my aunt so intensely penetrates my core and stirs feelings for which I have no words. It seems to me as though it were bliss, which raises itself above the earthly world and therefore is unable to find expression in earthly terms. But for that very reason it is quite impossible, when I hear such a singer, to break into loud admiration as the others do; I remain still and look into my inner core, where all of the outwardly faded tones still vibrate. And so I am called cold, without emotion, and an enemy of music.[47]

Hoffmann's protagonist, like Wackenroder, experiences something removed from earthly reality and located deep in his own interior experience, brought about through the physical medium of sound vibration. For Hoffmann, the condition engendered through this attunement is explicitly nondiscursive, "unutterable," and "not capable of expression in earthly terms," even while words like *Sehnsucht* and "bliss" stand in as approximations.[48] Among the

---

47. "Ich weiss wol, dass eine solche Stimme, ein solcher Gesang, wie der meiner Tante, so recht in mein Innerstes dringt, und sich da Gefühle regen, für die ich gar keine Worte habe: es ist mir, als sey das eben die Seligkeit, welche sich über das Irdische erhebt, und daher auch im Irdischen keinen Ausdruck zu finden vermag: aber eben deshalb ist es mir ganz unmöglich, höre ich eine solche Sängerin, in die laute Bewunderung auszubrechen, wie die Andern; ich bleibe still und schaue in mein Inneres, weil da noch alle die aussen verklungenen Töne widerstrahlen: und da werde ich kalt, empfindungslos, ein Musikfeind gescholten." E. T. A. Hoffmann, "Der Musikfeind," *Allgemeine musikalische Zeitung* (Leipzig), July 1, 1814, cols. 370–371.

48. In my emphasis on the aspects of immediacy and subject orientation in Wackenroder and Hoffmann, I mean to offer an alternative to the scholarship that has placed greater weight on the role of idealism and the sublime in the works of these authors. See, respectively, Mark Evan Bonds, *Music as Thought: Listening to the Symphony in the Age of Beethoven* (Princeton, NJ: Princeton University Press, 2006); and Kiene Brillenburg Wurth, "*Sehnsucht*, Music, and the Sublime," in *Musically Sublime: Indeterminacy, Infinity, Irresolvability* (New York: Fordham University Press, 2009), 47–71. In drawing attention to the use of attunement by these German romantics, I also mean to place them within the longer legacy of attunement affect theorists; this might be an alternative precursor for the productive metaphors of depth and interiority that are the subject of Holly Watkins's *Metaphors of Depth in German Musical Thought: E. T. A. Hoffmann to Arnold Schoenberg* (Cambridge: Cambridge University Press, 2011).

many intellectual commitments these writers held, one was a theory of attunement with a basis in the physical reality of sound vibration that engendered a single, subjective, nondiscursive transformation in the listener.

The evolution of the *Affektenlehre* from its earlier mimetic instantiations to the later attunement tradition is instructive. As it slowly changed from a theory of mimetic representation to a theory of sensation and autonomic process, the different manifestations of the *Affektenlehre* can be seen to have openly rehearsed their own internal contradictions. Theorists who penned mimetic *Affektenlehre* treatises posited homologies between the motions and forms of musical objects and the motions and forms of the affects in subjects. But these theorists' taxonomic efforts never cohered. Stumbling onto the inconsistencies and impossibilities of such a project, some melancholically lamented the loss of a once powerful but now forgotten *Affektenlehre* of the past, while others searched for alternative methods of explanation in the present. Theorists began to concentrate on the mediation between musical object and human subject, focusing their attention on the known properties of sound vibration and its capacity to create sympathetic resonances. They theorized the human body as an instrument, tuned and ready to ring in immediate response to music. These theorists ventured a new attunement *Affektenlehre*, which bypassed the traditional structure of signification and worked automatically on the human interior. And as this tradition developed and changed, the interior of that human subject became the penetrating focus of their theories. The original site of inquiry—the musical object—had been reduced to its vibrational transmission, and it was the human subject and its genres of affected response that became the primary site of the investigation. In the final stages of the *Affektenlehre* at the turn of the century, this affected subject was said to be moved to a singular, detached, and elevated state that was nearly indescribable in words. Corporeal, nondiscursive, immediate, and subject centered, affect once again avoided capture by the pen of the theorist, sharing properties and paradoxes with the ineffable.[49] This constant deferral is integral to many theories of affect, and it is generative of the patterns in their evolution.

The process traced in the genealogy that links the mimetic *Affektenlehre* to the attunement *Affektenlehre* is synecdochically linked to a much larger eighteenth-century transformation. This was, in Foucault's terms, a shift from representation to the modern human sciences, or—in Jacques Rancière's formulation, focusing specifically on the domain of art—from mimesis to aes-

49. See Gallope, *Deep Refrains*, esp. 10–32.

thesis.[50] Music and music theory played central roles in this dramatic reorgani-
zation. The debates concerning the ability of and method by which music had
the power to move its audiences forced critics to develop new, nonmimetic,
corporeal explanations of affect. But precisely because of the constantly shifting claims made concerning music and its supposed powers, scholars have not
always recognized how this art form and its theorists catalyzed the aesthetic
upheaval that took place during the eighteenth century.

Many accounts of this period and its transformations have emphasized the
burgeoning paradigm of expression, and rightly so.[51] This era saw the birth
of a new understanding of the artwork as the overflowing of an individual
artist's feelings. But this transformation can also be understood, more generally, as a shifting of focus to the interiority of subjects. Within the domain of
affect theory, this subject was often the reception point of affective transmission, understood now to take place between two subjects (the artist and the
beholder or auditor, for example). The repercussions of this transformation
were lasting in criticism, as the discourse on affect developed along disparate
vectors through the nineteenth century. In the physiological vein, scholars of
affect continued — like Planelli — to focus on the human subject's autonomic
processes and corporeal responses, focusing especially on the face; whereas
the concept of *Stimmung* eventually became, for Martin Heidegger, a kind of
attuned mood that has no object proper to it.[52] The attunement *Affektenlehre*
tradition itself eventually faded in prominence alongside musical romanticism. But these discourses are important precursors to contemporary affect

50. For Michel Foucault's classic accounts of this shift, see Foucault, *The Order of Things*
(1966), English trans. (1970; repr., New York: Routledge, 2002). Jacques Rancière traces the same
transformation in several texts, most notably in *Mute Speech: Literature, Critical Theory, and
Politics* (New York: Columbia University Press, 2011); and *Aisthesis: Scenes from the Aesthetic
Regime of Art* (New York: Verso, 2013).

51. See, for instance, M. H. Abrams, *The Mirror and the Lamp: Romantic Theory and the Critical Tradition* (Oxford: Oxford University Press, 1953); and also the narrative traced in Rancière's
Mute Speech. John Neubauer, in *The Emancipation of Music from Language: Departure from
Mimesis in Eighteenth-Century Aesthetics* (New Haven, CT: Yale University Press, 1986), proposes that we understand this shift from imitation to expression as a transformation interior to
the theory of mimesis. Further complicating this tricky matter of scholarly perspective is the fact
that eighteenth-century critics also quarreled about the meanings of imitation and expression
(and the applicability of these concepts to music). On this topic, see especially Barry, *Language,
Music, and the Sign*, 31–35.

52. See, for instance, Charles Bell, *Essays on the Anatomy and Philosophy of Expression*, 2nd
ed. (London: John Murray, 1824); and Charles Darwin, *The Expression of the Emotions in Man
and Animals* (New York: D. Appleton, 1886); for *Stimmung* in Martin Heidegger, see *Being and
Time*, trans. Joan Stambaugh, revised and with a foreword by Dennis J. Schmidt (Albany: SUNY
Press, 2010), 130–136; and concerning Heidegger see Wellbery, "Stimmung," 724–726.

theory, which tends to focus its attention on the immediate, corporeal, non-discursive, or precognitive responses of an affected individual.

Sense-Certainty: A Critique

Within the period that these historical theories flourished, there already existed a critical discourse that challenged the types of claims they made. Nowhere is this more clearly and elegantly set out than in the opening of G. W. F. Hegel's *Phenomenology of Spirit* (1807). In the first chapter of the section on consciousness — following the much-discussed preface to the *Phenomenology* — Hegel critically describes a form of sensation in which the subject apprehends the object directly, fully, and immediately. "Our approach to the object," Hegel writes, "must also be *immediate* or *receptive*; we must alter nothing in the object as it presents itself. In *ap*prehending it, we must refrain from trying to *com*prehend it."[53] *Affektenlehre* theorists proposed something of a troped version of this form of sensation, which Hegel called "sense-certainty."[54] In their claim that musical objects produced affective responses in listeners through sympathetic resonance, these theorists postulated for musical affect a kind of immediacy that bypassed concepts. For the attunement *Affektenlehre* theorists, to feel the vibration of sound was to have the affective response. The subject "has not as yet omitted anything from the object, but has the object before it in its perfect entirety."[55] As Hegel describes it, this is meant to be the richest kind of sense experience.

Sense-certainty is not a simplistic theory of sensation but rather a highly constructed idea; it is an elaborate attempt to escape from the complexities and problems of conceptual knowing.[56] As Robert Pippin explains of the critique of sense-certainty launched in the *Phenomenology of Spirit*, "Hegel's stroke is so broad here that commentators have identified many different historical objects of attack here (or potential objects), ranging from . . . Protagorean relativism, to Jacobi and the romantics on intuition, to sense-data phenomenalism (most clearly of a Humean variety)."[57] Pippin goes on to note

53. G. W. F. Hegel, *Phenomenology of Spirit*, trans. A. V. Miller (Oxford: Oxford University Press, 1977), § 90, p. 58.

54. I do not mean to suggest that Hegel was referring explicitly to the theorists of the *Affektenlehre* in his text but rather to the general outlook that their theories adopt. Nor am I the first to notice the surprising relevance of this passage in Hegel for theorizing the relationship between music and philosophy: see Gallope's account of its reception in *Deep Refrains*, 18–20.

55. Hegel, *Phenomenology of Spirit*, § 91, p. 58.

56. Hegel, *Phenomenology of Spirit*, § 109, pp. 64–65.

57. Robert Pippin, *Hegel's Idealism: The Satisfactions of Self-Consciousness* (Cambridge: Cambridge University Press, 1989), 118. Some musicologists have been keen to draw out the

that Hegel avoids identifying any particular historical author or tradition and instead explains the position abstractly. The wager of sense-certainty runs something like this: if we avoid any abstract thoughts and focus on our immediate, direct relation to the object before us — say, if we are simply attuned to this object through an autonomic process — we must know it in a way that will be richer and truer than in any way that involves conceptual generality. In the chapter on sense-certainty, Hegel is not mounting a critique of sensation but rather interrogating the idea that through it we have some certainty of the objects of our perception. He is demonstrating that we cannot rely on a notion of sense experience that construes subjects as simply passive recipients of stimuli from the outside world.[58]

Hegel's critique of sense-certainty unfolds in two basic steps. In the first, he describes the subject's attempt to fix an object as an object of perception. We can use an example of musical listening to better understand Hegel's argument: we hear music played, we sense it, some autonomic processes take place, perhaps we are attuned to it, and the musical object engenders an affect within us. What occurs here is a splitting in two. The subject (the listener) and the object (the music) are rendered distinct from each other. At this point, we realize that neither the subject nor the object is immediate to sensation but that they mediate each other, or make each other possible.[59] If we are willing to accept this initial mutual mediation, we then must ask the question of how we can be certain that we have the object before us. We can respond by simply saying that we hear this music right here and right now. We might even, in the style of an *Affektenlehre* theorist, indicate that the vibrations of this music have moved us to joy. But even upon indicating that this music is "here" and "now," we realize that we have made reference to universal concepts in order to account for our immediate experience of the music. Especially in the case of joy, we have invoked a complex concept. Suddenly, the particularity of the musi-

---

affinities between Hegel and his romantic predecessors, such as Hoffmann and Wackenroder; see in particular Bonds, *Music as Thought*. But I would underscore the antagonism between Hegel's critique of sense-certainty and the romantic conception of *Stimmung* registered in Gumbrecht, *Atmosphere, Mood*, Stimmung, 12–13. In this connection, it is also worth noting that recent commentators have recognized Hegel as a staunch critic of romanticism, despite his close ties to figures within that tradition. See especially Jeffrey Reid, *The Anti-Romantic: Hegel against Ironic Romanticism* (New York: Bloomsbury, 2014). For a discussion of Hegel's complex understanding of *Stimmung* — and to understand its distance from the attunement *Affektenlehre* — see Wallrup, *Being Musically Attuned*, 45–48.

58. See Quentin Lauer, *A Reading of Hegel's "Phenomenology of Spirit"* (1976; repr., New York: Fordham University Press, 1998), 45.

59. Lauer, *Reading*, 48.

cal object has taken on the form of universals: "here," "now," even "joy." What was once particular is now mediated through universals. As Hegel explains, once we want to say something about the immediacy of our sensation of the particular object, "then this is impossible, because the sensuous This that is meant cannot be reached by language, which belongs to consciousness, i.e. to that which is inherently universal. In the actual attempt to say it, it would therefore crumble away; those who started to describe it would not be able to complete the description, but would be compelled to leave it to others, who would themselves finally have to admit to speaking about something which *is not*."[60] The minute that we attempt to describe the affective immediacy of our listening experience, we end up relying on language, on universals, and we have to admit the impossibility of our task. Hegel's critique calls to mind the frustrations of early taxonomic *Affektenlehre* theorists like Rameau, who wrote that the project of a musical *Affektenlehre* "would demand more than the lifetime of a single individual," or Mattheson, who wrote, "that it is with the affects, especially, as it is with a bottomless sea: however much effort one might take to write something comprehensive about it, still only the least bit could be set down on the page, and infinitely more would remain unsaid."[61] This first move of sense-certainty initiates a powerful process of deferral — a process integral to affect theory.

Hegel considers a second step: What if we are certain of our sensation because we can be certain of the particularity of the subject — the *I* — that is sensing?[62] I am certain of my hearing of this musical object because I am certain of myself as a subject. As Hegel explains, "Its truth is in the object as *my* object, or in its being *mine* [*Meinen*]; it is, because *I* know it. Sense-certainty, then, though indeed expelled from the object, is not yet thereby overcome, but only driven back into the 'I.'"[63] But if certainty of the subject is all that can assure us of sense-certainty, we run into a problem similar to the first we encountered: all of the subject's experiences belong to the subject and are therefore identical in occurring for that individual. It is, therefore, the subject — the

---

60. Hegel, *Phenomenology of Spirit*, § 110, p. 66.

61. "C'est d'ailleurs une entreprise qui demanderoit peut-être plus que la vie d'un seul homme." Jean-Philippe Rameau, *Nouveau système de musique théorique* (Paris: Jean-Baptiste-Christophe Ballard, 1726), 43. "Anerwogen es mit den Affecten insonderheit eben die Bewandniß hat, als mit einem unergründlichen Meer, so daß, wie viel Mühe man sich auch nehmen mögte, etwas vollständiges hierüber auszufertigen, doch nur das wenigste zu Buche gebracht, unendlich viel aber ungesagt bleiben . . . anheimgestellet werden dürffte." Johann Mattheson, *Der vollkommene Capellmeister* (Hamburg: Christian Herold, 1739), 19.

62. Hegel, *Phenomenology of Spirit*, § 100, p. 61.

63. Hegel, *Phenomenology of Spirit*, § 100, p. 61.

listener, the "I" listening—that we must determine as an object, though we
have no mechanism to do so. The object of the sensing self would again need
to be determined through an appeal to a universal.[64] Furthermore, sensation
for this subject is "all the same simple and indifferent to whatever happens in
it."[65] Even if we could determine the subject listening, the specific qualities of
the musical object are inconsequential. This second stage in Hegel's critique
of sense-certainty is reminiscent of the latter stage of the attunement *Affektenlehre*, in which theorists began to focus their attention almost entirely on the
listening subject. Musical objects are here collapsed into the subjects that perceive them. For a writer like Wackenroder, being attuned to music might even
mean experiencing something beyond the specific attributes of the musical
object. "I no longer hear the emotion that prevails in the piece," he writes.[66]
Once again, the elusive immediacy of the musical object as it occurs for the
listener is lost in an appeal to universality.

Concluding, Hegel writes, "It is clear that the dialectic of sense-certainty is
nothing else but the simple history of its movement or of its experience, and
sense-certainty itself is nothing else but just this history."[67] To enter into the
game of sense-certainty is to create a movement of constant deferral—the
same constant deferral that is at work in the musical *Affektenlehre* tradition.
A brief synopsis of its history works something like this: First, attempting to
capture the immediacy of musical affect with the tools of language, theorists
assembled intricate taxonomies of the musical affects. But their reliance on
universal concepts in these taxonomies proved inadequate to the immediacy
of affect; they realized that they would never be able to fully explain it or account for every different subjective experience. Theorists responded with new,
corporeal tools and focused on listeners and human interiors. They collapsed
the musical objects of the *Affektenlehre* into its subjects. But these subjects
themselves require determination through universals and blanch out the specificity of the musical experiences that were originally the focus of inquiry.

Once again affect escapes capture, therefore strengthening the notion that
affect is nondiscursive, immediate, corporeal, and opposed to language, to
the sign, and to conceptual universals. It is this fundamental movement that
also creates the history of affect theory. The twenty-first century's newfound
interest in affect is our most recent witness.

64. Hegel, *Phenomenology of Spirit*, § 102, p. 62; see the commentary in Pippin, *Hegel's
Idealism*, 121.

65. Hegel, *Phenomenology of Spirit*, § 102, p. 62.

66. Wackenroder to Tieck, May 5, 1792, in Wackenroder, *Werke und Briefe*, 368.

67. Hegel, *Phenomenology of Spirit*, § 109, p. 64.

Coda: Affect after the *Affektenlehre*

The Sense-Certainty of Contemporary Affect Theory

The sounds of the last chords in Beethoven's Fifth Symphony have faded in the hall, and a moment of silence hangs suspended in the air before the applause begins. Something has been stirred within you for certain, but just what and just how is extremely difficult to say. Later you might call it joy, or you might remember it as wonder or even sheer pleasure. But no matter how you attempt to describe it, something of that moment's gripping, visceral immediacy is lost in the act of linguistic capture. It is something about the way the symphony moved your body into a new orientation toward the world — something that exceeds the stiff intellectual categories traditionally used to describe the experience of art.

This, at least, is the important wager of contemporary affect theory: we have been missing a vital component of the manner in which subjects encounter events of feeling, and we can recover this dimension if we attend to the autonomic processes that modify the body before rationality treads in with its categories. During the past two decades, a huge resurgence of interest in affect has begun to address this perceived lack in criticism. The appeal of a new method directed toward an understudied facet of human experience is defining of this scholarship. It styles itself as fresh and experimental. But the phenomenon at its core — affect — has a long and complex intellectual heritage.

Contemporary affect theory, despite its proclamations of novelty, spends a great deal of time rehearsing conceptual problems inherited from affect's long history. While there is much in this mode of inquiry that is exciting and radically different from the methodologies that were popular only a few decades previous, there is also a great deal that affect theory can learn from its vibrant, and often musical, past. With the eighteenth-century manifestations of the musical *Affektenlehre* in the background, I aim to take a closer look at the forms and dynamics of contemporary affect theory. Reading for affect after the *Affektenlehre*, I propose to return historical dimensions to the practice of contemporary affect theory, addressing critiques both old and new.

When examined in the company of its antecedents, contemporary affect theory has a familiar ring to it. Recent theorists of affect, like the authors writing in the tradition of the attunement *Affektenlehre*, are keen to describe the material workings of a resonant, often corporeal conduit of transmission. Take the work of Alexander Cho, who theorizes affect in social media. Cho responds to Brian Massumi and others in describing affect as a "force or intensity, . . . an attunement between entities."[1] But he develops and elaborates this somewhat standard explanation, synthesizing it with Gilles Deleuze and Félix Guattari's notion of the refrain so as to account for the digital media propagation and dispersal of affects, ideas, and images. Cho offers "reverb" as a new, distinctive theoretical contribution: "a quality and a process, a way to understand the direction and intensity of the flows of affect."[2] Here, once again, a property of musical sound provides for affect theory a concrete method of delivery. Affect arrives from an unspecified outside, attuning the subject through a resonant, vibrational force. In a certain way, then, Cho has recovered—with contemporary amplification—a trope common in eighteenth-century music theory.

Cho's concept of reverb extends the atmospheric, musicalized poetics that a group of recent theorists have used to explain the subject's reception of affect. In this tradition, authors consistently describe the affects as arbitrarily floating into and subsequently attaching themselves to subjects. This is true for Eve Sedgwick, for whom shame "is not a discrete intrapsychic structure, but a kind of free radical that . . . attaches to and permanently intensifies or alters the meaning of—of almost anything."[3] The figure of the free radical is taken up in the work of Ben Anderson and is closely related to the often repeated claim that "affect is what sticks," in the words of Sara Ahmed.[4] The

---

1. Alexander Cho, "Queer Reverb: Tumblr, Affect, Time," in *Networked Affect*, ed. Susanna Paasonen, Ken Hillis, and Michael Petit (Cambridge, MA: MIT Press, 2015), 44.

2. Cho, "Queer Reverb," 53.

3. Eve Kosofsky Sedgwick, *Touching Feeling: Affect, Pedagogy, Performativity* (Durham, NC: Duke University Press, 2003), 62.

4. See Ben Anderson, *Encountering Affect: Capacities, Apparatuses, Conditions* (Farnham, UK: Ashgate, 2014), 6–7; Sara Ahmed, *The Promise of Happiness* (Durham, NC: Duke University Press, 2010), 230n1.

notion that affects drift into subjective experience and adhere there is sometimes combined with the construal of affect as vibrational transmission, as
in Gregory Seigworth and Melissa Gregg's formulation of affects as "those
resonances that circulate about, between, and sometimes stick to bodies and
worlds."[5] These theories focus on the force and chance of affective arrival and
the subsequent embedding of affect in the subject.

This atmospheric poetics retains much from the concept of *Stimmung*,
central to the attunement *Affektenlehre*, in which the human is thought of
as a string instrument ready to resonate with those vibrations that find their
way to it. This is what draws Hans Ulrich Gumbrecht's renewed theory of
Stimmung—adapted from Heidegger and the German romantics before
him—so close to contemporary theories of affect. "This immediacy in the
experience of past presents occurs," Gumbrecht explains, "without it being
necessary to understand what the atmospheres and moods mean; we do not
have to know what motivations and circumstances occasioned them. For what
affects us in the act of reading involves the present of the past in substance—
not a sign of the past or its representation."[6] Gumbrecht's method of reading
for *Stimmung* (atmosphere or mood in his translation) is quite similar to reading for affect in its emphasis on immediacy and its professed contradistinction
from sign and representation. But most important is the network of linkages
that Gumbrecht posits between vibration, material reality, and felt experience: "Without knowing exactly why it was so or precisely what 'feelings' were
involved, we can be sure that dramatists, actors, and spectators in seventeenth-
century Paris were obsessed with the grave, pathos-laden verse forms they
called the 'alexandrine.' In a literal sense, it was part of the city's material reality
at that time. . . . The sounds and rhythms of the words strike our bodies as they
struck the spectators of that time. Therein lies an encounter—an immediacy,
and an objectivity of the past-made-present—which cannot be undermined
by any skepticism."[7] For Gumbrecht, the fact that we can hear today the same
sounding vibrations of the poetry that were heard in seventeenth-century Paris
affords us a material, immediate return to the felt conditions under which that
poetry was written. Although he recognizes that the alexandrine form bears
some relationship to its "grave, pathos-laden" significance, he is more interested in its physical dimensions. Its vibrating resonances reach present and

5. Gregory J. Seigworth and Melissa Gregg, "An Inventory of Shimmers," in *The Affect Theory Reader*, ed. Seigworth and Gregg (Durham, NC: Duke University Press, 2010), 1.
6. Hans Ulrich Gumbrecht, *Atmosphere, Mood, Stimmung: On a Hidden Potential of Litera-ture*, trans. H. Erik Butler (Stanford, CA: Stanford University Press, 2012), 14.
7. Gumbrecht, *Atmosphere, Mood, Stimmung*, 13.

historical subjects directly, in a material fashion that Gumbrecht explicitly contrasts with signification.

More recently, Erik Wallrup has continued and extended to music Gumbrecht's revival of *Stimmung*. In *Being Musically Attuned: The Act of Listening to Music*, Wallrup advocates for a return to attunement — inflected through Heidegger — as a way of accounting for the immediacy of musical experience. Crucially, though, Wallrup's notion of attunement is explicitly nonidentical to affect, since in his view affects entail objects while attunements are states without objects proper to them.[8]

This renaissance of the attunement *Affektenlehre*'s figures and operations even extends, in the work of some critics, to descriptions of the vibrating nerves in the resonant human interior. As William Connolly, writing in *A World of Becoming*, has it, "Affect, in its most elementary human mode, is an electrical-chemical charge that jolts or nudges you toward positive or negative action before it reaches the threshold of feeling or awareness. Its action invoking pressure arrives before it takes the shape of culturally infused feelings, emotions, or moods. The affective charge, consisting of vibrations running through different parts of the nervous system, provides the initial fast, subliminal response to something arriving from the outside."[9] This passage contains striking similarities with discourses in the attunement *Affektenlehre* tradition. For critics now as for critics then, sound vibration's materiality and its relation to the human body have powerful explanatory appeal; they describe the transmission of affect to the subject in an immediate manner that is said to bypass the traditional structure of representation.

For the most part — and with some notable exceptions explored shortly — contemporary affect theory has lost its objects. The contemporary affect theories just considered and those similar to them are alike in their avoidance of elaborating anything determined or specific about the origin sources of the affects. Vibration, resonance, and the attuned subject do the work of explaining the mediation of affect, but we learn very little from these theories about the objects that might engender affective responses in the first place. To examine an object under the aegis of its potential to create an affective response — say, a painting, a drama, or a piece of music — would mean to investigate the way it signifies. But despite the availability of phenomenological groundings for semiotic theory, this attention to signification — or, further, representation — is

8. Erik Wallrup, *Being Musically Attuned: The Act of Listening to Music* (Farnham, UK: Ashgate, 2015), esp. 156–160.

9. William E. Connolly, *A World of Becoming* (Durham, NC: Duke University Press, 2011), 50.

for contemporary affect theorists at odds with the goal of reading for what can "strike us directly and without mediation," in Gumbrecht's terms.[10]

Contemporary affect theory's oft-stated aversion to systems of signification and representation has attracted some critical commentary.[11] Ben Anderson, in his nuanced *Encountering Affect: Capacities, Apparatuses, Conditions*, confronts the question directly in the fourth chapter under the section heading "How Is Affect Non-Representational?"[12] Anderson contests the notion that affects are unmediated and further objects to the idea that significations and representations have no role in their engendering. Rather, he suggests, affects exceed these systems. Anderson goes on to identify two ways in which theorists have traditionally construed affect as nonrepresentational: affect is either said to occur prior to its subsequent, cognitive capture in representational structures (a view he associates with William Connolly and Nigel Thrift, among others), or affect is equated with an autonomous intensity (a view he associates with Massumi in particular). In his corrective, Anderson does not disagree entirely with the assessment of affect's nonrepresentational character. Rather, he proposes, "affects are transpersonal rather than pre-personal. . . . The former term — transpersonal — attunes us to how bodily capacities are mediated through forces that exceed the person. The key question is how does a body's 'force of existing' emerge through encounters, or more specifically the press and presence of the multiplicity that make up an encounter."[13] Here Anderson, like Teresa Brennan in *The Transmission of Affect*, encourages us to see affects as mediated and shared between subjects.[14] Rather than ordered through the structure of signification, affect can be understood as shaped through the intersubjective dynamics of an encounter between individuals.

Contrast this broadening of the subject's role in affect with Eugenie Brinkema's innovative and critical response to contemporary affect theory in *The Forms of the Affects*. Brinkema endeavors to restore an analytic of form to the study of affect, specifically in close readings of film. Her working assumption is that the filmic forms have some homology with the forms of the affects; this thesis is redolent of the mimetic *Affektenlehre* tradition, in which specific

10. Gumbrecht, *Atmosphere, Mood*, Stimmung, 71; On phenomenological groundings for semiotic theory, see T. L. Short, *Peirce's Theory of Signs* (Cambridge: Cambridge University Press, 2007); and Thomas Turino, "Peircean Thought as Core Theory for a Phenomenological Ethnomusicology," *Ethnomusicology* 58, no. 2 (2014): 185–221.

11. See, for instance, Gary Tomlinson, "Sign, Affect, and Musicking before the Human," *boundary* 2 43, no. 1 (2016): 143–172.

12. Anderson, *Encountering Affect*, 84–93.

13. Anderson, *Encountering Affect*, 87.

14. Theresa Brennan, *The Transmission of Affect* (Ithaca, NY: Cornell University Press, 2004).

musical structures were said to imitate the workings of the affects and thereby evoke them in listeners. For Brinkema, however, this formal investigation "should be regarded as a de-contribution to spectatorship studies, an attempt to dethrone the subject and the spectator—and attendant terms, such as 'cognition,' 'perception,' 'experience,' even 'sensation'—for affect theory."[15] Her corrective to the overwhelming attention to the subject thus throws all of the weight back onto the form of the affecting object, avoiding any consideration of the mode by which affect is transferred between one and the next.

Brinkema's powerful counterexample highlights contemporary affect theory's reliance on a highly constructed tactic of sense-certainty. In it, theorists typically place emphasis, trust, and authority in the particularity of immediate sense perception and in the singular subjective experience of affect. These are deemed the richest forms of experience and are contrasted with abstract conceptual frameworks that these theorists ignore, distrust, or even denigrate.

But subjects are not simply passive corporeal recipients of affects that waft toward and vibrate them. Nor are affects entirely located in objective forms. Viewed comparatively and historically, affect theories can be seen to have oscillated between these various positions over time, slowly shifting from signifying objects in one period to sensing, affected subjects in another. There is something more fundamental in this diachronic motion, played out among the theories themselves, than there is in any of their particular claims. Perhaps there is an important theoretical insight to be derived from the historical shuttling between object signification and subject sensation that can inform or renew the way we conceptualize affect. What if historical theory and historical perspective were integrated into the movement of affect—a concept that has sometimes seemed as though it has no history?

Future Historical Theories

We need to restore diachronicity and movement to affect theory. While twenty-first-century models of affect focus predominantly on the affected subject, we need to return affecting objects to their former prestige within the theoretical framework. In our construal of the motion that takes place between affecting objects and affected subjects, we need, finally, to bring historical perspective to affect theory, not only because historical theories allow us to tread the path between object and subject but also because we must understand

15. Eugenie Brinkema, *The Forms of the Affects* (Durham, NC: Duke University Press, 2014), 36.

this motion as mediated by histories of signification and the signification of history.

Such a proposal is not at all without precedent in contemporary affect theory. It builds, to begin with, on the impulse to understand affect as a dynamic passed between and among subjects — what Anderson describes as affect's transpersonal dimension and what Brennan calls its transmission.[16] If we broaden this framework slightly, we might imagine that subjects also transmit affects between each other through the use of objects as signifying mechanisms. While this would sacrifice the presumed immediacy of the exchange, it nevertheless would account for a great many more acts of affective communication. In addition, it could put affect theory into dialogue with recent work in actor-network theory — or, in a different vein, with object-oriented feminism — through the recognition of the agentive properties accorded to objects in these exchanges.[17] Objects, then, are one vital node in a network of affective motions.

This much at least is already recognized in the work of both Jonathan Flatley and Sianne Ngai, to whose robust models of affect we need only supplement a more thoroughgoing consideration of affect theory's history. The work of both of these authors is filled with close, formal readings of the affective qualities and capacities of aesthetic objects. Flatley, explicating the role that objects play within affect theory, observes a basic "subject-object confusion" in the transmission of affect. "That is," he writes, "it is often difficult to tell whether the affect originates in the object or the affect produces the object. Am I interested in this because it is interesting or because I have interest that needs to go somewhere?"[18] For Flatley, then, affect does not operate unidirectionally along an axis that connects objects to subjects; rather, it somehow exists in a movement between them. Interest, in this particular example, is neither a fixed component of the affecting object nor a singular, immediate facet of a subject's experience.

The location of affect in the interchange between object and subject is a signal component of what Sianne Ngai calls "tone" in her landmark study

16. Anderson, *Encountering Affect*, 87; Brennan, *Transmission of Affect*.

17. See, for example, Bruno Latour, *Reassembling the Social: An Introduction to Actor-Network-Theory* (Oxford: Oxford University Press, 2005); on object-oriented feminism, see Katherine Behar, "An Introduction to OOF," in *Object-Oriented Feminism*, ed. Behar (Minneapolis: University of Minnesota Press, 2016), 1–36.

18. Jonathan Flatley, *Affective Mapping: Melancholia and the Politics of Modernism* (Cambridge, MA: Harvard University Press, 2008), 17.

Ugly Feelings. By "tone," Ngai means to indicate a text's "global or organizing affect, its general disposition or orientation toward its audience and the
world."[19] Tone, in Ngai's account, is limited neither to the representations
contained within a literary text nor to the felt responses of its readers. "For we
can speak of a literary text whose global or organizing affect is disgust," she
writes, "without this necessarily implying that the work represents or signifies
disgust, or that it will disgust the reader (though in certain cases it may also
do so). Exactly 'where,' then, is the disgust?"[20] The answer is that it resides
in tone itself, which is the very mediation or movement between the text and
its reader. "Tone *is* the dialectic of objective and subjective feeling that our
aesthetic encounters inevitably produce," she suggests.[21] Tone, like sound
vibration in theories both contemporary and historical, serves as the material
foundation of affective encounter, providing the movement between subject
and object.

     With Ngai's suggestion of tone as mediation in mind, one might expect
that a fully developed theory of tones could do serious work at answering
some of the basic questions of affect. And so it is with an inflection through
the tonal theories of the eighteenth-century musical *Affektenlehre* that we can
gain some fresh perspective: critics continually call on the vibrations of tones
in order to explain the mediation of affect precisely because both affect and
sound are material and yet mysterious. This is why music — the art of tones —
has historically been embroiled in conceptual dilemmas resembling those of
affect theory. Since early modernity, theorists have variously claimed that both
music and affect are composed of formal dimensions that can be delineated
with some precision but also that they inhere in excess, in nondiscursive,
corporeal sensation that cannot be adequately captured with the tools of rationality. Music and affect are contested zones within criticism; this is what links
the history of affect theory so tightly with music and why we need a perspective from historical theories of tones in order to understand affect. Both music
and affect can be conceptualized dialectically, in ways that do not diminish
either their material appeal to our senses or their mediation by concepts and
universals.

     The movement of affect theory, then, is not only a shuttling between object
and subject. It is also a diachronic movement that replays within contemporary theory elements from the history of affect. When theorists begin to claim
that affect exceeds all terminologies, all specified linkages between object and

19. Sianne Ngai, *Ugly Feelings* (Cambridge, MA: Harvard University Press, 2005), 28.
20. Ngai, *Ugly Feelings*, 29–30.
21. Ngai, *Ugly Feelings*, 30 (emphasis in original).

subject, all systems of signification, they are rehearsing a commonplace that is familiar in the histories of both affect theory and music theory: the material is defined by that which exceeds capture, and this most enigmatic element spurs on yet further efforts to stand in its thrall, to describe it, to examine it, and indeed to capture it. Brinkema apprehends this phenomenon clearly, and although she writes specifically about film studies, what she says applies to twenty-first-century affect theory in general. "This concept of 'affect' that is all formless-feeling/what-is-not-structure thus has become a general term for any resistance to systematicity, a promised recovery of contingency, surprise, play, pleasure, and possibility. . . . It is the exuberantly generative nature of this negative term more than positive formulations that has mobilized a renewed interest in affect for the past thirty years in film studies. 'Affect' in this general sense is the negative ontology of the humanities."[22] In Brinkema's understanding, the force with which theorists have set affect against other methodologies and modes of understanding is what imbues the concept with power.

But affect is not the only conceptual domain that has been understood to operate as a kind of negative ontology or limit point within systems of human knowledge. This place was once occupied by music, a fact to which d'Alembert's "Discours préliminaire" to the *Encyclopédie* testifies. D'Alembert, we will recall, concludes his elaborate taxonomy of all human knowledge with a consideration of the arts, covering first those associated with the natural sign (painting, sculpture, and architecture) and then those of the arbitrary sign (poetry). Music, the last element of human knowledge to be considered, presents d'Alembert with a dilemma. Music seems neither limited to representations of sounding objects — which would render it a natural sign — nor to function quite like a discourse or language, which would make it an arbitrary sign. Rather, it overspills these categories of representation and threatens, in its excess, to devolve into sheer vibrating nonsense: "All music that does not paint something is only noise, and without the habituation that changes everything, it would create hardly more pleasure than a collection of harmonious and sonorous words stripped of order and connection."[23] Despite his protestations, one wonders at the role of pleasure in d'Alembert's insistence that music ought to conform to the structures of the mimetic doctrine. The pleasure of

---

22. Brinkema, *Forms of the Affects*, 30–31.

23. "Toute Musique qui ne peint rien n'est que du bruit; & sans l'habitude qui dénature tout, elle ne feroit guere plus de plaisir qu'une suite de mots harmonieux & sonores dénués d'ordre & de liaison." Jean le Rond d'Alembert, "Discours préliminaire," in *Encyclopédie ou dictionnaire raisonné des sciences, des arts et des métiers, par une société de gens de lettres*, ed. Denis Diderot and d'Alembert, vol. 1 (Paris: Briasson et Le Breton, 1751), xii.

listening to music that "neither expresses . . . nor paints"—to borrow a phrase from d'Alembert's contemporary Élie-Catherine Fréron—is precisely what has given the encyclopedist pause over the art form. Its surplus, its perceived inability to square with the categories of representation, is what makes it an attractive matter of feeling.

D'Alembert and his eighteenth-century colleagues suggest a way forward for affect theory. These earlier theorists, in the grand efforts they made at identifying the modalities through which music creates affect in its auditors, revealed something fundamental about how materials function in sign systems. Music, for d'Alembert, has not yet devolved into senseless sounds. It has been saved from this only by of the "habituation that changes everything" (*l'habitude qui dénature tout*): the sonorous material of music has come to signify because custom and practice have denatured it, have imbued it with meaning. This was, indeed, one of the premises from which early eighteenth-century theorists of the mimetic *Affektenlehre* departed. Heinichen's introduction to *Der General-Bass in der Composition* responds to the growing systematicity with which musical sounds were linked to intended significations in the operas of the day. His treatise links the formal structures of music with the intended affects on the basis of conventionality. A 12/8 siciliana invokes a pastoral scene and a 3/8 dance signifies frivolity because these forms are so consistently and so regularly related within the multimedia practice of early opera. Documents like Heinichen's *Der General-Bass in der Composition* and Mattheson's *Der vollkommene Capellmeister* bear witness to this moment of formal conventionality. In order better to understand affect theory, we must remember the gambit these theorists set out and the subsequent debates they created.

The forms of material objects, like musical sounds, signify at least in part because of their historical associations. Through this signification, they have the ability to stir affective responses in their audiences. This is the final diachronic movement we must restore to contemporary affect theory: not only must we account for the ways in which forms of affecting objects acquire the ability to signify through tradition and custom, but we must also recall how this historical dynamic continues to unfold and to revise itself. The rhythms, meters, and harmonies of the finale to Beethoven's Fifth Symphony have historically signified the heroic, but they might well also come to signify hegemony or fear or shame. Mattheson and Rameau both met with frustration in their efforts to capture the relationship between musical materials and their intended affects. This endeavor appeared endless to both of them, since "however much effort one might take to write something comprehensive about it, still only the least bit could be set down on the page, and infinitely more would remain unsaid," as Mattheson pointed out.[24]

What the objectless, nonrepresentational style of affect ultimately misses is the opportunity to assess the complex and still poorly understood ways that relations between objects and subjects are mediated by ideology. An affect theory without representation is an affect theory without ideology critique. Paying close scrutiny to the objects of affect theory is a difficult task. In order to do it, affect theorists must either describe something definite about the qualities of these objects in a premodern way or admit that the transmission of affect from an object to a subject is always mediated in some fashion. It is impossible, for example, to have an unmediated encounter with Beethoven's Fifth Symphony. The corporal, vibrational, and generally materialist explanations of affective mediation do not supplant the role of ideology — they obscure it. If in 1992 Lawrence Grossberg could suggest, "Affect is the missing term in an adequate understanding of ideology," I now rather think that ideology is the missing term in an adequate understanding of affect.[25]

The movement of history itself guarantees new and different associations between the forms of affecting objects and their ideologically inflected significations. There is no moment at which this diachronic motion abates. Significations are constantly in flux. This means that the work of an affect taxonomy is never done, and affect theorists are tempted to conclude that taxonomy or even rationality is the wrong way to approach the always-excessive affects. Affect theorists then begin to collapse affect into the force of its impact on the affected subject or to emphasize the material modes of mediation by which it reaches the subject's sensorium. Affect begins to resemble d'Alembert's unintelligible music: all vibration and sensation but devoid of sense and signification. This is not only to miss the objects and forms that play a role in engendering affect but also to miss the historical movement that has traced and retraced this very circuit.

If future affect theories are to become historical, they will want to take account of the evolution of this system. To restore diachronicity and movement to affect theory is to acknowledge the constantly shifting ways that the forms of affecting objects have come to signify and therefore to afford affective

24. "Wie viel Mühe man sich auch nehmen mögte, etwas vollständiges hierüber auszufertigen, doch nur das wenigste zu Buche gebracht, unendlich viel aber ungesagt bleiben . . . anheimgestellet werden dürffte." Johann Mattheson, *Der vollkommene Capellmeister* (Hamburg: Christian Herold, 1739), 19.

25. Lawrence Grossberg, *We Gotta Get Out of This Place* (New York: Routledge, 1992), 82.

responses in audiences through history. It is also to understand the impetus behind affect theory's slow changes in emphasis from affecting object to affected subject. Theorists have much to gain from the historical conflicts that have arisen over these elements, particularly those that involve the linked and equally vexed domain of musical sound. As d'Alembert, completely baffled at the end of his taxonomy of all human knowledge, suggested, "all that one may conclude is that after having created an art of learning music, one should also create an art of listening to it."[26] To listen again, artfully, to affect theory's torrid history is to hear its distant musical antecedents and to heed their lessons.

26. "Mais tout ce qu'on en doit conclurre, c'est qu'après avoir fait un art d'apprendre la Musique, on devroit bien en faire un de l'écouter." D'Alembert, "Discours préliminaire," xii.

Acknowledgments

There is pleasure in reminiscing on acts of generosity that others have extended to you, so it is rather fitting to conclude a book about affect theory in this way. I cannot, however, adequately appreciate in print the friends and mentors who have helped to make the writing of this book a great and stimulating joy. Nor will I be able to achieve comprehensiveness in these thanks. But what follows is my best attempt, with the recognition that it must be incomplete.

I would like to extend deep gratitude to several institutions that helped to make this book possible: first to the Stanford Humanities Center, where — during one blissful fellowship year — I wrote most of it; to Wesleyan University for continued research support through the entire project and to the Wesleyan Center for the Humanities for a fellowship semester nearer to the completion of the project; to the Society for Music Theory for a vital publication subvention grant; to the Staatsbibliothek zu Berlin, where I typed some of the manuscript's first words; to the New York Public Library for precious space in the center of Manhattan; to the Green Library and Music Library at Stanford, the Sterling Memorial Library and the Beinecke Library at Yale, the Butler Library at Columbia, and the Bobst Library at NYU, all of which provided important resources for this project.

At Wesleyan, I am incredibly fortunate to have such supportive and inspiring colleagues in the music department. Warm thanks to Jane Alden, Balu Balasubrahmaniyan, Neely Bruce, Eric Charry, John Dankwa, Ron Ebrecht, Kate Galloway, I. Harjito, Jay Hoggard, Ron Kuivila, Paula Matthusen, David Nelson, Nadya Potemkina, Mark Slobin, Tyshawn Sorey, Sumarsam, and Su Zheng. Like many books, this one first took shape in graduate seminars that I was lucky enough to teach: two at Wesleyan and one in the music department at Harvard. I will forever be in the debt of the many brilliant students who helped me to develop my ideas.

During the early stages of this book's formulation, Lauren Berlant and Sianne Ngai generously invited me to contribute my work on comic opera to "Comedy: An Issue," which convened at the University of Chicago's Neubauer Collegium for Culture and Society. I cannot thank Lauren and Sianne enough for their encouragements and critiques, which pushed my essay in new directions (it appears here in revised and expanded form as chapter 2); and many thanks to Glenda R. Carpio and Anca Parvulescu for helping me to think through thorny issues related to mimesis. Also important during this early stage were the regular meetings of the New York Seminar on Music and Mimesis working group, which consisted of James Currie, Stephen Decatur Smith, and Daniel Villegas Vélez. I cannot thank you three enough for our conversations.

The project first took discernable shape while I was an external faculty fellow at the Stanford Humanities Center. My heartfelt thanks go to the center's director, Caroline Winterer, and associate director, Andrea Davies. I am grateful to my entire cohort of 2016–2017 fellows, particularly to Katy Meadows and Willie Costello for conversations on Kant and Hegel. Janaki Bakhle deserves special mention for spending so much time in helping me to articulate the stakes of my argument. While I was in California, I had a formative experience as a participant of the "Musical Pasts" consortium meeting at UC Berkeley. I am very thankful to Alan Tansman for the generous invitation to provide a keynote address and to Martha Feldman, Nick Mathew, Roger Parker, and Gary Tomlinson for extremely important feedback during that meeting.

During the process of writing, I tried out portions of the material in invited talks at the University of Pittsburgh, Columbia University, Stony Brook University, UC San Diego, Northwestern University, the University of Chicago, Dartmouth College, Stanford University, UC Santa Barbara, UC Berkeley, the University of Toronto, the Peabody Institute of Johns Hopkins University, and the Max Planck Institute for Empirical Aesthetics in Frankfurt. Countless exceptional interlocutors helped me to refine my ideas, to situate the interventions, and to explain the inner workings of the narrative I present here. I am extremely grateful for these invitations and for the chance to work through the intellectual issues with such generous communities of thinkers.

So many people in my queer intellectual family have contributed to this project in intensive conversations, in debates, through their own work, or in reading portions of the manuscript and responding generously and critically. Thank you to Marco Aresu, Daniel Callahan, Thomas Christensen,

Amy Cimini, Suzannah Clark, Andy Curran, Helen Kim, Natasha Korda, Clara Latham, Nathan John Martin, Michael Meere, Caleb Mutch, Victoria Pitts-Taylor, Marcel Przymusinski, Carmel Raz, Alex Rehding, Sergio Rigoletto, Michael Roth, Rafael Walker, Kari Weil, Courtney Weiss-Smith, Anna Zayaruznaya, and Emily Zazulia; if writing can sometimes feel lonely and isolating, you all helped me to feel like a part of something larger than myself. Toward the end of the writing process, I was fortunate to take part in the community at the Wesleyan Center for the Humanities. Special thanks to Natasha Korda, the director, and to my fellow fellows Katie Brewer Ball, Tushar Irani, Jill Morawski, Catherine Damman, Heather Vermeulen, Anna Apostolidis, Elean Harris-Bauer, Sam Morreale, and Isabel Steckel. Two research assistants who worked with me very closely deserve thanks for their invaluable contributions: Victoria Ding at Stanford and Belén Rodriguez at Wesleyan. I have also been incredibly lucky to work with a team of consummate professionals at Fordham University Press who appreciate and understand my work. Many thanks in particular to Tom Lay, Eric Newman, and my copy editor, Andrew Katz.

Then there are those to whom I owe a great deal of appreciation because of the incredible amount of work they selflessly committed to this book project. The first group is of my musicological mentors, whose unflagging support keeps me going: Mark Butler, Gary Tomlinson, Emily Dolan, and Jairo Moreno. Your influence is deeply felt in these pages. My heartfelt gratitude to Michael Gallope, whose response to the project at an early stage steered me in the right direction; also to the anonymous reader for Fordham who likewise provided invaluable feedback; to Scott De Orio, with whom I shared some beautiful time at the origins of this project and who helped me to refine it; to Craig Comen, my eighteenth-century partner in crime who provided detailed feedback on the entire manuscript; to Mark Schulte, who has my deep appreciation for all of our conversations and for his help in editing; to my colleague Daniel Smyth, who also read an entire draft and who helped me with so many vital philosophical and logical details; to Gavin Steingo, with whom I have the most productive debates and without whom I would not be an academic; and to David Halperin, who has been extremely influential in my thinking at all levels, from the theoretical interventions to the minute details of prose and translation. I cannot thank you enough, David, for being my inspiration and guide.

My family has offered me endless support and love, always taking interest in my work. I cannot adequately express how lucky I feel to have them in my life. My deep thanks to Henry and Lorraine T. Grant, Daniel Grant, and Jean Triggiani.

While I was writing the bulk of this manuscript in California, a very special group of people showed me new things and helped me to trace the circuit of this book's logic and energy. Thank you to Billy Kelaher, Dan Fettig, Scott Fettig, David Guttierez, Dylan Chouinard, Eric Shen, Casey McKerchy, Landry Whitted, Luke Salinas, John Espiritu (also to HQ!), Joshua Carroll, Merredith Lloyd, Justin Potter, Kenny DeSoto, Kris Baylon, Ali Mafi, Matthew Card, and Richard Kim.

And finally, to James Kim, who shared each day with me. In so many ways this book is about you: you are joy, you are wonder, you are passion. An academic book is a strange gift, but nevertheless, I dedicate this book to you, for teaching me to feel.

The Introduction to this book is an expanded and revised version of "Music Lessons on Affect and Its Objects," which first appeared in *Representations* 144 no. 1 (2018). I am very grateful to the editorial board for its feedback on the piece and also to the University of California Press for allowing me to incorporate it into this book. An earlier version of chapter 2 likewise appeared in *Critical Inquiry* 43 no. 2 (2017), a special issue on comedy edited by Lauren Berlant and Sianne Ngai. My gratitude to the editors and the editorial board for their formative help with the piece and also to the University of Chicago Press for permission to include the work here.

Bibliography

Abbate, Carolyn. "Music — Drastic or Gnostic?" *Critical Inquiry* 30, no. 3 (2004): 505–536.

Abbate, Carolyn, and Roger Parker. *A History of Opera: The Last Four Hundred Years*. London: Allen Lane, 2012.

Abrams, M. H. *The Mirror and the Lamp: Romantic Theory and the Critical Tradition*. Oxford: Oxford University Press, 1953.

Agawu, Kofi. *Music as Discourse: Semiotic Adventures in Romantic Music*. New York: Oxford University Press, 2009.

———. *Playing with Signs: A Semiotic Interpretation of Classic Music*. Princeton, NJ: Princeton University Press, 1991.

Ahern, Stephen. "Nothing More than Feelings? Affect Theory Reads the Age of Sensibility." *Eighteenth Century* 58, no. 3 (2017): 281–295.

Ahmed, Sara. "Happy Objects." In *The Affect Theory Reader*, edited by Melissa Gregg and Gregory J. Seigworth, 29–51. Durham, NC: Duke University Press, 2010.

———. *The Promise of Happiness*. Durham, NC: Duke University Press, 2010.

Allanbrook, Wye Jamison. *Rhythmic Gesture in Mozart: "Le nozze di Figaro" and "Don Giovanni."* Chicago: University of Chicago Press, 1983.

———. *The Secular Commedia: Comic Mimesis in Late Eighteenth-Century Music*. Berkeley: University of California Press, 2014.

Allison, Henry. *Kant's Theory of Taste*. Cambridge: Cambridge University Press, 2001.

Anderson, Ben. *Encountering Affect: Capacities, Apparatuses, Conditions*. Farnham, UK: Ashgate, 2014.

André, Yves Marie. *Essai sur le beau*. Paris: Hippolyte-Louis Geurin and Jacques Guerin, 1741.

Apel, Willi. *Harvard Dictionary of Music*, 2nd ed. Cambridge, MA: Harvard University Press, 1972.

Barbier, Antoine-Alexandre. *Dictionnaire des ouvrages anonymes*. Paris: Paul Daffis, 1879.

Barry, Kevin. *Language, Music, and the Sign: A Study in the Aesthetics, Poetics, and Poetic Practice from Collins to Coleridge*. Cambridge: Cambridge University Press, 1987.

Batteux, Charles. *Les beaux arts réduits à un même principe*. Paris: Durand, 1746.

Baumgarten, Alexander Gottlieb. *Meditationes philosophicae de nonnullis ad poema pertinentibus*. Halle: Grunert, 1735. Modern edition, edited by Benedetto Croce, Naples: Vecchi, 1900.

Beattie, James. "An Essay on Poetry and Music, as They Affect the Mind: Written in the Year 1762." In *Essays*, vol. 2, 3–205. Edinburgh: William Creech; London: E. & C. Dilliy, 1776.

Behar, Katherine. "An Introduction to OOF." In *Object-Oriented Feminism*, edited by Katherine Behar, 1–36. Minneapolis: University of Minnesota Press, 2016.

Bell, Charles. *Essays on the Anatomy and Philosophy of Expression*. 2nd ed. London: John Murray, 1824.

Bennett, Jane. *Vibrant Matter: A Political Ecology of Things*. Durham, NC: Duke University Press, 2010.

Bergson, Henri. *Laughter: An Essay on the Meaning of the Comic*. Translated by Cloudesley Brereton and Fred Rothwell. New York: Macmillan, 1914.

Berlant, Lauren. *Cruel Optimism*. Durham, NC: Duke University Press, 2011.

Bonds, Mark Evan. *Absolute Music: The History of an Idea*. New York: Oxford University Press, 2014.

———. *Music as Thought: Listening to the Symphony in the Age of Beethoven*. Princeton, NJ: Princeton University Press, 2006.

Boyer, Pascal. *L'Expression musicale, mise au rang des chimères*. 1779. Reprint, Geneva: Minkoff, 1973.

Brennan, Theresa. *The Transmission of Affect*. Ithaca, NY: Cornell University Press, 2004.

Brinkema, Eugenie. *The Forms of the Affects*. Durham, NC: Duke University Press, 2014.

Bucciarelli, Melania. *Italian Opera and European Theatre, 1680–1720: Plots, Performers, Dramaturgies*. Turnhout: Brepolis, 2000.

Buelow, George J. "Johann Mattheson and the Invention of the *Affektenlehre*." In *New Mattheson Studies*, edited by George J. Buelow and Hans Joachim Marx, 393–407. Cambridge: Cambridge University Press, 1983.

Bukofzer, Manfred F. *Music in the Baroque Era: From Monteverdi to Bach*. New York: Norton, 1947.

Ceballos, Sara Gross. "François Couperin, *Moraliste*?" *Eighteenth-Century Music* 11, no. 1 (2014): 79–110.

———. "Keyboard Portraits: Performing Character in the Eighteenth Century." PhD diss., University of California Los Angeles, 2008.

Chabanon, Michel Paul Guy de. *Observations sur la musique, et principalement sur la metaphysique de l'art*. Paris: Pissot, 1779.

Charlton, David. *Opera in the Age of Rousseau*. Cambridge: Cambridge University Press, 2012.

Cho, Alexander. "Queer Reverb: Tumblr, Affect, Time." In *Networked Affect*, edited by Susanna Paasonen, Ken Hillis, and Michael Petit, 43–58. Cambridge, MA: MIT Press, 2015.

Christensen, Thomas. "The *corps sonore*." In *Rameau and Musical Thought in the Enlightenment*, 133–168. Cambridge: Cambridge University Press, 1993.

Cimini, Amy. "How to Do Things with Dualism: The Political Expedience of the Musical Mind-Body Problem." In "Baruch Spinoza and the Matter of Music: Toward a New Practice of Theorizing Musical Bodies," 21–84. PhD diss., New York University, 2011.

Clark, Jane, and Derek Connon. *"The Mirror of Human Life": Reflections on François Couperin's "Pièces de Clavecin."* Huntingdon, UK: King's Music, 2002.

Clark, Michael. "Humor and Incongruity." In *The Philosophy of Laughter and Humor*, edited by John Morreall, 139–155. Albany: SUNY Press, 1987.

Connolly, William E. "Critical Response I: The Complexity of Intention." *Critical Inquiry* 37, no. 4 (2011): 791–798.

———. *A World of Becoming*. Durham, NC: Duke University Press, 2011.

Cook, Elisabeth. "Challenging the *Ancien Régime*: The Hidden Politics of the 'Querelle des Bouffons.'" In *La "Querelle des Bouffons" dans la vie culturelle française du XVIIIe siècle*, edited by Andrea Fabiano, 139–160. Paris: CNRS Éditions, 2005.

Cooper, Anthony Ashley. *Characteristics of Men, Manners, Opinions, Times*. 1711. Edited by Lawrence E. Klein. Cambridge: Cambridge University Press, 1999.

Coriando, Paola-Ludovika. *Affektenlehre und Phänomenologie der Stimmungen: Wege einer Ontologie und Ethik des Emotionalen*. Frankfurt: Vittorio Klostermann, 2002.

Couperin, François. *Pièces de clavecin . . . premier livre*. Paris: Ballard, 1713.

Dahlhaus, Carl. *The Idea of Absolute Music*. Translated by Roger Lustig. Chicago: University of Chicago Press, 1989.

d'Alembert, Jean le Rond. "Discours préliminaire." In *Encyclopédie ou dictionnaire raisonné des sciences, des arts et des métiers, par une société de gens de lettres*, edited by Denis Diderot and Jean le Rond d'Alembert, vol. 1, i–xlv. Paris: Briasson et Le Breton, 1751.

———. "Fragment sur l'opéra." ca. 1752. In *Oeuvres et correspondances inédites de d'Alembert*, edited with notes and appendix by Charles Henry. Paris: Perrin, 1887.

———. *Oeuvres*. 5 vols. Paris: Belin, 1821–1822.

Darwin, Charles. *The Expression of the Emotions in Man and Animals*. New York: D. Appleton, 1886.

Decker, Gregory J. "Colonizing Familiar Territory: Musical Topics, Stylistic Level and Handel's Cleopatra." *Opera Journal* 47, no. 2 (2014): 3–32.

———. "Pastorals, Passepieds, and Pendants: Interpreting Characterization through Aria Pairs in Handel's *Rodelinda*." *Music Theory Online* 19, no. 4 (2013). http://mtosmt.org/issues/mto.13.19.4/mto.13.19.4.decker.html.

Deleuze, Gilles. "The Shame and the Glory: T. E. Lawrence." In *Essays Critical and Clinical*, translated by Daniel W. Smith and Michael A. Greco, 115–125. Minneapolis: University of Minnesota Press, 1997.

Descartes, René. *Les passions de l'âme*. Paris: Henry Le Gras, 1649.

Diderot, Denis. *Denis Diderot's "Rameau's Nephew": A Multi-Media Edition*. Translated by Kate E. Tunstall and Caroline Warman. Edited by Marian Hobson. Cambridge, UK: Open Book, 2014. www.openbookpublishers.com/product/216/

———. *Le rêve de d'Alembert*. In *Œuvres philosophiques*, edited by Michel Delon with Barbara de Negroni, 343–409. Paris: Gallimard, 2010.

———. *Lettre sur les sourds et muets: À l'usage de ceux qui entendent & qui parlent*. 1751.

———. *Paradoxe sur le comédien*. 1773. Edited by Stéphane Lojkine. Paris: Armand Colin, 1992.

———. *Principes de la philosophie morale; ou Essai de M. S*** sur le mérite et la vertu, avec réflexions*. Amsterdam: Zacharie Chatelain, 1745.

———. *Rameau's Nephew and Other Works*. Translated by Jacques Barzun and Ralph H. Bowen. Indianapolis: Hackett, 1956.

Dill, Charles. *Monstrous Opera: Rameau and the Tragic Tradition*. Princeton, NJ: Princeton University Press, 1998.

Dolan, Emily I. *The Orchestral Revolution: Haydn and the Technologies of Timbre*. Cambridge: Cambridge University Press, 2013.

Dubiel, Joseph. "Senses of Sensemaking." *Perspectives of New Music* 30, no. 1 (1992): 210–221.

Dubos, Jean-Baptiste. *Réflexions critiques sur la poésie et sur la peinture*. Vol. 1. Paris: Jean Mariette, 1719.

Edelstein, Dan. *The Enlightenment: A Genealogy*. Chicago: University of Chicago Press, 2010.

Elferen, Isabella van. "Affective Discourse in German Baroque Text-Based Music." *Tijdschrift voor muziektheorie* 9, no. 3 (2004): 217–233.

Engel, Johann Jakob. *Ueber die musikalische Malerey*. Berlin: Christian Friedrich Voß und Sohn, 1780.

Fabiano, Andrea, ed. *La "Querelle des Bouffons" dans la vie culturelle française du XVIIIe siècle*. Paris: CNRS Éditions, 2005.

Feldman, Martha. "Music and the Order of the Passions." In *Representing the Passions: Histories, Bodies, Visions*, edited by Richard Evan Meyer, 37–67. Los Angeles: Getty Research Institute, 2003.

———. *Opera and Sovereignty: Transforming Myths in Eighteenth-Century Italy*. Chicago: University of Chicago Press, 2007.

Flatley, Jonathan. *Affective Mapping: Melancholia and the Politics of Modernism.* Cambridge, MA: Harvard University Press, 2008.

Forkel, Johann Nikolaus. *Allgemeine Geschichte der Musik.* Vol. 1. Leipzig: Schwickertschen Verlage, 1788.

Foucault, Michel. *The Order of Things.* 1966. English translation. 1970. Reprint, New York: Routledge, 2002.

Freeman, Robert S. *Opera without Drama: Currents of Change in Italian Opera, 1675–1725.* Ann Arbor: UMI Research Press, 1981.

Fréron, Elie-Catherine. "Les spectacles de Paris, ou Calendrier historique et chronologique des théâtres." In *L'Année littéraire, ou Suite des lettres sur quelques écrits de ce temps*, vol. 1, 159–167. Amsterdam: Lambert, 1756.

Fux, Johann Joseph. *Gradus ad Parnassum.* Vienna: Peter van Ghelen, 1725.

Gallarati, Paolo. *Musica e maschera: Il libretto italiano del setteccento.* Turin: EdT, 1984.

Gallope, Michael. *Deep Refrains: Music, Philosophy, and the Ineffable.* Chicago: University of Chicago Press, 2017.

Gebauer, Gunter, and Christoph Wulf. *Mimesis: Culture–Art–Society.* Translated by Don Reneau. Berkeley: University of California Press, 1995.

Goethe, Johann Wolfgang. *Johann Wolfgang Goethe zwischen Weimar und Jena.* 2 vols. Vols. 8–9 of *Sämtliche Werke: Briefe, Tagebücher und Gespräche*. Frankfurt am Main: Deutscher Klassiker Verlag, 1999.

Gottsched, Johann Christoph. *Auszug aus des Herrn Batteux schönen Künsten aus dem einzigen Grundsatze der Nachahmung hergeleitet . . .* Leipzig: Bernhard Christoph Breitkopf, 1754.

Grant, Roger Mathew. *Beating Time and Measuring Music in the Early Modern Era.* New York: Oxford University Press, 2014.

———. "Peculiar Attunements: Comic Opera and Enlightenment Mimesis." *Critical Inquiry* 43, no. 2 (2017): 550–569.

Gravina, Gian Vincenzo. *Della tragedia.* Vol. 1. Naples, 1715.

Grimm, Friedrich Melchior. "Poeme lyrique." In *Encyclopédie ou dictionnaire raisonné des sciences, des arts et des métiers, par une société de gens de lettres*, edited by Denis Diderot and Jean le Rond d'Alembert, vol. 12, 823–836. Paris: Briasson et Le Breton, 1765.

Grossberg, Lawrence. *We Gotta Get Out of This Place.* New York: Routledge, 1992.

Gumbrecht, Hans Ulrich. *Atmosphere, Mood, Stimmung: On a Hidden Potential of Literature.* Translated by H. Erik Butler. Stanford, CA: Stanford University Press, 2012.

Halliwell, Stephen. *The Aesthetics of Mimesis: Ancient Texts and Modern Problems.* Princeton, NJ: Princeton University Press, 2002.

Halperin, David. "What Is Sex For?" *Critical Inquiry* 43, no. 1 (2016): 1–31.

Hamilton, John T. *Music, Madness, and the Unworking of Language.* New York: Columbia University Press, 2008.

Handel, George Frideric. *Giulio Cesare.* Edited by Walter Gieseler. Kassel: Bärenreiter, 1972.

Hanslick, Eduard. *Vom Musikalisch-Schönen: Ein Beitrag zur Revision der Ästhetik der Tonkunst.* Leipzig: Rudolph Weigel, 1854.

Hardt, Michael. "Foreword: What Affects Are Good For." In *The Affective Turn: Theorizing the Social*, edited by Patricia Clough with Jean Halley, ix. Durham, NC: Duke University Press, 2007.

Hartley, David. *Observations on Man, His Frame, His Duty, and His Expectations.* London: S. Richardson, 1749.

Haynes, Bruce, and Geoffrey Burgess. *The Pathetick Musician: Moving an Audience in the Age of Eloquence.* Oxford: Oxford University Press, 2016.

Heartz, Daniel. *From Garrick to Gluck: Essays on Opera in the Age of Enlightenment.* Edited by John A. Rice. Hillsdale, NY: Pendragon, 2004.

———. "Locatelli and the Pantomime of the Violinist in *Le Neveu de Rameau*." *Diderot Studies* 27 (1998): 115–127.

Hegel, G. W. F. *Phenomenology of Spirit.* Translated by A. V. Miller. Oxford: Oxford University Press, 1977.

Heidegger, Martin. *Being and Time.* Translated by Joan Stambaugh. Revised and with a foreword by Dennis J. Schmidt. Albany: SUNY Press, 2010.

Heinichen, Johann David. *Der General-Bass in der Composition.* Dresden: Heinichen, 1728.

Herder, Johann Gottfried. *Kalligone.* Vol. 1. Leipzig: Johann Friedrich Hartknoch, 1800.

Hiller, Johann Adam. "Abhandlung von der Nachahmung der Natur in der Musik." In *Historisch-Kritische Beyträge zur Aufnahme der Musik*, by Friedrich Wilhelm Marpurg, vol. 1, 515–543. Berlin: J. J. Schützens Witwe, G. A. Lange, 1754.

Hoffmann, E. T. A. "Der Musikfeind." *Allgemeine musikalische Zeitung* (Leipzig), July 1, 1814.

———. "Recension." *Allgemeine musikalische Zeitung* (Leipzig), July 4–11, 1810.

Holden, John. *An Essay towards a Rational System of Music.* Glasgow: Robert Urie, 1770.

Hollinghurst, Alan. *The Swimming-Pool Library.* New York: Vintage Books, 1989.

Horkheimer, Max, and Theodor W. Adorno. *Dialectic of Enlightenment.* Translated by John Cumming. New York: Continuum, 1989.

Hosler, Bellamy. *Changing Aesthetic Views of Instrumental Music in 18th-Century Germany.* Ann Arbor, MI: UMI Research Press, 1981.

Hultquist, Aleksondra. "Introductory Essay: Emotion, Affect, and the Eighteenth Century." *Eighteenth Century* 58, no. 3 (2017): 273–280.

Hume, David. *"A Dissertation on the Passions" and "The Natural History of Religion": A Critical Edition.* Edited by Tom L. Beauchamp. Oxford, UK: Clarendon, 2007.

———. *Four Dissertations.* London: A. Millar, 1757.

Hunter, Mary. "Topics and Opera Buffa." In *The Oxford Handbook of Topic Theory*, edited by Danuta Mirka, 61–89. Oxford: Oxford University Press, 2014.

Hyppolite, Jean. *Genesis and Structure of Hegel's "Phenomenology of Spirit."* Translated by Samuel Cherniak and John Heckman. Evanston, IL: Northwestern University Press, 1974.

Johnston, Keith James. "È caso da intermedio! Comic Theory, Comic Style, and the Early Intermezzo." PhD diss., University of Toronto, 2011.

Junker, Carl Ludwig. "Tonkunst." In *Betrachtungen über Mahlerey, Ton- und Bildhauerkunst*, 63–69. Basel: Karl August Serini, 1778.

Kane, Brian. *Sound Unseen: Acousmatic Sound in Theory and Practice.* Oxford: Oxford University Press, 2014.

Kant, Immanuel. *Critik der Urtheilskraft.* Berlin: Lagarde und Friederich, 1790. Facsimile edition, with an introduction by Lewis White Beck. London: Routledge/Thoemmes, 1994.

———. *Critique of Judgment.* Translated by Werner S. Pluhar. Indianapolis: Hackett, 1987.

Kennaway, James, ed. *Music and the Nerves, 1700–1900.* New York: Palgrave Macmillan, 2014.

Kerman, Joseph. *Opera as Drama.* 1956. Reprint, Berkeley: University of California Press, 1988.

Kintzler, Catherine. *Poétique de l'opéra français de Corneille à Rousseau.* Paris: Minerve, 1991.

Kircher, Athanasius. *Musurgia universalis.* Rome: Eredi di Francesco Corbelletti, 1650.

Kramer, Lawrence. *Classical Music and Postmodern Knowledge.* Berkeley: University of California Press, 1996.

Krause, Christian Gottfried. *Von der musikalischen Poesie.* Berlin: Johann Friedrich Voß, 1752.

Kretzschmar, Hermann. "Allgemeines und Besonderes zur Affektenlehre." *Jahrbuch der Musikbibliothek Peters* 18 (1911): 63–77; 19 (1912): 65–78.

Latour, Bruno. *Reassembling the Social: An Introduction to Actor-Network-Theory.* Oxford: Oxford University Press, 2005.

Lauer, Quentin. *A Reading of Hegel's "Phenomenology of Spirit."* New York: Fordham University Press, 1976; third printing, 1998.

Launay, Denise, ed. *La querelle des bouffons: Texte des pamphlets.* 3 vols. Geneva: Minkoff, 1973.

Le Guin, Elisabeth. *Boccherini's Body: An Essay in Carnal Musicology.* Berkeley: University of California Press, 2006.

Lessing, Gotthold Ephraim. *Laokoon: Oder über die Grenzen der Mahlerey und Poesie.* Vol. 1. Berlin: Christian Friedrich Voß, 1766.

———. *Werke und Breife.* Vol. 3, *Werke, 1754–1757.* Edited by Conrad Wiedemann. Frankfurt am Main: Deutscher Klassiker Verlag, 2003.

Leys, Ruth. *The Ascent of Affect: Genealogy and Critique*. Chicago: University of Chicago Press, 2017.

Lippman, Edward A., ed. *Musical Aesthetics: A Historical Reader*. Vol. 1. Hillsdale, NY: Pendragon, 1986.

Loughridge, Deirdre. *Haydn's Sunrise, Beethoven's Shadow: Audiovisual Culture and the Emergence of Musical Romanticism*. Chicago: University of Chicago Press, 2016.

Lully, Jean-Baptiste. *Armide*. Edited by Lois Rosow. Hildesheim: Georg Olms, 2003.

Maillart, Pierre. *Les tons ov discovrs svr les modes de mvsique, et les tons de l'eglise, et la distinction entre iceux*. Tournay: Charles Martin, 1610.

Mandelbaum, Eric. "Associationist Theories of Thought." In *The Stanford Encyclopedia of Philosophy*, Summer 2017 Edition, edited by Edward N. Zalta. Accessed June 12, 2018. https://plato.stanford.edu/archives/sum2017/entries/associationist-thought.

Marcello, Benedetto. *Il teatro alla moda . . .* Venice, 1720. Facsimile edition, Milan: Ricordi, 1883.

Martello, Pier Jacopo. *Della tragedia antica e moderna*. Rome: Francesco Gonzaga, 1715.

Massumi, Brian. "Notes on the Translation." In *A Thousand Plateaus: Capitalism and Schizophrenia*, by Gilles Deleuze and Félix Guattari, xvii. Minneapolis: University of Minnesota Press, 1987.

——. *Parables for the Virtual: Movement, Affect, Sensation*. Durham, NC: Duke University Press, 2002.

Mattheson, Johann. *Das neu-eröffnete Orchestre*. Hamburg: Mattheson and Benjamin Schillers Witwe, 1713.

——. *Der vollkommene Capellmeister*. Hamburg: Christian Herold, 1739.

McAuley, Tomas. "Rhythmic Accent and the Absolute: Sulzer, Schelling, and the Akzenttheorie." *Eighteenth-Century Music* 10, no. 2 (2013): 277–286.

McClary, Susan. "In Praise of Contingency: The Powers and Limits of Theory." *Music Theory Online* 16, no. 1 (2010). www.mtosmt.org/issues/mto.10.16.1/mto.10.16.1.mcclary.html.

Mendelssohn, Moses. "Ueber das Erhabene und das Naïve in den schönen Wissenschaften." In *Moses Mendelssohns philosophische Schriften*, vol. 2, 153–240. Berlin: Christian Friedrich Voß, 1771.

Mersenne, Marin. *Harmonie universelle*. Paris: Sébastien Cramoisy, 1636–1637.

Mirka, Danuta. Introduction to *The Oxford Handbook of Topic Theory*, edited by Danuta Mirka, 1–57. Oxford: Oxford University Press, 2014.

——, ed. *The Oxford Handbook of Topic Theory*. Oxford: Oxford University Press, 2014.

Morellet, André. *De l'expression en musique*. Paris, 1770.

——. *Mélanges de littérature et de philosophie du 18e siècle*. Vol. 4. Paris: Le Bailly, Libraire, 1836.

Morris, William Edward, and Charlotte R. Brown. "David Hume." In *The Stanford*

Encyclopedia of Philosophy, Spring 2017 Edition, edited by Edward N. Zalta. Accessed April 4, 2017. https://plato.stanford.edu/archives/spr2017/entries/hume/.

Moshaver, Maryam. "Rameau, the Subjective Body, and the Forms of Theoretical Representation." *Theoria* 23 (2016): 113–128.

Muratori, Ludovico Antonio. *Della perfetta poesia italiana*. Vol. 2. Modena: Bartolomeo Soliani, 1706.

Neubauer, John. *The Emancipation of Music from Language: Departure from Mimesis in Eighteenth-Century Aesthetics*. New Haven, CT: Yale University Press, 1986.

Ngai, Sianne. *Our Aesthetic Categories: Zany, Cute, Interesting*. Cambridge, MA: Harvard University Press, 2012.

———. *Ugly Feelings*. Cambridge, MA: Harvard University Press, 2005.

Oliver, Richard A. *The Encyclopedists as Critics of Music*. New York: Columbia University Press, 1947.

O'Sullivan, Simon. "The Aesthetics of Affect: Thinking Art beyond Representation." *Angelaki* 6, no. 3 (2001): 125–135.

Palisca, Claude. "Moving the Affections through Music: Pre-Cartesian Psycho-Physiological Theories." In *Number to Sound: The Musical Way to the Scientific Revolution*, edited by Paolo Gozza, 289–308. Dordrecht: Kluwer, 2000.

Pergolesi, Giovanni Battista. *La serva padrona*. Vol. 3 of *Opera omnia di Giovanni Battista Pergolesi*, edited by Francesco Caffarelli. Rome: Gli Amici della Musica da Camera, 1941.

———. *Livietta e Tracollo*, translated and edited by Charles C. Russell. In *Complete Works/Opere Complete*, edited by Gordana Lazarevich, vol. 6. Stuyvesant, NY: Pendragon, 1991.

Phemister, Pauline. "Ideas." In *The Oxford Handbook of Philosophy in Early Modern Europe*, edited by Desmond M. Clarke and Catherine Wilson, 142–159. Oxford: Oxford University Press, 2011.

Pinch, Trevor, and Karin Bijsterveld, eds. *The Oxford Handbook of Sound Studies*. Oxford: Oxford University Press, 2012.

Pippin, Robert. *Hegel's Idealism: The Satisfactions of Self-Consciousness*. Cambridge: Cambridge University Press, 1989.

Planelli, Antonio. *Dell' opera in musica*. Naples: Donato Campo, 1772.

Pluche, Noël-Antoine. *Le spectacle de la nature, ou entretiens sur les particularités de l'histoire naturelle, qui ont paru les plus propres à rendre les Jeunes-Gens curieux, & à leur former l'esprit*. Vol. 7. Paris: Veuve Estienne et Fils, 1747.

Purcell, Henry. *Dido and Aeneas*. Edited under the supervision of the Purcell Society by Margaret Laurie. Borough Green, UK: Novello, 1979.

Quéro, Dominique. "Rire et comique à l'Académie royale de musique: La querelle du 'bouffon'?" In *La "Querelle des Bouffons" dans la vie culturelle française du XVIIIe siècle*, edited by Andrea Fabiano, 57–72. Paris: CNRS Éditions, 2005.

Rameau, Jean-Philippe. *Génération harmonique, ou traité de musique théorique et pratique*. Paris: Prault fils, 1737.

———. *Nouveau système de musique théorique*. Paris: Jean-Baptiste-Christophe Ballard, 1726.

———. *Observations sur notre instinct pour la musique et sur son principe*. Paris: Prault fils, Lambert, Duchesne, 1754.

———. *Traité de l'harmonie*. Paris: Jean-Baptiste-Christophe Ballard, 1722.

Rancière, Jacques. *Aisthesis: Scenes from the Aesthetic Regime of Art*. New York: Verso, 2013.

———. *Mute Speech: Literature, Critical Theory, and Politics*. New York: Columbia University Press, 2011.

Ratner, Leonard. *Classic Music: Expression, Form, and Style*. New York: Schirmer Books, 1980.

Raz, Carmel. "'The Expressive Organ within Us': Ether, Ethereality, and Early Romantic Ideas about Music and the Nerves." *19th-Century Music* 38, no. 2 (2014): 115–144.

Reddy, William M. *The Navigation of Feeling: A Framework for the History of Emotions*. Cambridge: Cambridge University Press, 2001.

Reid, Jeffrey. *The Anti-Romantic: Hegel against Ironic Romanticism* (New York: Bloomsbury, 2014).

Rinaldo di Capua. *La zingara*. Edited by Eva Riccioli Orecchia. Florence: Edizioni Musicali Otos, 1969.

Roach, Joseph. *The Player's Passion: Studies in the Science of Acting*. Ann Arbor: University of Michigan Press, 1993.

Roger, Joseph-Louis. *Traité des effets de la musique sur le corps humain*. 1758. Translated by Étienne Sainte-Marie. Paris: Brunot; Lyon: Reymann et Compe and J. Roger, 1803.

Rosand, Ellen. "The Descending Tetrachord: An Emblem of Lament." *Musical Quarterly* 65, no. 3 (1979): 346–359.

———. "*Il lamento*: The Fusion of Music and Drama." In *Opera in Seventeenth-Century Venice*, 361–386. Berkeley: University of California Press, 1990.

Rothfuss, Joan. *Topless Cellist: The Improbable Life of Charlotte Moorman*. Cambridge, MA: MIT Press, 2014.

Rousseau, Jean-Jacques. "Essai sur l'origine des langues." In *Œuvres completes de J. J. Rousseau, citoyen de Genève*, vol. 8, 137–231. Geneva, 1782.

———. *Lettre sur la musique françoise*. Paris, 1753.

———. "Sonate." In *Dictionnaire de musique*, 459–460. Paris: Duchesne, 1768.

———. "Sonate." In *Encyclopédie ou dictionnaire raisonné des sciences, des arts et des métiers, par une société de gens de lettres*, edited by Denis Diderot and Jean le Rond d'Alembert, vol. 15, 348. Paris: Briasson et Le Breton, 1765.

Ruetz, Caspar. "Sendschreiben eines Freundes an den andern über einige Ausdrücke des Herrn Batteux von der Musik." In *Historisch-Kritische Beyträge zur Aufnahme der Musik*, by Friedrich Wilhelm Marpurg, vol. 1, 273–311. Berlin: J. J. Schützens Witwe, G. A. Lange, 1754.

Saint-Mard, Rémond de. *Réflexions sur l'opéra*. The Hague: Neaulme, 1741.

Scheibe, Johann Adolph. *Der critische Musicus.* Vol. 1. Hamburg: Thomas von Wierings Erben, 1737–1738.

Schenker, Heinrich. *Der Tonwille: Pamphlets/Quarterly Publications in Witness of the Immutable Laws of Music.* 1921–1924. Edited by William Drabkin. Vol. 2. New York: Oxford University Press, 2004.

Sedgwick, Eve Kosofsky. *Touching Feeling: Affect, Pedagogy, Performativity.* Durham, NC: Duke University Press, 2003.

Sedgwick, Eve Kosofsky, and Adam Frank. *Shame and Its Sisters: A Silvan S. Tomkins Reader.* Durham, NC: Duke University Press, 1995.

———. "Shame in the Cybernetic Fold: Reading Silvan Tomkins." *Critical Inquiry* 21, no. 2 (1995): 496–522.

Seigworth, Gregory J., and Melissa Gregg. "An Inventory of Shimmers." In *The Affect Theory Reader,* edited by Gregory J. Seigworth and Melissa Gregg, 1–25. Durham, NC: Duke University Press, 2010.

Serjeantson, R. W. "The Soul." In *The Oxford Handbook of Philosophy in Early Modern Europe,* edited by Desmond M. Clarke and Catherine Wilson, 119–141. Oxford: Oxford University Press, 2011.

Short, T. L. *Peirce's Theory of Signs.* Cambridge: Cambridge University Press, 2007.

Spinoza, Baruch. *Ethica.* In *Opera im Auftrag der Heidelberger Akademie der Wissenschaften,* edited by Carl Gebhardt. Heidelberg: Universitætsbuchhandlung, 1925.

———. *Spinoza: The Complete Works.* Translated by Samuel Shirley, edited with introduction and notes by Michael L. Morgan. Indianapolis: Hackett, 2002.

Sterne, Jonathan. *The Audible Past: Cultural Origins of Sound Reproduction.* Durham, NC: Duke University Press, 2003.

———, ed. *The Sound Studies Reader.* New York: Routledge, 2012.

Strohm, Reinhard. "Introduction: The *Drama per Musica* in the Eighteenth Century." In *Dramma per Musica: Italian Opera Seria of the Eighteenth Century,* 1–29. New Haven, CT: Yale University Press, 1997.

Sulzer, Johann Georg. *Allgemeine Theorie der schönen Künste.* 2 vols. Leipzig: M. G. Weidmanns Erben und Reich, 1771–1774).

Terada, Rei. *Feeling in Theory: Emotion after the "Death of the Subject."* Cambridge, MA: Harvard University Press, 2001.

Terrasson, Abbé Jean. *Dissertation critique sur l'Iliade d'Homère.* Vol. 1. Paris: François Fournier and Antoine-Urbain Coustelier, 1715.

Tevo, Zaccaria. *Il musico testore.* Venice: Antonio Bortoli, 1706.

Thomas, Downing. *Aesthetics of Opera in the Ancien Régime, 1647–1785.* Cambridge: Cambridge University Press, 2002.

———. "Rameau's *Platée* Returns: A Case of Double Identity in the *Querelle des bouffons.*" *Cambridge Opera Journal* 18, no. 1 (2006): 1–19.

Thrift, Nigel. *Non-Representational Theory: Space, Politics, Affect.* New York: Routledge, 2008.

Tomkins, Silvan S. *Affect, Imagery, Consciousness: The Complete Edition.* 2 vols.

New York: Springer, 2008. Volumes 1 and 2 were originally published 1962 and 1963, and volumes 3 and 4 were originally published in 1991 and 1992.

Tomlinson, Gary. *Metaphysical Song: An Essay on Opera*. Princeton, NJ: Princeton University Press, 1999.

———. "Musicology, Anthropology, History." *Il saggiatore musicale* 8, no. 1 (2001): 21–37.

———. "Sign, Affect, and Musicking before the Human." *boundary 2* 43, no. 1 (2016): 143–172.

Trower, Shelley. *Senses of Vibration: A History of the Pleasure and Pain of Sound*. London: Continuum, 2012.

Tunley, David. *François Couperin and "The Perfection of Music."* Aldershot, UK: Ashgate, 2004.

Turino, Thomas. "Peircean Thought as Core Theory for a Phenomenological Ethnomusicology." *Ethnomusicology* 58, no. 2 (2014): 185–221.

Usher, James. *Clio; or, A Discourse on Taste*. London: T. Davies, 1767.

Van den Toorn, Pieter. *Music, Politics, and the Academy*. Berkeley: University of California Press, 1995.

Verba, Cynthia. *Music and the French Enlightenment: Rameau and the "Philosophes" in Dialogue*. 2nd ed. Oxford: Oxford University Press, 2016.

Vion, Charles Antoine. *La musique pratique et theorique*. Paris: Jean-Baptiste-Christophe Ballard, 1742.

Wackenroder, Wilhelm Heinrich. *Sämtliche Werke und Briefe*. Edited by Silvio Vietta and Richard Littlejohns. Vol. 2. Heidelberg: Carl Winter Universitätsverlag, 1991.

———. *Werke und Briefe*. Edited by Gerda Heinrich. Munich: Carl Hanser, 1984.

Waeber, Jacqueline. "Jean-Jacques Rousseau's 'Unité de Mélodie.'" *Journal of the American Musicological Society* 62, no. 1 (2009): 79–143.

Wallrup, Erik. *Being Musically Attuned: The Act of Listening to Music*. Farnham, UK: Ashgate, 2015.

Watkins, Holly. *Metaphors of Depth in German Musical Thought: E. T. A. Hoffmann to Arnold Schoenberg*. Cambridge: Cambridge University Press, 2011.

Webb, Daniel. *Observations on the Correspondence between Poetry and Music*. London: J. Dodsley, 1769.

Weiss, Piero, and Pier Jacopo Martello. "Pier Jacopo Martello on Opera (1715): An Annotated Translation." *Musical Quarterly* 66, no. 3 (1980): 378–403.

Wellbery, David. *Lessing's Laocoon: Semiotics and Aesthetics in the Age of Reason*. Cambridge: Cambridge University Press, 1984.

———. "Stimmung." In *Historisches Wörterbuch Ästhetischer Grundbegriffe*, edited by Karlheinz Barck et al., vol. 5, 703–733. Stuttgart: Metzler, 2003.

Wentz, Jed. "Gaps, Pauses and Expressive Arms: Reconstructing the Link between Stage Gesture and Musical Timing at the Académie Royale de Musique." *Journal for Eighteenth-Century Studies* 32, no. 4 (2009): 607–623.

Wessel, Frederick T. "The Affektenlehre in the Eighteenth Century." PhD diss., Indiana University, 1955.

Wilbourne, Emily. *Seventeenth-Century Opera and the Sound of the Commedia dell'Arte*. Chicago: University of Chicago Press, 2016.

Winckelmann, Johann Joachim. *Gedanken über die Nachahmung der Griechischen Werke in der Malerey und Bildhauerkunst*. Dresden und Leipzig: Verlag der Waltherischen Handlung, 1756.

Wood, Caroline. "Orchestra and Spectacle in the 'Tragédie en Musique,' 1673–1715: Oracle, 'Sommeil' and 'Tempête.'" *Proceedings of the Royal Musical Association* 108 (1981–1982): 25–46.

Wurth, Kiene Brillenburg. "*Sehnsucht*, Music, and the Sublime." In *Musically Sublime: Indeterminacy, Infinity, Irresolvability*, 47–71. New York: Fordham University Press, 2009.

Zarlino, Gioseffo. *Le istitutioni harmoniche*. Venice: Francesco de i Franceschi Senese, 1558.

Index

Abrams, M. H., 14
actor-network theory, 137
actors, Diderot on, 84n69
adherence, affect and, 132–133
Adorno, Theodor, 25
aesthetics: Diderot on, 83n68
affect: Cho on, 132; definitional issues, 1, 1n1, 26; dialectics of, 23–26, 63, 136; Diderot on, 83; eighteenth-century theory on, 4–15; indescribability of, 23–24, 59–60, 129, 140–141; transmission of, 7–8, 135, 137
affective attunement, 22–23, 115–127; development of, 13–15; Diderot on, 81–85; Fréron on, 75–80; and instrumental music, 103–107
affective experience, Deleuze on, 18
affect theory: and instrumental music, 86–107; and music theory, 2–3, 26–28, 63, 138; recommendations for, 136–142; terminology in, 26; turn toward, 1–2, 19, 131, 139. See also contemporary affect theory; nineteenth-century affect theory
Affektenlehre, 3–4, 10; definitional issues, 46–47; evolution of, 125–127, 130; historical treatment of, 46–47; opera and, 29–60. See also attunement Affektenlehre; mimetic Affektenlehre
Ahern, Stephen, 3n4
Ahmed, Sara, 132
alexandrine, Gumbrecht on, 133
Allanbrook, Wye J., 99
L'Amphibie (Couperin), 86–89, 96

amphibious style, 91, 91n12, 96–103
ancients: and moderns, 69, 69n24; and power of music, 40–42; Zarlino on, 48
Anderson, Ben, 132, 135
André, Yves Marie, 77–78
arbitrary sign, 8–9, 105
arias, 35; "A Serpina penserete," 64–65; "Piangerò," 37–39
Aristoxenus, 53
L'Arlequine (Couperin), 88
Armide (Lully), 29–33, 40, 56–58
"A Serpina penserete" (Pergolesi), 64–65
associationist philosophy, 78–79
attunement: Chabanon on, 122; contemporary affect theory on, 20; Wallrup on, 134
attunement Affektenlehre, 15, 108–130; comic opera and, 62–63

Barry, Kevin, 116n22
Batteux, Charles, 69, 94–95, 102–104
Baumgarten, Alexander Gottlieb, 6
Beattie, James, 120
Beethoven, Ludwig, Fifth Symphony, 1, 108–110, 123–124, 131
Bell, Charles, 16
Bennett, Jane, 18n51
Bergson, Henri, 66n14, 68
Berlant, Lauren, 21
bliss: Hoffman on, 123–124; Wackenroder on, 124–125
body. See corporeality; instrument, human
La bondissante (Couperin), 88–89

ROGER MATHEW GRANT is Associate Professor of Music at Wesleyan University. He is the author of *Beating Time and Measuring Music in the Early Modern Era* (Oxford, 2014, pbk 2017), which won the 2016 Society for Music Theory Emerging Scholar Award.

CPSIA information can be obtained
at www.ICGtesting.com
Printed in the USA
JSHW010550131219
2960JS00008B/28